Designing Embedded Networking Applications

Essential Insights for Developers of
Intel® IXP4XX Network Processor Systems

Peter Barry
Gerard Hartnett

INTEL
PRESS

This book is printed on acid-free paper. ⊗

Publisher: Richard Bowles
Editor: Lynn Putnam
Managing Editor: David B. Spencer
Text Design & Composition: Wasser Studios
Graphic Art: Wasser Studios (illustrations), Fresh Interactive (cover)

Printed in the United States of America

10 9 8 7 6 5 4 3 2 1

First printing, May 2005

To my wife Viviane, my children Brianna and Jason, and my parents John and Anne.

– Peter

For my wife Luci, my children Clíodhna and Hannah, and my parents Larry and Pauline.

– Ger

Contents

Chapter 10 **Performance Tuning   241**

Preface

The best way to become acquainted with a subject is to write a book about it.

—Benjamin Disraeli

Is this book for you? Chances are good that you are reading this book because you have already decided to use the IXP4XX network processor. Maybe you have been asked to develop a product or to evaluate the processor for your next generation designs. Maybe you are teaching a university course on embedded networking applications or using an IXP4XX network processor in a research project.

We expect you have already downloaded some of the IXP4XX product line data sheets and reference manuals from the Intel Developer Web site, listed in "References." This extensive product documentation is freely available and provides detailed information on the processors. The documentation, while comprehensive, is a little daunting at first. One of the goals of this book is to distill the documentation down to its essence, highlighting the information that is important to all designers and software engineers, then providing you with a roadmap through the more detailed information on the Web site.

Even if you do not plan to use an IXP4XX network processor, we believe you still could find useful general information in this book to help you design embedded network applications.

A Guide to the Rest of the Book

You do not have to read this book page-by-page from start to finish. You can read some chapters independently. Other chapters depend on material presented in previous chapters. Some readers might be interested in system design details; others might want to know the details of a particular API. Here are our recommended approaches to reading this book.

System architects. If you are looking to apply the IXP4XX network processor in a specific product or family of products, read Chapter 2, which covers the processor's hardware. You should then read Chapters 3 and 4 for details on system design and operating system choices. You should also read Chapter 5, which provides a good overview of the software architecture. You can skip or skim Chapter 6 as it describes a detailed example that uses the Ethernet software component. You should read Chapter 7, which describes the high-level design of a number of IXP4XX network processor applications, both from platform and software perspectives. Skip Chapter 8, unless you are designing a multimedia application. Skim Chapter 9 concentrating on the specific components your application uses. You can skip Chapter 10, which focuses on performance and code tuning.

Software developers and test engineers. If you are a software engineer, developing software applications for the IXP4XX network processor, you are the core audience for this book and you should read most of it. Skim Chapter 2 for an overview of the hardware. Chapter 3 gives you a concise overview of the physical layer interfaces that connect to the IXP4XX network processor and can correspond to the network view of your product. Chapter 4 is essential reading because it situates the IXP4XX network processor in the context of the RTOS you have selected. Chapters 5–8 are also essential reading. These chapters describe the software architecture in the context of an application. If you are developing a device driver, Chapter 6 will be of particular interest. You can select the parts of the Chapter 9 that are of interest to you in developing your application. Chapter 10 presents a broad spectrum of tuning techniques, from bottleneck identification to general network processing tuning. It also contains sections on the Intel XScale® core and IXP4XX network processor-specific tuning. Finally, Chapter 11 answers some frequently asked questions.

Technical project leaders or managers. If you are leading a team that is developing an application on the IXP4XX network processor, consider following this route through the book. Read the initial sections of Chapter 2, which describes the features of the IXP4XX product line. You can skim Chapters 3 and 4, which detail system design and operating system choices. You can skim Chapter 5, which provides a good overview of the software architecture. You can skip Chapter 6, which describes a detailed example using the Ethernet software component. You should read Chapter 7, which describes the high-level design of a number of IXP4XX network processor applications, both from platform and software perspectives. Skip Chapter 8 unless your application deals with multimedia. You can also skip Chapters 9 and 10.

Conventions

Throughout the book, the terms byte, half-word, word, and long-word represent 8, 16, 32, and 64 bits of data, respectively.

Many of the code examples refer to the demonstration code examples that you receive when you download the IXP400 software from the Intel Developer Web site, listed in "References." We call these code examples *codelets*. The following is an example of the code format used in the book.

Transmit-Done Callback

The transmit-done callback returns the buffer to the original receive port. Error check code has been removed to simplify the example.

```
1    void myPortTxDoneCallback (UINT32 cbTag,
2                               IX_OSAL_MBUF* mBufPtr)
3    {
4      if(cbTag == IX_ETH_PORT_1 )
5      {
6         ixEthAccPortRxFreeReplenish(IX_ETH_PORT_2, mBufPtr);
7      }
8      else
9      {
10        ixEthAccPortRxFreeReplenish(IX_ETH_PORT_1, mBufPtr);
11     }
12
13   }
```

Lines 1-2:

These lines are the transmit-done callback entry point, which is registered with the Ethernet Access component.

Lines 4-10:

Check the callback tag and call the replenish function for the appropriate port.

Each line of code has a number for easy reference.

File names take the form: src/include/IxEthAcc.h. These names are relative to the path in which you installed the software. For example, if you installed the software in /usr/local/4XX then you can find the Ethernet access header in /usr/local/4XX/src/include/IxEthAcc.h.

Acknowledgements

We owe a debt of gratitude to a large number of people for their help and encouragement during the writing of this book. First, we would like to thank the men and women in Intel's software engineering, silicon engineering, product marketing, technical marketing, and program management teams for developing such a terrific book-worthy product. We would like to thank all of the people outside of Intel who have designed such imaginative and ingenious applications with this processor.

In particular, we'd like to thank all of the people who reviewed this book and provided us with much valuable feedback: Brian Aherne, Conor Aylward, Ian Betts, Dirk Blevins, Kelly Block, Mark Burkley, Paul Burkley, Dani Carles, Shailesh Chaudhry, Stephen Dolan, Mike Hogg, Brian Keating, Pierre Laurent, Lee Booi Lim, Jean-Jacques Loesch, Dave Lyons, Teodor Mihai, Uday Naik, Hu Ningxin, Ruairí Ó hAilín, Robert Ranslam, Mickey Sartin, Chen Yong Seow, John Twomey and Chengda Yang. Without their comments and suggestions, this book would be less accurate and more incomprehensible.

We would like to thank Duke Tallam for his strong support and guidance during the course of writing this book.

We would like to thank our senior management in IPD, including Jonathan Walsh and Doug Davis, for recognizing the importance of this work and funding it.

We would like to thank Raj Yavatkar and Jim Finnegan for "encouraging" us to write the book in the first place. We would also like to thank our editors David Spencer and Lynn Putnam for taking a couple of wet-behind-the-ears engineers and guiding them from idea to camera-ready copy on numerous early morning phone calls to Ireland.

Last but far from least, we'd like to thank our families, for putting up with the clatter of late night keyboards, short weekends, and missed bedtime stories. This would not have been possible without your love, patience, and support.

—Peter Barry and Gerard Hartnett

Chapter 1

Why Use Intel® IXP4XX Network Processors?

Developing a new system or product is always a challenge. It might seem daunting to look at the broad range of interfaces and accelerators the Intel® IXP4XX silicon and software provides. You could then feel further overwhelmed by the range and combinations of choices you have in powerful real-time operating systems (RTOSs), software stacks, and third-party vendors. However, we have already helped a number of companies bring successful products through design to high-volume production. These products are now in use in homes, offices, factories, and telecommunications infrastructure around the globe. You might even use a product powered by an Intel IXP4XX Network Processor on your next visit to a coffee shop.

Our goal in this book is to provide you with the kind of practical knowledge you need to design and ship your own products using this proven technology.

Whether you are looking to use the series of IXP4XX network processors to build a USB-powered virtual private network (VPN) dongle, a wireless-enabled voice-over-IP (VoIP) access point, an industrial controller, or a communications line card, this book is your guide. The IXP4XX product line excels in a large range of applications, supports a plethora of integrated networking interfaces, and provides enough headroom and processor cycles to enable your high-performance software designs.

The IXP4XX designation represents all of the processors in the IXP4XX product line, which includes the IXP420, IXP421, IXP422, IXP423, IXP425, IXP455, IXP460, and IXP465. The information contained in this book applies to all these network processors, except where noted. Chapter 2 describes the IXP4XX network processor architecture in detail.

The IXP4XX product line contains a powerful general-purpose processor, the Intel XScale® core; one or more network processor engines (NPEs); and a number of communications interfaces, including UTOPIA, Ethernet, TDM, and PCI, along with bulk/asymmetric cryptographic accelerators. While Intel uses the term "network processor" for this class of product, others might use the term "communications processor."

Intel supplies software libraries, called Intel IXP400 software, which provide easy-to-use abstractions of the interfaces and accelerators. If you want to learn how to build high-performance systems by combining these libraries with an RTOS, networking stack, and your own application code, this book will take you systematically through the process.

The IXP4XX Product Line

When you use the IXP4XX network processors, you can add and extend your product's network services by adding or modifying software. When designing your communications product, you need to choose a technology that balances the following dimensions for your product:

- *Flexibility*. How easy is it to modify the system and design for changing requirements?

- *Integration/Cost*. How many discrete devices does your system design require? What is the cost of the bill of materials (BOM)?

- *Time-to-market*. How long does it take to develop a solution?

- *Performance*. Does the technology support your product's performance requirements?

- *Power*. What is the power budget for the system design?

You have a choice of solution technologies that optimize these dimensions differently. These solution technologies include network processors, general-purpose processors, system-on-a-chip (SoC) integration, and application-specific integrated circuits (ASICs).

Network Processors versus Alternatives

A general-purpose processor certainly provides the flexibility needed in communications systems. Tools and operating systems exist that allow you to write code for an embedded general-purpose processor, and they are typically programmable in a standard programming language like C or C++. They also aid time-to-market through the availability of design collateral and pre-integrated software applications from third-party vendors. However, general-purpose processors usually have serious shortcomings when it comes to the integration and performance aspects of your system design. Typically, they do not include integrated media access control interfaces (MACs) or interfaces to ATM PHY devices (UTOPIA). So, to provide these functions, you would need to add discrete components to your board or system design, increasing the BOM cost of the overall solution. Similarly, when it comes to performance, a general-purpose processor might consume a large percentage of its available cycles running algorithms that are more suited to hardware implementation. For example, cryptographic algorithms, such as block ciphers and hashes, are notorious consumers of clock cycles in general-purpose implementations.

At the other end of the scale, you could design an ASIC to implement the functionality in your product. A well-executed ASIC design should give you excellent performance and optimize the cost of the product when you build very large volumes. However, time-to-market and flexibility challenges offset the potential gains. The initial ASIC design cycle can be a year or more, and the length of iteration cycles can make it difficult to keep up with the rate of changes in required functionality and services.

Another alternative is taking a generic synthesizable reduced instruction set computer (RISC) core and combining it with interface logic from one or more silicon IP vendors. This approach improves the flexibility and time-to-market disadvantages compared to an ASIC. The programmable RISC core provides flexibility. The product should have good performance and manufacturing cost characteristics. However, the development and validation cost can still be high and the cumulative license fees could make this approach prohibitive for large volume applications.

We believe the IXP4XX network processors provide a compelling balance of these dimensions for a large number of product categories.

The IXP4XX network processors tackle the performance problem by combining a high-performance Intel XScale core with one or more independent network-oriented processors, called NPEs. These independent processors execute Intel-provided microcode to offload processing from the main Intel XScale core, leaving more processor headroom for your application code. Secondly, IXP4XX network processors include a number of fixed-function hardware accelerators for complex algorithms, such as bulk cryptography and HDLC processing. The NPEs and Intel IXP400 software libraries provide this functionality to the Intel XScale core and your application code. The integrated interfaces reduce the overall BOM cost of your systems when compared to a general-purpose processor.

The IXP4XX network processors are suited to applications where aggregate system throughput is in the region of 200 megabits per second. Overall system throughput will depend on the complexity and performance of the code you add. For higher throughput applications, you should consider using the IXP2XXX product line (Johnson and Kunze 2003).

For time-to-market, you can then develop an application that runs on the Intel XScale core using standard tool chains, the C programming language, and an RTOS such as Linux[†], VxWorks[†], and Windows[†] CE. These RTOSs usually contain higher-level functionality ranging from Internet protocol (IP) networking stacks to firewall features to HTTP servers. In addition, many third-party companies provide applications, such as VoIP gateways, enterprise wireless access points, and network-addressed storage applications (NAS) that have already been integrated and optimized to take advantage of the IXP4XX network processor silicon and software architecture.

Finally, IXP4XX processors provide you with scalability and the ability to reuse designs across your product range. The IXP4XX product line extends from low-cost devices to high-performance, highly integrated devices. Using the range of IXP4XX network processors can provide you with levels of reuse at the board/system and software levels that can significantly boost your product quality and time-to-market capabilities.

Intel® IXP4XX Network Processor Architecture

Technology is dominated by two types of people: those who understand what they do not manage, and those who manage what they do not understand.

— Anonymous

The Intel® IXP4XX product line offers a range of different processors, each with their own characteristics and features. This chapter provides you with a comparative view of each.

By understanding the processor's architecture and available features, you can choose the right processor for your project and make optimal use of the processor's performance and features.

Overview of the Processor Family

The block diagram of an IXP4XX network processor in Figure 2.1 shows a superset of all of the functionality and features of processors in the IXP4XX product line. All of these processors have an Intel XScale® core general-purpose CPU and one or more network processing engines (NPE).

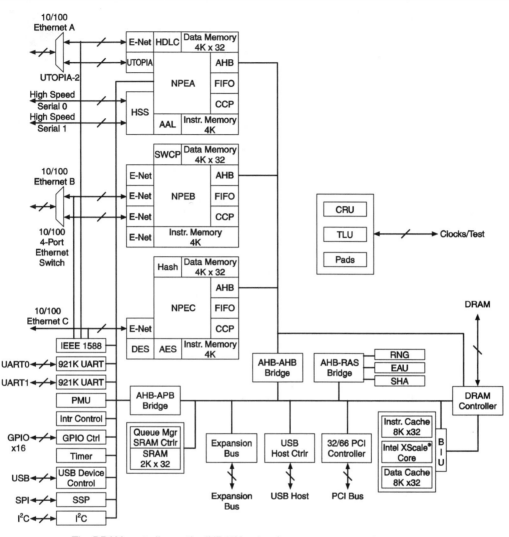

The DRAM controller on the IXP42X network processors supports synchronous dynamic random access memory (SDRAM). The IXP45X and IXP46X network processors support double data rate type 1 (DDR-1). The IXP46X network processors support error correction code (ECC) on DDR.

Figure 2.1   Chip Level Block Diagram

Starting from the top left of Figure 2.1, these are the main features of the processor:

- *Network Processing Engine A.* The NPE A contains UTOPIA interfaces and coprocessors to accelerate ATM applications. It contains high-speed-serial (HSS) interfaces for T1/E1, pulse code modulation (PCM), and multi-vendor integration protocol (MVIP) applications. It also contains a high-level data link control (HDLC) co-processor. On some members of the processor family NPE A also contains an Ethernet co-processor and media access control (MAC) functionality.

- *Network Processing Engine B.* The NPE B contains Ethernet co-processors. On some members of the product line, it contains four MACs and a co-processor to accelerate switching functionality on the NPE.

- *Network Processing Engine C.* The NPE C contains an Ethernet co-processor and, in some members of the processor product line, contains co-processors for bulk cryptographic algorithm acceleration.

- *Peripheral Interfaces.* These interfaces include two serial interfaces (UART) and a USB-device interface. Also supported are general-purpose I/O (GPIO) pins that you can use as software-controllable inputs or outputs. When configured as an input, you can use changes in the pin state to trigger an interrupt to the Intel XScale core. In addition, some pins are capable of generating clocks.

- *Queue Manager.* The queue manager is used typically to transfer information between the NPEs and Intel XScale core.

- *Expansion Bus, USB-Host, and PCI.* The expansion bus, USB-host, and peripheral component interconnect (PCI) controllers all sit on the AHB bus. The expansion bus is an extension of the internal memory bus and allows you to connect devices with a memory interface to the IXP4XX network processor. You would typically use the expansion bus to connect flash memory or a custom device like an ASIC to the processor. The USB-host controller is available on the IXP45X and IXP46X product lines only. You can use the PCI interface to connect devices, such as wireless chip sets and graphics cards, to the IXP4XX network processor.

■ *Intel XScale Core.* Located at the bottom right of Figure 2.1, the Intel XScale core contains instruction and data caches. This processor executes your code. The core supports both big-endian and little-endian operation.

■ *Memory Controller Interfaces to DRAM.* The memory controller interface is an SDRAM controller on the IXP42X product line and a DDR controller on the IXP45X and 46X product lines.

The Intel® IXP420 Network Processor

You can use the Intel IXP420 Network Processor in many low-cost applications from home gateways, small office/home office (SOHO) routers, and wireless access points to industrial control and networked imaging applications.

It contains:

■ Intel XScale core at 266, 400, and 533 megahertz commercial temperature and 266 megahertz extended temperature

■ Two NPEs and two integrated 10/100 Base-T Ethernet MACs with MII interface

■ 33/66 megahertz PCI v2.2 host and option interface for glueless connection of up to four devices

■ DRAM controller supporting from 8 to 256 megabytes of synchronous dynamic random access memory (SDRAM)

■ USB version 1.1 device controller

■ Two high-speed UARTS at up to 921 kilobaud each

■ Sixteen GPIO pins

■ 16-bit configurable expansion bus

■ Low system power consumption (1.0–1.5 watt typical)

The Intel IXP421 and IXP423 Network Processors

The Intel IXP421 and IXP423 Network Processors add features to the IXP420 to support voice applications. You can use these processors in high-performance and cost-sensitive data and voice over IP (VoIP) applications ranging from residential gateways, integrated access devices (IADs), and small office IP/PBX systems.

The main differences from the IXP420 network processor are:

- The Intel XScale core runs at 266 megahertz only

- The Intel IXP400 DSP software library, which runs on a co-processor attached to the Intel XScale core, supports 2–4 channels of voice processing

- Two HSS ports to connect to SLIC/CODEC or T1/E1 for VoIP applications

- A UTOPIA 2 interface supports up to four xDSL PHYs (ADSL, G.SHDSL, or VDSL)

- The IXP421 network processor contains one Ethernet MAC and one NPE. The IXP423 network processor contains two MACs and two NPEs.

The Intel IXP422 Network Processor

The Intel IXP422 Network Processor adds features to the IXP420 network processor to support security applications, including wireless access points, residential gateways, VPN firewall appliances, and security-enabled SME routers and switches.

The main differences from the IXP420 network processor are:

- The Intel XScale core runs at 266 megahertz only

- Integrated hardware acceleration of popular bulk cryptography algorithms (SHA-1, MD5, DES, 3DES, AES)

The Intel IXP425 Network Processor

The Intel IXP425 Network Processor combines the features of the IXP420, IXP421, and IXP422 network processors into a single device. Its Intel XScale core is available in speeds of up to 533 megahertz. It combines integration and support for multiple WAN and LAN technologies in a common architecture designed to meet requirements for high-end gateways, VoIP applications, wireless access points, SME routers, switches, security devices, mini-DSLAMs (digital subscriber line access multiplexers), xDSL line cards, industrial control, and networked imaging applications.

The Intel IXP455 Network Processor

The IXP455 network processor adds the following features to the IXP425 network processor.

- Supports 32 megabytes to 1 gigabyte of double data rate type 1 (DDR-1) memory

- USB 1.1 host controller

- Support for a full-duplex synchronous serial interface. It supports the National Semiconductor Microwire[†], Texas Instruments synchronous serial protocol (SSP), and Motorola serial peripheral interface (SPI) protocol.

- A lead-free package option

- Acceleration support for asymmetric cryptographic algorithms

- An enhanced expansion bus, which includes bus mastering, ZBT SRAM support, and 32-bit mode of operation features

The Intel IXP46X Network Processors

The IXP46X product line adds the following features to the IXP45X network processors. The IXP46X product line contains just the IXP460 and IXP465 network processors at the time of writing.

■ Intel XScale core at 266, 400, 533, and 667 megahertz commercial temperature and 266 megahertz extended temperature

■ ECC support on DDR

■ IEEE 1588[†] hardware-assist support

Summary of the Intel IXP4XX Product Line

Table 2.1 summarizes the features of the full product line.

Table 2.1   IXP4XX Product Line Summary

Feature	IXP420	IXP421	IXP422	IXP423	IXP425	IXP455	IXP460	IXP465
Intel XScale Core Speed	266, 400, 533	266	266	266	266, 400, 533	266, 400, 533	266, 400, 533, 667	266, 400, 533, 667
SDRAM 8MB–256MB	✓	✓	✓	✓	✓			
DDR 32MB–1GB						✓	✓	✓
ECC							✓	✓
DSP support		✓		✓	✓	✓		✓
Ethernet MACs	2	1	2	2	2	2	2	5/6
ATM		✓		✓	✓	✓		✓
HSS/HDLC		✓		✓	✓	✓		✓
Crypto B=Bulk A=Asym			B		B	B & A		B & A
USB 1.1 D=Device H=Host	D	D	D	D	D	H & D	H & D	H & D
IEEE 1588							✓	✓

The Intel XScale® Microarchitecture

The Intel XScale core is the central processor on all IXP4XX network processors. It is a reduced instruction set computer (RISC). ARM Ltd has defined a number of ARM[†] architecture versions (Seal 2000). The Intel XScale core is ARM V5TE compatible, implements the ARM version 5 architecture definition, the Thumb instruction set extensions (T variants), and enhanced DSP instructions (E variants). The core on the IXP4XX network processors does not provide a floating-point (FP) co-processor.

It might interest you to know that the Intel XScale core-related information in this book is applicable to other Intel XScale core-based products such as the Intel PCA processors—Intel PXA27X, PXA26X, and PXA255 processor families; and Intel I/O processors—Intel IOP321, IOP310, and IOP315 chipsets.

The Intel XScale core incorporates an extensive list of architecture features that allow it to achieve high performance at very low power consumption. This rich feature set allows programmers to select the appropriate configuration to obtain the best performance for their application. Many of the architectural features added to Intel XScale core help hide memory latency, which often is a serious impediment to high-performance processors. Intel XScale core features include:

■ A 32-kilobyte instruction cache, which is a piece of very fast memory used to store the most recently used processor instructions.

■ A 32-kilobyte data cache, which is a piece of very fast memory used to store the most-recently-used data.

■ A 2-kilobyte mini data cache avoids "thrashing" of the main data cache for frequently changing data streams.

■ The memory management unit provides logical-to-physical address translation, access permissions/protection, instruction and data cache attributes. In addition, the Intel XScale core memory management unit (MMU) provides extensions to control coalescing within the write buffer. This ability allows the MMU to be used to optimize the performance of access to general-purpose memory and peripherals.

■ The eight-entry write buffer allows the core to continue execution while data is being written to memory. It also supports coalescing (merging) multiple writes to the same half cache line to improve overall memory performance.

■ The core has the ability to continue instruction execution even while the data cache is retrieving data from external memory.

■ The data cache allocation policy can be configured as read allocate or read/write allocate to obtain the best performance for each application.

■ A Branch Target Buffer (BTB) is provided. It stores the target address of branch type instructions and predicts the next address based on the history of branches taken. The instruction at the predicted memory address is prefetched, which improves the overall performance of the XScale core.

■ Intel XScale core performance counters are provided in coprocessor 14 of the Intel XScale core. These counters can be used to obtain key performance data such as the data cache hit rate.

■ A multiply-accumulate (MACC) co-processor performs two simultaneous 16-bit SIMD multiplies with 40-bit accumulation for efficient media processing. The multiply and accumulate instructions are cornerstone operations in digital signal processing.

Figure 2.2 shows the Intel XScale microarchitecture.

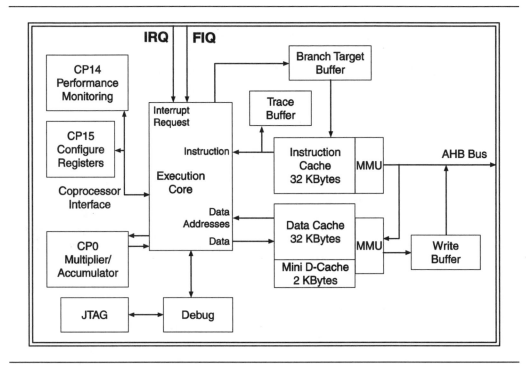

Figure 2.2 Intel XScale® Microarchitecture

Programming Model

The Intel XScale microarchitecture uses the ARM version 5TE instruction set architecture programming model that handles 8-bit, 16-bit, and 32-bit data types and operates in one of seven processor modes: user, system, supervisor, abort, undefined instruction, fast interrupt, and normal interrupt. The microarchitecture provides 16 general-purpose 32-bit registers (R0-R15) where R13 is the stack pointer (SP), R14 is the link register (LR), which is used to save the return address of subroutines, and R15 is the program counter (PC). It also supplements its 16 general registers and current program status register (CPSR) with 20 mode-dependent "shadow" registers listed in Table 2.2. The modes of the processor normally correlate to different states of the operating systems. For example, in Linux a user-level process would run in user mode, the kernel would run in supervisor mode, and the interrupt handlers would run in IRQ mode. The mechanism predominately used to change the mode is a processor exception.

Table 2.2   Mode-Dependent "Shadow" Registers

User	System	Supervisor	Abort	Undefined	Normal Interrupt	Fast Interrupt
R0	R0	R0	R0	R0	R0	R0
R1	R1	R1	R1	R1	R1	R1
R2	R2	R2	R2	R2	R2	R2
R3	R3	R3	R3	R3	R3	R3
R4	R4	R4	R4	R4	R4	R4
R5	R5	R5	R5	R5	R5	R5
R6	R6	R6	R6	R6	R6	R6
R7	R7	R7	R7	R7	R7	R7
R8	R8	R8	R8	R8	R8	R8
R9	R9	R9	R9	R9	R9	R9
R10	R10	R10	R10	R10	R10	R10
R11	R11	R11	R11	R11	R11	R11
R12	R12	R12	R12	R12	R12	R12
SP	SP	SP_SVC	SP_ABORT	SP_UNDEF	SP_IRQ	SP_FIQ
LR	LR	LR_SCV	LR_ABORT	LR_UNDEF	LR_IRQ	LR_FIQ
PC	PC	PC	PC	PC	PC	PC
CPSR	CPSR	CPSR	CPSR	CPSR	CPSR	CPSR
		SPSR_SVC	SPSR_ABORT	SPSR_UNDEF	SPSR_IRQ	SPSR_FIQ

The "shadow" registers (shaded in Table 2.2) for the supervisor, abort, undefined instruction, normal interrupt (IRQ), and fast interrupt (FIQ) modes provide fast context switching by precluding the need to first save general registers. Upon entry into any of the supervisor, abort, undefined instruction, IRQ, or FIQ modes, the CPSR is "saved" in the mode-related saved program status register (SPSR). The user mode and system mode use the same registers. Unlike the user mode, the system mode has privileges that allow it to change the CPSR to select processor mode, turn on/off normal and fast interrupts, and select the thumb instruction set. The core mode can be changed under program control (privileges permitting) and on entry to an exception. Table 2.3 shows the exceptions supported by the core, the address of the exception handler, and the mode of the processor when the exception type is entered.

Table 2.3   Intel XScale® Core Exceptions

Exception Type	Vector Address	Mode	Comment
Reset	0x0	Supervisor	When the reset signal is de-asserted, the processor starts execution at this vector in supervisor mode with interrupts disabled.
Undefined Instructions	0x4	Undefined	The processor transfers execution to this vector if it executes an undefined instruction. Undefined instructions can be used to extend the instruction set through software emulation. They might be encountered due to error conditions in your program or might be used deliberately.
Software Interrupt	0x8	Supervisor	Execution of the software interrupt instruction (SWI) causes this exception. Operating systems use this instruction to transfer from user to supervisor mode.
Prefetch Abort	0xC	Abort	Memory abort during an instruction cycle fetch. A memory abort can be returned by the MMU or external devices. The MMU returns a memory abort if an attempt is made to execute from an address that is not mapped or does not have the required privilege.

(continued)

Table 2.3   Intel XScale® Core Exceptions *(continued)*

Exception Type	Vector Address	Mode	Comment
Data Abort	0x10	Abort	An abort during a data memory cycle. The abort is generated by the MMU or memory subsystem.
			The Intel XScale core can be configured to generate data aborts for unaligned data transfers.
			A number of abort models are defined by ARM. The Intel XScale core uses the base restored abort model.
Normal Interrupt	0x14	Interrupt	The IRQ vector is executed when the IRQ line is asserted to the Intel XScale core. The IRQ line is generated by the IXP4XX network processor's interrupt controller block. The line is asserted while any unmasked normal interrupts are active.
Fast Interrupt	0x1C	Fast Interrupt	The FIQ vector is executed when the FIQ line is asserted to the Intel XScale core. The FIQ line is generated by the IXP4XX network processor's interrupt controller block. The line is asserted while any unmasked FIQ interrupts are active.

When the core processes an exception, the LR and CPSR are saved into their corresponding shadow version. The CPSR mode bits are updated to reflect the new mode, and the program counter is set to the vector address.

The exception vector address can be either normal, as shown in Table 2.3, or high. When the vector addresses are high, you must add 0xFFFF0000 to the address shown. When the IXP4XX network processor first starts, the normal vector addresses are used. Some ARM processor core-based devices allow you to map the location of the exception table when the chip comes out of reset. In this case, the startup code must be located at the physical address 0xFFFF0000.

You can configure the Intel XScale core to raise a data abort for unaligned memory access. Unaligned accesses occur when a 32-bit access is performed on an address that is not a multiple of four or when a 16-bit access is performed on addresses that are not a multiple of two. Some operating systems provide an unaligned data abort handler. When an unaligned data access occurs, the exception handler performs the appropriate number of aligned reads/writes to memory and updates the Intel XScale core registers, obviously resulting in a performance penalty. In general, your code should not perform any unaligned data access. Some other architectures do not have such a performance penalty. You should give due consideration to alignment of data when porting code from such architectures.

Intel XScale Core Interrupts

The Intel XScale core provides two external interrupts: IRQ and FIQ. Each interrupt line is connected to the IXP4XX network processor's interrupt controller block. The interrupt controller block collects inputs from all interrupt sources on the chip and routes them to either the IRQ or FIQ input. All IRQ and FIQ interrupts can be disabled by writing to the CPSR registers. Individual interrupts are masked at the interrupt controller block. Having only two interrupt sources to the core is seen as a limitation sometimes, but the nesting of interrupts can be supported in software. The Intel IXP400 software provides functions to enable and disable core interrupts.

Memory Management Unit

The Intel XScale core implements the memory management unit (MMU) architecture specified in the ARM reference manual (Seal 2000).

A function of the MMU is to translate logical addresses used within the processor to actual physical addresses. This function is essential in some operating systems, such as Linux, where each user process usually has the same logical address but is mapped to different physical memory addresses. The MMU also provides memory protection. This mechanism prevents processes from directly accessing the memory of the kernel or other processes. Finally, the MMU provides memory attributes for the logical memory addresses. Caches use these attributes to identify how to handle a transaction appropriately.

Information is supplied to the MMU controller in the form of a translation table. The translation table base register (Co-processor 15—register 2) points to the physical address of the first-level translation table. The translation table consists of 4000 first-level descriptors and optionally second-level descriptors. Descriptors provide information on the address translation, access permissions, and caching options for a range of physical memory addresses to the MMU. The first-level descriptors are a single word long (32 bits). The entire first-level table occupies 16 kilobytes of memory. Each entry can be one of the following shown in Figure 2.3

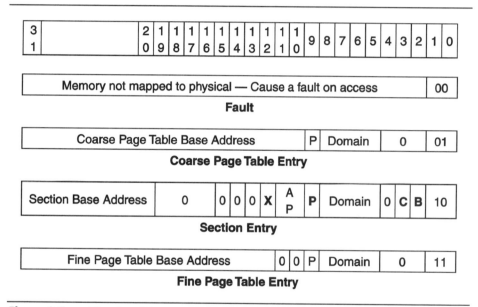

Figure 2.3   First-level Descriptor Entries

The description of the second level descriptors is available in the appropriate developer manual listed in "References." The translation and attributes of memory can be defined at a granularity of 1-megabyte sections, 64-kilobyte large pages, 4-kilobyte small pages, or 1-kilobyte tiny pages. The finer the granularity, the larger the table needed. The translation look-aside buffer (TLB) is used to cache the memory translation for the most recently used translations. The finer the granularity of the MMU entries, the more likely the TLB does not contain a cached copy for the translation required. When a translation is not available in the TLB, the Intel XScale core performs an MMU table walk to obtain the translation. Frequent TLB misses degrade the performance of the application.

A table of 16 kilobytes fully describes memory in 1-megabyte blocks using section entries in the page table, whereas a table of approximately 16 megabytes is needed to fully describe memory using tiny pages. The operating system typically defines the granularity of page tables used.

Figure 2.4 shows a section translation of a virtual address to a physical address. This type of translation is the simplest. The translation replaces bit 20 to bit 31 of the virtual address, with the section base address (bit 20 to bit 31) read from the MMU table to produce the physical address.

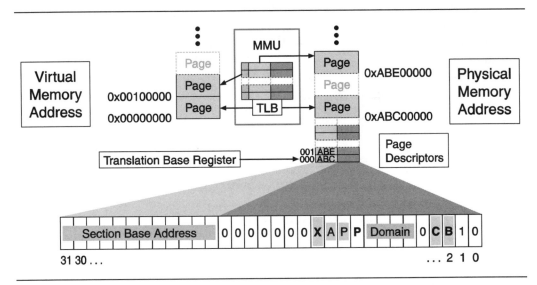

Figure 2.4   Virtual-to-Physical Address Translation Using Section Descriptors

The MMU controller reads the first-level table entries and, if necessary, the second-level entry to find the appropriate translation and attributes for a particular memory region. The process is known as "walking the table" and is performed in hardware. Associated with all MMU translations are the following attribute bits:

■ *Cachable*—'C' bit

■ *Bufferable*—'B' bit

- *eXtension*—Called the "X" bit, this Intel XScale core-specific bit modifies the operation of cacheable (C) and bufferable (B) bits.

- *Domain* bits. The descriptor domain bit along with the domain register in CP15 provides a very quick way to manipulate memory access controls without requiring an MMU table updated along with TLB management.

- *Proprietary*—Called the "P" bit, this bit is specific to the Intel XScale core and is used in little endian mode to control different endian conversion modes.

The attribute bits are provided to each cache when they are accessed. The resultant behavior depends on which cache is being accessed and the value of the cacheable (C), bufferable (B), and extension (X) bits.

Processor Exceptions

The processor vector addresses are virtual-memory addresses. The use of the MMU allows the exception vectors to be resident anywhere in physical memory. Vectors are usually placed in SDRAM to allow updates by the operating system. In most cases, the vector address has enough room for only one instruction. This instruction is usually a branch instruction to the code segment that handles the exception. Unlike some other RISC processor architectures, the MMU remains enabled on transition to the different processor modes.

On processor reset, the MMU is disabled. For the device to boot up, an exception vector must be located at physical address zero.

Instruction Cache

The instruction cache utilizes only the MMU C attribute bit. If the C bit is clear, the instruction cache considers a code fetch from that memory to be non-cacheable and will not fill a cache entry. If the C bit is set, fetches from the associated memory region are cached.

Data Cache and Write Buffer

If the MMU is disabled, all data accesses will be non-cacheable and non-bufferable. This same behavior occurs when the MMU is enabled and a data access uses a descriptor with X, C, and B all set to zero.

The X, C, and B bits determine when the processor should place new data into the data cache. The cache places data into the cache in lines (also called blocks). The *line-allocation policy* dictates how the cache decides when it should put new data into the cache. If the line-allocation policy is read-allocate and the cache is enabled, all load operations in cacheable pages that miss the cache request a 32-byte cache line from external memory and allocate it into either the data cache or mini-data cache. Store operations that miss the cache do not cause a line to be allocated. If read/write-allocate is in effect, load or store operations that miss the cache request a 32-byte cache line from external memory if the cache is enabled.

The other set of policies determined by the X, C, and B bits is the *write policy*. The cache-write policy defines what happens when a write operation occurs. A write-through policy instructs the data cache to keep external memory coherent by performing stores to both external memory and the cache. A write-back policy updates external memory only when a line in the cache is flushed (explicitly by the programmer) or needs to be replaced with a new line. Generally, write-back provides higher performance because it generates less data traffic to external memory and the memory controllers are optimized for burst memory access, which is more likely with write-back mode. Table 2.4 shows the effect for each combination of C, B, and X bits.

Table 2.4   MMU Cache Attributes

Attributes			Cacheable	Bufferable	Write Policy	Line Allocation	Notes
X	C	B					
0	0	0	N	N	—	—	Stall until complete*.
0	0	1	N	Y	—	—	Typically used for peripherals.
0	1	0	Y	Y	Write Through	Read Allocate	
0	1	1	Y	Y	Write Back	Read Allocate	Mainly used for general-purpose memory.
1	0	0	—	—	—	—	Unpredictable, do not use.
1	0	1	N	Y	—	—	Writes do **not** coalesce into buffers.
1	1	0	Allocate to mini data cache	—	—	—	Cache policy is determined by MD field of auxiliary control register in CP15. Useful for memory that is invalidated frequently, such as memory used for packet data.
1	1	1	Y	Y	Write Back	Read/Write Allocate	

*Stall until complete — Normally, the processor continues executing after a data access if no dependency on that access is encountered. With X=C=B=0, the processor stalls execution until the data access completes. This stall guarantees that the data access has taken effect by the time execution of the data access instruction completes.

Memory Operation Ordering

In certain circumstances, it is important to enforce a specific memory transaction ordering from the Intel XScale core to the rest of the chip and external devices. You can enforce the ordering of these transactions by using a *fence*. A fence memory operation is one that guarantees all memory operations issued prior to the fence execute before any memory operations issued after the fence. Thus, software can issue a fence to impose a partial ordering on memory accesses. Table 2.5 shows memory operations that impose a fence.

Table 2.5   Memory Operations That Impose a Fence

Memory operation	X Bit	C Bit	B Bit
Load	Don't Care	0	Don't Care
Store	1	0	1
Load or Store	0	0	0

Translation Look-aside Buffers

To accelerate virtual-to-physical address translation, the Intel XScale core uses both an instruction translation look-aside buffer (TLB) and a data TLB to cache the latest translations. Each TLB holds 32 entries. Not only do the TLBs contain the translated addresses, but also the access rights for memory references. If an instruction or data TLB miss occurs, a hardware translation-table-walking mechanism is invoked to translate the virtual address to a physical address. Once translated, the physical address is placed in the TLB along with the access rights and attributes of the page or section. These translations can also be locked down in either TLB to guarantee the performance of critical routines.

Instruction Cache

The Intel XScale core instruction cache enhances performance by reducing the number of instruction fetches from external memory. The cache provides fast execution of cached code. Figure 2.5 shows the cache organization and how the instruction address is used to access the cache. The instruction cache is available as a 32-kilobyte, 32-way set, associative cache. The size of each set is 1,024 bytes. Each set contains 32 ways. Hennessy and Patterson (2003) give details on processor cache (ways and sets) architectures. Each way of a set contains eight 32-bit words and one valid bit, which are referred to as a line. The replacement policy is a round-robin algorithm, and the cache also supports the ability to lock code into the cache at line granularity. The instruction cache is virtually addressed and virtually tagged. All actions on the cache under program control must specify a virtual address.

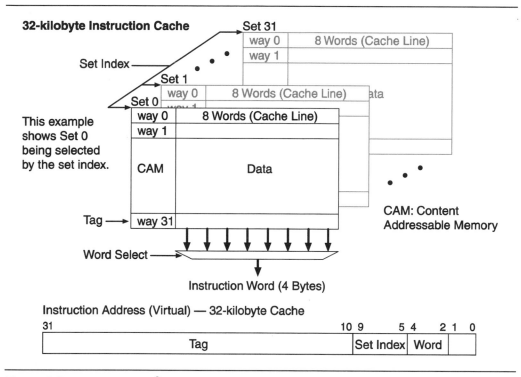

Figure 2.5   Intel XScale® Core 32-Kilobyte Instruction Cache

When the cache is enabled, it compares every instruction request address against the addresses of instructions that it is currently holding. If the cache contains the requested instruction, the access "hits" the cache, and the cache returns the requested instruction. If the cache does not contain the requested instruction, the access "misses" the cache. The cache requests an eight-word, also known as a line, fetch from external memory that contains the requested instruction. As the fetch returns instructions to the cache, the instructions are placed in one of two fetch buffers and the requested instruction is delivered to the instruction decoder within the Intel XScale core.

Locking Instruction Cache Entries

It is unlikely that your entire application will fit into the core instruction cache. As a result, the cache contents are updated continuously to keep it populated with the most recently used code. As a system designer, you might know of code segments that are critical to the performance of your application. The Intel XScale core allows you to lock specific code segments into the instruction cache.

Up to 28 (of the 32) ways in each set can be locked. Hardware ignores the lock command if software is trying to lock all the lines in a particular set. Ways 29 to 32 never can be locked. When you request all of the ways in a particular set to be locked, the instruction cache line is still allocated into the cache but the lock is ignored. The round-robin pointer stays at way 32 for that set. Cache lines can be locked into the instruction cache by initiating a write to co-processor 15. To lock down the code, you must ensure it meets these requirements:

■ The routine used to lock lines down in the cache must be placed in non-cacheable memory, which means the MMU is enabled. As a result, no fetches of cacheable code should occur while locking instructions into the cache.

■ The code being locked into the cache must be cacheable.

■ The instruction cache must be enabled and invalidated prior to locking down the lines.

Failure to follow these requirements will produce unpredictable results when accessing the instruction cache. The following code segment shows how a routine, called "lockMe," can be locked into the instruction cache.

Instruction Cache Locking

```
1       lockMe: ; This is the code that will be locked
2               ; into the instruction cache
3       mov r0, #5
4       add r5, r1, r2
5       . . .
6       lockMeEnd:
7
8       ; System programmers should ensure that the code to
9       ; lock instructions into the cache does not reside
10      ; closer than 128 bytes to a non-cacheable/cacheable page
11      ; boundary. If the processor fetches ahead
12      ; into a cacheable page, then the requirement to keep
```

```
13       ; the locking routine in non cacheable memory
14       ; would be violated.
15
16       codeLock: ; here is the code to lock the "lockMe" routine
17       ldr r0, =(lockMe AND NOT 31)   ; r0 gets a pointer to the
18                                      ; first line we should lock
19       ldr r1, =(lockMeEnd AND NOT 31); r1 contains a pointer
20                                      ; to the last line we
21                                      ; should lock
22       lockLoop:
23       mcr p15, 0, r0, c9, c1, 0   ; lock next line of code
24                                   ; into ICache
25       cmp r0, r1                  ; are we done yet?
26       add r0, r0, #32             ; advance pointer to
27                                   ; next line
28       bne lockLoop                ; if not done,
29                                   ; do the next line
```

Data Cache

The Intel XScale core data cache enhances performance by reducing the number of data accesses to and from external memory. The two data cache structures in the core are a 32-kilobyte data cache and a 2-kilobyte mini-data cache. An 8-entry write buffer and a 4-entry fill buffer are also implemented to decouple the core instruction execution from external memory accesses, which increases overall system performance.

The data cache is a 32-kilobyte, 32-way set, associative cache. The 32-kilobytes cache has 32 sets. Hennessy and Patterson (2003) give details on processor cache (ways and sets) architectures. Each set contains 32 ways. Each way of a set contains 32 bytes (one cache line) and one valid bit. Every line also has two dirty bits, one for the lower 16 bytes and the other one for the upper 16 bytes. When a store hits the cache, the dirty bit associated with it is set. The replacement policy is a round-robin algorithm. Keep this in mind when you are tuning or selecting algorithms for performance. The cache supports the ability to reconfigure portions of the data cache as randomly accessible memory (RAM). When it is configured as such, data can be managed directly by the Intel XScale core software as it no longer functions as a cache. Figure 2.6 shows the cache organization and how the data address is used to access the cache. Cache policies can be adjusted for particular regions of memory by altering page attribute bits in the MMU descriptor that controls that memory.

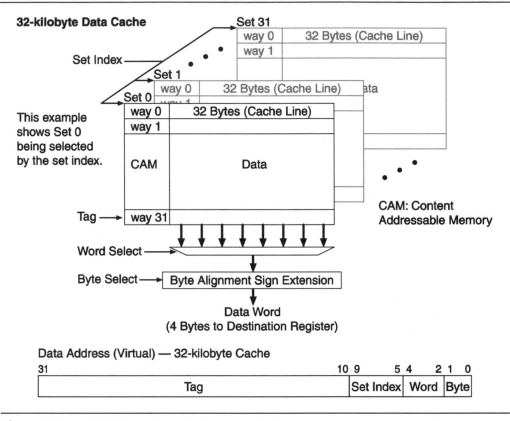

Figure 2.6   32-Kilobyte Data Cache Organization

The data cache is virtually addressed and virtually tagged. As a result, all cache operations under program control must specify a virtual address. The data cache supports write-back and write-through caching policies. The data cache always allocates a line in the cache when a cacheable read miss occurs and allocates a line into the cache on a cacheable write miss when write allocate is specified by its page attribute. Page attribute bits also determine whether a line is allocated into the data cache or mini-data cache.

The size of the mini-data cache is two kilobytes. The 2-kilobyte mini data cache has 32 sets and is two-way set associative. Each way of a set contains 32 bytes (one cache line) and one valid bit. Every line also has two dirty bits, one for the lower 16 bytes and the other one for the upper 16 bytes. When a store hits the cache, the dirty bit associated with it is set. The replacement policy is a round-robin algorithm.

Data Cache Operation

When the data/mini-data cache is enabled for an access, the data/mini-data cache compares the address of the request against the addresses of data that it is currently holding. If the line containing the address of the request is resident in the cache, the access "hits" the cache. As the cache memory is much faster than external memory, the access that hits the cache has much lower latency than an access that misses the cache. For a load memory operation, the cache returns the requested data to the destination register and, for a store operation, the data is stored into the cache. The data associated with the store may also be written to external memory if write-through caching is specified for that area of memory. If the cache does not contain the requested data, the access "misses" the cache, and the sequence of events that follows depends on the configuration of the cache, the configuration of the MMU, and the page attributes.

Cacheability

Data at a specified address is cacheable given the following conditions:

■ The MMU is enabled.

■ The cacheable attribute (C) bit is set in the descriptor in the MMU table for the accessed address.

■ The data and/or mini-data cache is enabled.

The following sequence of events occurs when a cacheable load operation misses the cache:

■ A 32-byte (cache line) external memory read request is made.

■ A line is allocated in the cache to receive the 32 bytes of data. A round-robin pointer determines the line selected. The line chosen might contain a valid line previously allocated in the cache. In this case, both dirty bits are examined, and if set, the dirty data is written back to external memory as 16-byte burst operations.

■ When the data requested by the load is returned from external memory, it is immediately sent to the destination register specified by the load.

■ As data returns from external memory, it is written into the cache in the previously allocated line.

A load operation that misses the cache and is not cacheable makes a request from external memory for the exact data size of the original load request.

The Intel XScale core supports write-back caching or write-through caching, controlled through the MMU page attributes. When write-through caching is specified, all store operations are written to external memory even if the access hits the cache. This feature keeps the external memory coherent with the cache; that is, no dirty bits are set for this region of memory in the data/mini-data cache. However, write-through does not guarantee that the data/mini-data cache is coherent with external memory, which is dependent on the system level configuration; specifically, if another master such as an NPE updates the external memory, the cache is not directly aware of the event, and thus coherence is lost. When write-back caching is specified, a store operation that hits the cache does not generate a write to external memory, thus reducing external memory traffic.

Intel XScale Core Write Buffer

The Intel XScale core employs an 8-entry write buffer, each entry containing up to 16 bytes. The write buffer performs two separate functions. It helps to prevent the core from stalling. It does this by allowing the core to write to the buffer and then continue executing instructions. In addition, it reduces the overall memory bus traffic by coalescing multiple single word writes to memory to a burst write operation, which is more efficient.

Stores to external memory are first placed in the write buffer and subsequently taken out when the bus is available. The write buffer supports the coalescing of multiple store requests to external memory. An outgoing store can coalesce with any of the eight entries.

When the Intel XScale core writes to memory, make sure external memory is up to date (consistent) before an external device accesses it. You may need to explicitly drain the write buffer. The Intel XScale core co-processor 15 provides instructions to drain the write buffer.

Branch Target Buffer

The branch target buffer (BTB) stores the history of branches that have executed along with their targets. The Intel XScale core uses this information to start fetching instructions at the branch target address earlier than it would if branch prediction were not enabled.

The Intel XScale core uses dynamic branch prediction to reduce the penalties associated with changing the flow of program execution. The core features a BTB that provides the instruction cache with the target address of branch type instructions. The BTB is implemented as a 128-entry, direct-mapped cache. The BTB is always disabled on reset. Software can enable the BTB through the BTB enable (Z) bit in the co-processor 15's register zero. In general, enabling the BTB improves the performance of the software.

Intel XScale Core Configuration

Registers within the co-processors (CP) in the Intel XScale core control its configuration. Co-processors are mechanisms defined by the ARM architecture to extend the capabilities of the core. The co-processors are assigned numbers from zero to fifteen. The Intel XScale core in the IXP4XX product line contains the following co-processors:

- System control co-processor (co-processor 15)
- Performance monitor and debug unit co-processor (co-processor 14)
- MACC co-processor (co-processor 0)

The system control co-processor (co-processor 15) configures the endianness, MMU, caches, branch target buffer enable, alignment exception, write buffer coalescing, and other system attributes. Where possible, the definition of co-processor 15 follows the definition of the ARM products. The MRC (move to ARM register from co-processor) and MCR (move to co-processor from ARM register) co-processor instructions provide access to the co-processors. Any access to co-processor 15 in user mode or with LDC (load co-processor) or STC (store co-processor) co-processor instructions causes an undefined instruction exception.

Each co-processor contains a number of registers. Co-processor registers are uniquely addressed by the register number and an additional parameter supplied in the instruction known as opcode_2. The syntax for the MRC and MCR instructions is as follows:

```
MCR    <coproc>,<opcode_1>,<Rd>,<CRn>,<CRm>,{<opcode_2> }

MRC    <coproc>,<opcode_1>,<Rd>,<CRn>,<CRm>,{<opcode_2> }
```

`<coproc>`	The name of the co-processor. The convention is to use p0 to p15.
`<opcode_1>`	A co-processor specific parameter
`<Rd>`	The source or destination ARM register
`<CRn>`	The co-processor register
`<CRm>`	Additional co-processor register
`<opcode_2>`	A co-processor specific parameter

Table 2.6 shows the CP15 registers and the example instructions that access each co-processor register. Details of these registers are in the appropriate developer manual listed in "References." The table is provided to illustrate the range of controls available in CP15.

Table 2.6   Intel XScale Core CP15 Registers

Register	Opcode_2	Access	Description	Example Instruction
0	0	Read/ Write ignored	Chip ID	mrc p15, 0, r0, c0, c0,0
0	1	Read/ Write ignored	Cache type	mrc p15, 0, r0, c0, c0,1
1	0	Read/Write	Control register	mcr p15, 0, r1, c1, c0,0
1	1	Read/Write	Auxiliary control	mcr p15, 0, r1, c1, c0,1
2	0	Read/Write	Translation table base	mrc p15, 0, r0, c0, c0,0
3	0	Read/Write	Domain access control	mrc p15, 0, r0, c0, c0,0
4	0	Unpredictable	Reserved	mrc p15, 0, r0, c4, c0,0
5	0	Read/Write	Fault status	mrc p15, 0, r0, c5, c0,0
6	0	Read/Write	Fault address	mrc p15, 0, r0, c6, c0,0

(continued)

Table 2.6   Intel XScale Core CP15 Registers *(continued)*

Register	Opcode_2	Access	Description	Example Instruction
7	0	Read-unpredictable / Write	Cache operations	Drain write buffer mcr p15, 0, r0, c7, c10, 4 Invalidate Data Cache line mcr p15, 0, r0, c7, c6, 1
8	0	Read-unpredictable / Write	TLB operations	Invalidate instruction and data TLB mcr p15, 0, r1, c8, c7,0 Invalidate data TLB entry mcr p15, 0,r0, c8, c6,1
9	0	Read/Write	Cache lock down	Fetch and Lock Instruction cache line mcr p15, 0,r0, c9, c1, 0
10	0	Read-unpredictable / Write	TLB lock down	Translate and Lock Instuction TLB entry mcr p15, 0, r0, c10, c4, 0
11–12	0	Unpredictable	Reserved	
13	0	Read/Write	Process ID (PID)	mrc p15, 0, r0,c13,c0,0
14	0	Read/Write	Breakpoint registers	Access instruction Breakpoint control mrc p15,0, r0,c14,c8,0
15	0	Read/Write	Co-processor access control	mcr p15,0, r0, c15, c1,0

Multiply and Accumulate (MACC) Co-Processor

The Intel XScale core adds a DSP co-processor to increase the performance and precision of multimedia (audio and video) processing algorithms. The Intel IXP400 DSP software makes extensive use of the MACC co-processor to provide VoIP CODECs, echo cancellers, tone detection, and tone generation.

The co-processor performs multiply and accumulate operations. It contains a 40-bit accumulator and provides eight new co-processor instructions.

Several new instructions that were added to the architecture reference the 40-bit accumulator. MIA and MIAPH are multiply and accumulate instructions that reference the MACC 40-bit accumulator. MAR and MRA provide the ability to read directly and write the 40-bit accumulator within the MACC.

If multiple operating system processes are sharing the MACC, you must save the state and restore it on each operating system context switch.

Performance Monitoring Unit

The Intel XScale core provides a performance-monitoring unit (PMU). You can get detailed performance information about your application by making effective use of the PMU. It provides four 32-bit performance counters that allow four unique events to be monitored simultaneously. The PMU also implements a 32-bit core clock counter that can be used in conjunction with the performance counters; their main purpose is to count the number of core clock cycles, which is useful in measuring total execution time.

The counters can monitor either occurrence events or duration events. When counting occurrence events, a counter is incremented each time a specified event takes place. When measuring duration, a counter counts the number of processor clocks that occur while a specified condition is true. If any of the five counters overflow and interrupts are enabled, an interrupt request occurs. Each counter has its own interrupt request enabled. The counters continue to monitor events even after an overflow occurs, until disabled by software.

A full list of performance monitor events is available in the appropriate developer manual listed in "References." Table 2.7 shows some useful combinations to establish the efficiency of caches and TLBs.

Table 2.7   Common PMU Measurements

Mode	Event Select Counter 1	Event Select Counter 2
Instruction cache efficiency	Instruction count	Instruction cachemiss
Data cache efficiency	Data cache access	Data cache miss
Instruction fetch latency	Instruction cache cannot deliver instruction (cycle count during an Instruction cache miss or TLB miss)	Instruction cache miss
Stall/write back statistics	Data stall	Data Cache write back
Instruction TLB efficiency	Instruction count	I-TLB miss
Data TLB efficiency	Data Cache access	Data TLB miss

Note: The average core cycles per instruction (CPI) can be derived by dividing the core clock counter by the instruction count, where the core clock counter was used to measure total execution time of the test.

The efficiency of the cache or TLB for your application is obtained by dividing event counter 2 by event counter 1. For example, the instruction cache efficiency is calculated by dividing the instruction cache miss by the instruction count.

Bus Architecture

The IXP4XX product line uses a bus system called the Advanced Microcontroller Bus Architecture (AMBA) defined by ARM. A bus connects a number of devices. A bus master can initiate read or write transactions on the bus. A target can respond only to read or write requests.

AMBA defines a multilevel busing system, with a system bus and a lower-level peripheral bus. The IXP4XX network processor uses the AMBA high-speed bus (AHB) and the advanced peripheral bus (APB). See Figure 2.1 for a graphical representation of the internal buses.

The IXP4XX network processors contain two AHB buses and one APB. Bridges connect the three buses. The use of two AHB buses allows the processor to achieve better utilization of memory. In addition, instruction and data fetches from the Intel XScale core can be isolated to some extent from packet data traffic traveling between the NPEs and DRAM.

The AHB supports split transactions, which means a bus target can decide to split the transaction into request and reply phases allowing other bus masters to use the bus between these phases. This feature gives a higher bandwidth but usually means higher latency than a bus held for a full transaction. Hennessy and Patterson (2003) give more details on processor bus architectures. Bus masters must support split transactions but targets do not have to support them.

The NPEs can master a 133-megahertz, 32-bit AHB, named the North-AHB. The targets of this bus can be the DRAM controller or the AHB/AHB bridge.

The AHB/AHB bridge allows the NPEs to access the peripherals and internal targets on the South-AHB. Data transfers by the NPEs to the South-AHB are targeted predominately at the queue manager.

Most of the traffic on the North-AHB is packet data targeted to the DRAM controller. Descriptors and pointers to this data are then sent to the core via the queue manager.

The South-AHB is a 133-megahertz, 32-bit bus, which can be mastered by the Intel XScale core, PCI controller DMA engines, USB host controller, AHB/AHB bridge, and the AHB/APB bridge DMA engines. The targets of this AHB can be the DRAM, PCI interface, queue manager, or the APB/AHB bridge.

The APB/AHB bridge allows access to peripherals attached to the APB.

The APB is a 66-megahertz, 32-bit bus that can be mastered by the AHB/APB bridge only. The targets of the APB can be the two UART interfaces, USB v1.1 device interface, all NPEs, the bus PMU, interrupt controller, general-purpose input/output (GPIO), and timers. The APB interface to the NPEs is used for code download and configuration.

Many of the AHB slaves support split transactions. However, the DRAM controllers do not. On the IXP42X network processors, the SDRAM controller supports two AHB interfaces. On the IXP45X and IXP46X network processors, the DDR controller supports three AHB interfaces, one for each AHB bus and one private interface for the core. Provisioning more than one AHB interface on the DRAM controllers means subsequent read accesses from other buses/interfaces can be initiated while a previous read completes, thereby reducing the gaps in the pipeline, effectively utilizing the DRAM bandwidth.

The IXP45X and IXP46X product lines incorporate a memory port interface (MPI) bus, a dedicated interface between the Intel XScale core, and the DDR1 DRAM. This interface is a 133-megahertz, 64-bit bus that is mastered by the Intel XScale core only. The only target of this interface is the DDR1 DRAM controller. The MPI supports multiple outstanding queues, split, and posted transactions. It improves Intel XScale core memory performance.

Typical Packet Transfer Scenarios

To help you put this chapter in context, look at the following packet transfer scenarios. The scenarios show the interaction of the main components of the system at a high level but do not detail cache interactions. You can find more detailed information on these components in Chapter 9.

Receive a Packet on a UTOPIA Interface and Forward to Ethernet

This scenario, shown in Figure 2.7, would occur in a product that contains a wide area network (WAN) interface, such as ADSL, and a local area network (LAN) interface, such as Ethernet.

1. A packet arrives from the Internet in the form of ATM cells on the UTOPIA interface. The NPE typically performs the low-level processing, examining the layer-2 ATM header and AAL5 trailer. It calculates and verifies checksums to determine whether the data should be accepted or dropped.

2. If it is acceptable, the NPE stores the packet in DRAM. In this scenario, the data is in the form of ATM cells carrying AAL5 packets. The NPE reassembles the packet in DRAM then checks the AAL5 trailer.

3. The NPE then puts a descriptor containing a pointer to the packet data in a queue on the queue manager.

4. Software on the Intel XScale core discovers the packet in the queue. It might have received an interrupt to indicate a non-empty queue or polled the queue.

5. The Intel IXP400 software running on the core manages the low-level handling of the descriptors on the queue manager. It calls a callback function typically in a device driver passing a packet descriptor to it.

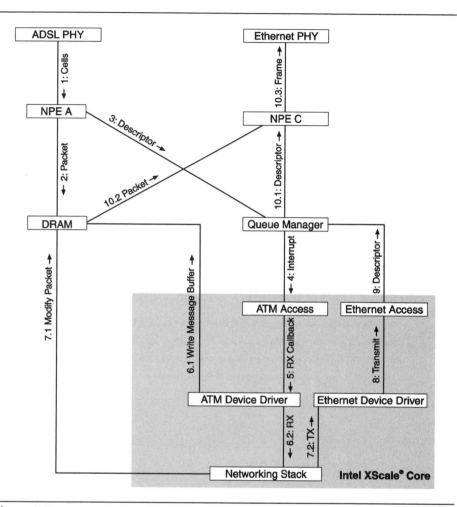

Figure 2.7 Receive UTOPIA Transmit on Ethernet

6. The device driver converts the packet into the appropriate message buffer format and writes it to DRAM. It then passes the packet into a networking stack running on the Intel XScale core.

7. The networking stack then examines the packet and decides to either consume the packet in the device or modify the packet removing encapsulation (7.1) and forward the packet for transmission to another interface (7.2).

8. The packet arrives in the Ethernet device driver for transmission to the LAN.

9. The Ethernet device driver passes the packet to the Ethernet transmit function in Intel IXP400 software, which puts a descriptor containing a pointer to the packet data into a queue.

10. The Ethernet NPE picks up the descriptor in the queue. It then reads the packet data from DRAM and pushes it into the Ethernet MAC. While transmitting the packet the Ethernet NPE can, if required, modify the packet to insert a virtual LAN (VLAN) header.

Receive Wireless, Encrypt then Transmit Ethernet

The scenario shown in Figure 2.8 might occur when the product you are designing receives wireless LAN traffic from a wireless card connected to the IXP4XX network processor through the PCI interface, encrypts the traffic using IPSec, and transmits it over an Ethernet WAN uplink.

1. The wireless card transfers the received frame over the PCI into DRAM (1.1). When it has transferred a certain number of frames, it generates an interrupt (1.2).

2. The wireless device driver running on the core handles the interrupt and reads a ring of descriptors from the wireless device (2.1). Each descriptor represents a buffered packet and contains a pointer to the packet data. The device driver converts each frame from 802.11 format and passes it into the networking stack running on the core (2.2).

3. The networking stack or application decides the packet needs encryption. It calls the IPSec/crypto stack (3.1), which then calls Intel IXP400 software to send the packet for encryption (3.2).

4. Intel IXP400 software sends a descriptor for the packet to a queue.

5. The NPE reads the descriptor from the queue (5.1) and then reads the packet from DRAM (5.2). It generates and stores the encrypted packet in another DRAM location (5.3) and generates a signature for the packet. It then sends a message to a queue to notify Intel IXP400 software on the core when the packet encryption is complete (5.4).

6. Intel IXP400 software calls the IPSec/crypto stack to inform it the packet encryption has completed.

7. The application or networking stack decides to forward the packet for transmission on another interface.

8. The packet arrives in the Ethernet device driver for transmission to the WAN.

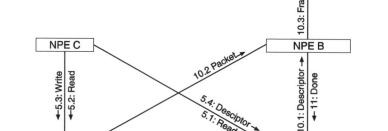
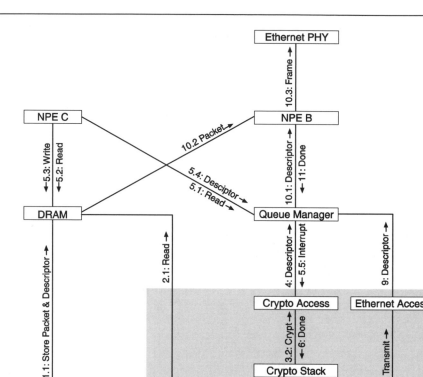

Figure 2.8   Receiving Wireless, Encryption then Ethernet Transmission

9. The Ethernet device driver passes the packet to the Ethernet transmit function in Intel IXP400 software, which puts a descriptor containing a pointer to the packet data into a queue.

10. The Ethernet NPE picks up the descriptor in the queue (10.1). It then reads the packet data from DRAM (10.2) and pushes it into the Ethernet MAC (10.3).

11. The NPE then returns the descriptor to a queue for packets whose transmission has completed. These descriptors then can be recycled by higher-level software.

Chapter **3**

Systems and Platform Design

This chapter describes the Intel® IXP4XX Network Processors in the context of overall system and platform design. The chapter concentrates on the specifics that are common across all application designs.

The chapter is primarily intended for system architects and software designers. It covers the different interfaces and the associated board-level components that accompany the IXP4XX network processor-based platforms.

Intel IXP4XX Network Processor Development and Reference Platforms

Many development and reference platforms incorporating the IXP4XX network processor are commercially available, some from Intel and others from independent hardware vendors (IHVs). Each platform is developed with a specific purpose in mind. The development boards that Intel produces are typically intended to show customers how to use the devices, facilitate evaluation of the product by making all interfaces available in an accessible form, and serve as a platform they can use to develop their application prior to having their own proprietary board available. This type of development platform is general purpose and not likely to be the form factor (board size) that you are designing. Intel produces two general-purpose reference platforms to demonstrate the IXP4XX product line.

- *Intel IXDP425 development platform*—supports IXP42X network processors

- *IXDP465 development platform*—supports the IXP45X and IXP46X network processors

Figure 3.1 shows a photograph of an Intel IXDP465 development platform.

Figure 3.1   IXDP465 Development Platform

Numerous platforms based on the IXP42X network processor are developed by IHVs. These platforms, called "reference designs," are typically focused on a specific market segment. They have a small form factor and only the interfaces required by the target application. Some examples of such reference designs are:

■ *Coyote Gateway Reference Design by ADI Engineering.* This reference design provides everything needed to develop an ADSL wireless residential gateway with voice support. The platform provides two voice lines, ADSL PHY, a 4-port Ethernet switch, one Ethernet WAN link, and two mini-PCI slots. In addition, ADI Engineering has developed the *Pronghorn Intel IXP425 802.11 OEM Application Platform*, the *Monte Jade IXDPG425 Reference Platform*, and the *Diamondback Intel IXP425 Network Security Appliance OEM Application Platform*.

■ *MERCURY Single Board Computer by Arcom Control Systems.* This platform is a PC/104 compatible single board computer based on the 533-megahertz Intel IXP425 network processor with the Intel XScale® core. It provides two 100-BaseT Ethernet ports, four USB 2.0 ports, a CompactFlash† connector and four serial ports. Its target market is industrial control applications.

■ *Avila Network Platform by Gateworks Corporation.* This platform is designed for wired and wireless network routers, bridges, and access points. It provides up to four Type III Mini PCI slots, two 10/100 BaseT Ethernet ports, USB 2.0, a serial port, and a battery backed real-time clock.

■ *E2BRAIN EB425 from KONTRON Modular Computers.* This platform includes four asynchronous serial interfaces, two synchronous serial interfaces, two 10/100-BaseT Ethernet ports, Controller Area Network (CAN) Interface, a real-time clock, and an ATM UTOPIA connector. The platform is targeted at embedded applications.

If you are using a third-party reference platform to develop your software, you should select an IXP4XX network processor platform that closely matches your needs to reduce the overall effort in migrating software to your own system once it becomes available.

Anatomy of the IXDP465 Development Platform

Although the IXDP425 and IXDP465 development platforms are very similar, we have chosen to limit our description to the IXDP465. The IXDP465 development platform is designed to be modular. As a result, the platform supports all variants of the IXP45X and IXP46X network processors and allows you to rapidly develop your own interface modules and products. The platform consists of three types of module or board:

■ *Processor module.* The processor module contains an IXP465 network processor. This processor contains a superset of all of the features in the IXP45X and IXP46X product lines. It contains all the available interfaces and operates at the highest speed of 677 megahertz. The module contains 128 megabytes of DDR Type 1 DRAM memory.

■ *Base board.* The base board provides standard connectors for all interfaces on the IXP4XX network processor, a place to plug in all the appropriate modules, and nonvolatile storage for the platform. The nonvolatile storage consists of 16 megabytes of flash memory and a 512-byte serial EEPROM that is accessed via the inter-integrated circuit (I^2C) bus. An FPGA is used to act as a virtual set of jumpers between the various I/O signals on the board and the associated GPIO pins. You should not require this FPGA in your design.

■ *Interface modules.* Although some of the IXP4XX network processor interfaces are directly accessible on the base board (universal serial bus [USB] and universal asynchronous receiver-transmitter [UART]), others are supported via the interface modules. Four module types are available: Ethernet PHY, ADSL, voice POTS module, and T1/E1 framer module.

Figure 3.2 is a diagram of the IXDP465 development platform.

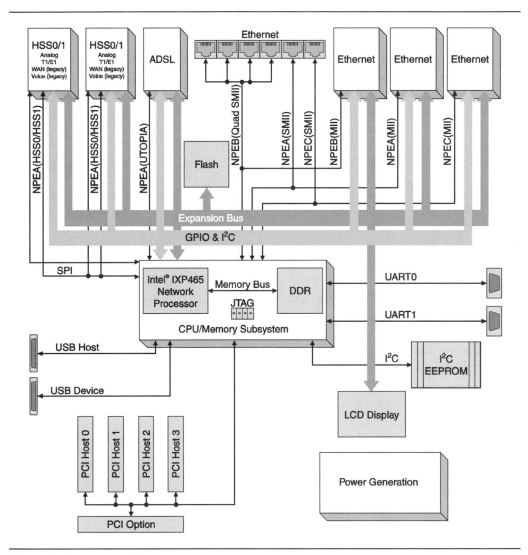

Figure 3.2   IXDP465 Development Platform Diagram

Core Interfaces

The following section covers the processor's core interfaces. The Intel XScale core requires these interfaces to boot up and start executing code.

DRAM Memory

To perform any useful work, all processors need memory. During processor development, Intel must project what the commodity memory technology will be during the lifetime of the network processors. With that in mind and the fact the IXP42X network processor and the IXP45X and IXP46X network processors were released several years apart, it should not surprise you that each part supports a different memory technology. The IXP42X product line supports a technology known as SDRAM, specifically PC 133 SDRAM. It can support from 8 megabytes to 256 megabytes. The IXP45X and IXP46X network processors are more recent, and they support DDR memory. The DDR Type 1 SDRAM operates at 266 megahertz and supports ECC. The DDR controller supports a memory footprint from 32 megabytes all the way up to 1 gigabyte.

Even though the clock frequency of DDR memory technology has doubled from its predecessor, a system using DDR memory technology may not double in performance. Although the memory throughput is improved significantly, the latency to memory has improved by about 10 percent.

The use of DDR memory gives an increase of approximately 10 percent performance. This performance improvement is directly related to the reduction in latency to memory.

In addition to supporting a particular memory technology and size, the memory controllers on embedded devices have to define how that memory can be arranged. Each controller supports different configurations of memory. Table 3.1 shows some configurations supported by the IXP465 network processor.

Table 3.1   Example Memory Configurations for the Intel® IXP465 Network Processor

Total Memory	128MBit Device	256MBit Device	512MBit Device	1024MBit Device
32Mbytes	2 chips 8Mx16			
64Mbytes	4 chips 16Mx8			
128Mbytes	8 chips 16Mx8	4 chips 32Mx8	2 chips 32Mx16	
256Mbytes		8 chips 32Mx8	4 chips 32Mx16	2 chips 64Mx16
512Mbytes			8 chips 64Mx8	4 chips 128Mx8
1024Mbytes				8 chips 128Mx8

The decision as to which memory to populate is usually a tradeoff between the higher price of high-density memory parts and the amount of space you have available on the board. When you are designing a system where performance is critical, you must go to the next level of analysis, as there are differences in the page size and number of open pages supported by the different configurations.

The memory controller is configured by the boot code prior to accessing the DRAM. The IXP45X and IXP46X network processors support error-correcting code (ECC) memory. This memory type can automatically fix single-bit errors and identify two-bit errors in the memory array. If you have ECC-enabled memory, it must be *scrubbed* before your program or operating system uses it. Scrubbing is a process where the boot loader writes a known value into all of the memory. This process allows the controller to set the ECC protection bits to the correct value for each memory location. If you read a memory location before it has been scrubbed, you are likely to get an ECC error indication. The memory controller initialization and scrubbing is typically done from startup code running in your nonvolatile storage.

Flash Memories

All embedded processor platforms need some form of nonvolatile storage to allow the processor to boot. Flash memory is typically used for this purpose because it can be erased and re-written under program control. Once the Intel XScale core is reset, it begins fetching instructions from memory address zero. The internal decode logic of the chip decodes these instruction fetches to access chip select 0. Nonvolatile storage must be connected to this chip select for the platform to boot.

Flash memory contains the boot code for the processor. Each operating system has its own boot code. RedBoot[†] is used to boot Linux, Eboot to boot Windows[†] CE, and VxWorks[†] bootrom to boot VxWorks. In addition to the boot code, flash memory typically contains the operating system, some memory for a flash file system, and storage of platform information such as the MAC address for Ethernet interfaces. The traditional boot-up mechanism is as follows: the boot loader initializes the memory and chip selects, copies the kernel image from flash to DRAM, and then transfers control from the boot loader to the kernel. Flash memory is considerably slower than DRAM and, as a result, the performance of the kernel is much higher when executed from DRAM. In some embedded systems, the kernel images are executed directly in flash, known as *execute in place.*

Although the platform could support execute in place, this model is not supported in Intel boot loaders/BSPs because the flash interface is considered too slow for this purpose. In addition to loading kernel images from flash memory, kernel images can also be downloaded from a server via the Ethernet interface. You would use this configuration during development as it allows you to test your code without the time-consuming process of programming the flash memory each time you need to run a different image. Figure 3.3 shows the flash memory map used on a RedBoot-based platform.

The IXP4XX product line supports multiple configurations of flash memory. All our reference designs ship with Intel StrataFlash® memory. The drivers to read and write from this memory are provided within each of the boot loaders and BSPs.

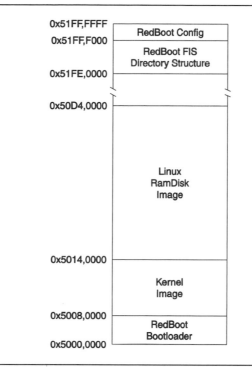

Figure 3.3   Example Memory Map for RedBoot and Linux System

The IXP4XX product line supports operation of the flash memory in 8-bit, 16-bit, and 32-bit modes. That is, the flash memory connects 8, 16, or 32 data bits to the expansion bus controller. The IXP42X network processors support a maximum of 16 megabytes of flash memory in 8-bit or 16-bit mode on each chip select. With the addition of 32-bit mode per chip select on the IXP45X and IXP46X network processors, 32 megabytes of flash memory are supported. You can also use additional chip selects to decode additional flash memory, if required. You should use chip select 1, chip select 2, and so on for any additional memory; otherwise, the flash memory will not be contiguous in the memory map and will be more difficult to use and partition in the BSPs.

Because the IXP4XX network processors support 8-bit, 16-bit, and 32-bit flash modes, some mechanism is needed to configure the internal chip select block to indicate the attached flash configuration. This mechanism is provided by the devices configuration straps, which are described below.

The XScale core instruction width is 32 bits, and flash memory can be connected in 8-bit, 16-bit, or 32-bit modes The flash memory must be programmed in such a way that the core processor receives valid instructions. As an example, for 16-bit flash mode you must swap the bytes within each half-word (16 bits) before you program the flash device. Customers frequently ask us how we program the flash devices. We typically use a JTAG in-circuit emulator (ICE) debugger to program the devices, and a trick we have learned is to dump the flash memory in word mode (32 bits) using the ICE. If you see a 0x0E in the most significant byte of the word, you can be reasonably confident that the flash has been programmed with the correct byte ordering. The reason the values are typically 0x0E is that almost all ARM instructions start with that value.

Configuration Straps

A number of items must be configured on the IXP4XX network processors before they start executing. The expansion bus address lines are used to configure these options during processor initialization. At the deassertion of reset, logic in the chip reads the values on these pins to determine board configuration. Table 3.2 shows the different configuration options. You can find details on each option in the appropriate developer manual listed in "References."

Table 3.2   Expansion Bus Strapping Options

Expansion Bus Address	IXP42X	IXP45X and IXP46X	Description
bit 0	8/16_FLASH bit	8/16_FLASH bit	Specifies the data bus width of the flash memory device. For IXP45X and IXP46X the 32_FLASH bit overrides this setting.
bit 1	PCI_ HOST	PCI HOST	Configures the PCI controller as PCI bus host. 0 = PCI as non-host 1 = PCI as host
bit 2	PCI_ARB	PCI_ARB	Enables the PCI controller arbiter 0 = PCI arbiter disabled 1 = PCI arbiter enabled

(continued)

Table 3.2 Expansion Bus Strapping Options *(continued)*

Expansion Bus Address	IXP42X	IXP45X and IXP46X	Description
bit 3	Reserved	Reserved	
bit 4	PCI_CLK	PCI_CLK	Sets the clock speed of the PCI interface
			0 = 33 MHz
			1 = 66 MHz
bit 5	Unused	EXP_DRIVE	Expansion bus low/high drive strength
			0 = low drive
			1 = high drive
bit 6	Unused	EXP_ARB	Configures the expansion bus arbiter
			0 = External arbiter for expansion bus
			1 = Expansion bus controller arbiter enabled
bit 7	Unused	32_FLASH	1 = 32-bit data bus
			0 = 8/16 bit data bus based on 8/16_FLASH bit
bit 8	Unused	USB_HOST_CLOCK	Controls the USB clock select
			1 = USB host/device clock is generated internally
			0 = USB device clock is generated from GPIO pin zero and USB host clock is generated from GPIO pin one.
bit 9	Unused	EXP_MEM_DRIVE	1 = Expansion bus drive strength is determined by EXP_DRIVE (bit 5)
			0 = Expansion bus drive strength is medium drive. If EXP_MEM_DRIVE is set to 0, EXP_DRIVE bit must be 1.

(continued)

Table 3.2   Expansion Bus Strapping Options *(continued)*

Expansion Bus Address	IXP42X	IXP45X and IXP46X	Description
bit 10	Unused	IOWAIT_CS0	1 = EX_IOWAIT_N is sampled during the read/write expansion bus cycles.
			0 = EX_IOWAIT_N is ignored for read and write cycles to chip select 0 if EXP_TIMING_CS0 is configured to Intel mode.
bit 11-16	Reserved	Reserved	
bit 17-20	Customer Use	Customer Use	The values sampled on reset are available in a register. You can use this to provide platform information to the system software.
bit 21-23	Clock Speed	Clock Speed	You can use these straps to select the frequency that the core operates. Note: You can only request a speed equal or slower than the part's capabilities.
bit 24-30	MEM_MAP	MEM_MAP	Location of expansion bus in memory map space:
			0 = Located at "50000000" (normal mode)
			1 = Located at "00000000" (boot mode)

Clocks

The IXP4XX product line requires either a 33.33-megahertz or 33.00-megahertz reference clock. Logic within the chip uses this reference clock to generate all core and most internal peripheral clocks. This reference clock can be a crystal, oscillator, or PLL chip.

A clock running at twice the speed of the reference clock feeds all peripherals on the chip. As a result, the timers within the chip count at 66.66 megahertz or 66.00 megahertz. To ensure the timers are accurate, the code developed to control the on-chip timers needs to be aware of the reference clock provided to the device.

The PCI controller requires either a 33.00-megahertz or 66.00-megahertz clock which is also provided to the PCI bus. This clock is usually supplied by an external oscillator; however, if the bus speed is 33.00 megahertz, the clock may be generated by a GPIO pin.

The media-independent interface (MII), HSS, and UTOPIA interfaces all need to be supplied with the appropriate clocks on your board.

The IXP4XX network processor can optionally provide the expansion bus clock on GPIO pin 14.

Although some interfaces require similar frequency oscillators—for example, the expansion bus and PCI—separate inputs to the chip are provided for each to allow oscillator frequencies to be altered on each interface independently. The reference platforms provide a large number of jumpers that allow you to configure the source of clocks. For example, jumpers allow you to select the PCI clock as internal 33-megahertz, 33-megahertz oscillator, or 66-megahertz oscillator.

JTAG In-Circuit Emulator (ICE)

The processor also has a JTAG interface that is used to provide debug control to a JTAG in-circuit emulator (ICE) debugger. We strongly recommend that you supply a connector on your board to allow the connection of a JTAG ICE, such as ARM Multi-ICE, Macraigor Raven[†], EPI Majic[†], Wind River Systems visionPROBE[†]/visionICE[†] or other JTAG debuggers. The ICE allows you to program the flash and debug your programs. It is especially useful during the development of board initialization code. It provides complete visibility of the Intel XScale core registers and external memory.

General IXP4XX Network Processor Interfaces

The following section describes how each of the chip interfaces is used on the reference platforms.

Expansion Bus

The expansion bus is an extension of the internal memory bus. It allows you to connect devices with a memory interface to the IXP4XX network processors. Attached devices usually provide a set of registers to control their operation. When attached to the expansion bus, the devices are visible in the processor's memory map where your application can perform read and write memory operations to the registers within the attached device.

The IXP45X and IXP46X network processors provide eight chip selects, allowing you to have up to eight devices on the expansion bus without any additional logic to control the devices. The IXDP425 and IXDP465 development platforms include the following devices on the expansion bus:

■ Flash memory

■ ADSL module

■ High-speed serial (HSS) module

■ Hex or LCD display

■ Ethernet PHY module

The expansion bus is split into individual chip selects. Each chip select is memory mapped to the Intel XScale core. To access the devices attached to chip selects, you simply read or write the memory address. Each attached device has a specific number of data bits on its memory interface. In general, you should perform reads and writes that correspond to the width of the device. The IXP45X and IXP46X network processors also allow the expansion bus to be used by external bus masters. That is, you could connect an external device such as an ASIC, and it has the ability to access the DRAM memory attached to the network processor. Table 3.3 shows the specific assignment of chip selects used on the development platform.

Table 3.3   IXP45X and IXP46X Network Processor Platform Chip Selects and
Associated Addresses

Chip Select	Assignment	Address
CS0	Bootrom flash	0x5000,0000
CS1	ADSL/UTOPIA module	0x5200,0000
CS2	LCD display and GPIO mapping FPGA	0x5400,0000
CS3	HSS0/HSS1	0x5600,0000
CS4	MII-0 module	0x5800,0000
CS5	MII-1 module	0x5A00,0000
CS6	HSS1/HSS0	0x5C00,0000
CS7	MII-2 module	0x5E00,0000

Note: Each chip select is programmed to occupy 32 megabytes of address space. The default mode of IXP45X and IXP46X network processors is to operate in a backward compatible mode to the IXP42X network processors, in which each chip select occupies 16 megabytes of space.

The IXDP465 development platform provides a 16-digit LCD display on CS2. These LCDs are very useful for software debug during early development of BSPs and applications. They provide a very low-impact mechanism for indicating your program's progress. Output on the LCD is achieved simply by writing a value to a specific memory address.

The remaining chip selects are routed to the modules to provide accessibility to any memory-mapped registers on the modules.

You may have noticed that two devices are attached to CS2 (the LCD and an FPGA). To access each device, additional logic decodes address lines on the expansion bus to identify which device should be active.

GPIO

GPIOs are pins on the IXP4XX network processors that are under software control. They can be configured as inputs or outputs. When configured as an input, you can use changes in the pin state to trigger an interrupt to the processor core. Additionally, some are capable of generating clocks such as the expansion bus clock.

The GPIO pins are used for many purposes on the development platform. To facilitate numerous combinations of modules and applications an FPGA routes GPIO signals to I/O signals—any GPIO to any I/O—on the board. This routing eliminated the need for a large number of jumpers as was the case on the IXDP425 reference platform. Registers within the FPGA can be programmed to configure the GPIO to I/O associations. The FPGA is connected to CS2. It is unlikely that your design will require such an FPGA. It is more common to map the GPIO pins directly to the function required.

Universal Asynchronous Receiver Transmitter

The IXP4XX network processors provide two *universal asynchronous receiver-transmitter* (UART) interfaces. UART interfaces are usually connected to an RS232 serial port via a transceiver device. The serial port itself is usually a DB9 connector—the same connector that you can find on your PC. Both UARTs are identical in the features they provide. UART one is traditionally defined as the console port for BSPs and kernels. The feature list is as follows:

- All standard baud rates from 1,200 baud to 921,600 baud

- Parity—odd, even, and none

- Stop bit—1, 1½ , or 2

- Modem flow-control signals—clear to send (CTS) and request to send (RTS)

The register map and capabilities of the UARTs are almost identical to that provided by the de facto 16550 UART standard. Minor differences result from the fact that the IXP4XX network processor provides larger FIFOs than the de facto 16550 UART—increased from 16 bytes to 64 bytes. Intel provides serial drivers for each of the operating systems supported—Linux, VxWorks, and Windows CE.

These drivers support both software and hardware flow control. The CTS and RTS signals are automatically controlled by the UART when hardware flow control is in use. The drivers do not support the full array of modem control signals—such as data terminal ready, data set ready, ring indicator, and data carrier detect—in the UART. Use standard GPIO pins if such support is required.

You cannot connect the UART pins directly to a standard RS232 serial port, as the voltage levels are incompatible. The IXP4XX network processor reference designs connect via a MAXIM RS232 transceiver. The transceiver converts the RS232 differential +/- 12-volt signals into 3.3-volt signals for the UART. Even if you do not require an external serial port on your production system, we recommend that at a minimum you place the UART header (UART transmit, receive, and power) on your board. You can then build a simple transceiver board to provide serial access to your board without wasting real estate for a transceiver and connector on your production board. Serial access is very useful to facilitate debug of your platform. Figure 3.4 shows the connections between the network processor UART pins and an RS232 connector.

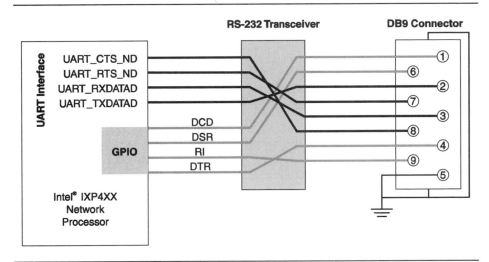

Figure 3.4   Full Modem RS232 Setup

The UARTs include a programmable baud rate generator that is clocked from an internally generated 14.7456-megahertz clock. The register values to set the baud rate are all derived from this input clock. This clock does not vary with processor speed.

Media-independent Interface

The media-independent interface (MII) is an interface between an Ethernet media access control (MAC) and the physical layer device (PHY). MII is defined in the 802.3[†] standard (IEEE 2002b). The MACs are internal to the IXP4XX network processors, and the PHYs are external to them and must be populated on your reference board.

The MACs provide two interfaces within the chip. The MAC control registers are memory mapped and the data path is via the NPEs. The IXP42X network processors have at most two internal MACs. On the IXP45X and IXP46X network processors, the number of MACs has been increased to six.

The IXP42X network processor supports the MII standard. In addition, Intel has introduced support for two reduced-pin count interfaces on the IXP45X and IXP46X network processors. These de facto standard interfaces are serial media independent interface (SMII) and source synchronous serial media independent interface (SS-SMII).

All variants of the MII interfaces can be logically separated into two parts. The first is the data path from MAC to PHY and the second is a PHY control interface to the PHY(s). The data path must be configured to match the PHY setup. For example, if the PHY mode is 100 megabits per second half duplex, the MAC MII interface must be configured to operate at 100 megabits per second and monitor the collision signals from the PHY. The control interface consists of a shared bus from the IXP4XX network processor to all attached Ethernet PHYs. The shared bus consists of two signals MDC and MDIO. Each PHY has a unique address on the control bus. Figure 3.5 shows the first of two configuration examples connecting the processor to Ethernet PHYs and an Ethernet switch.

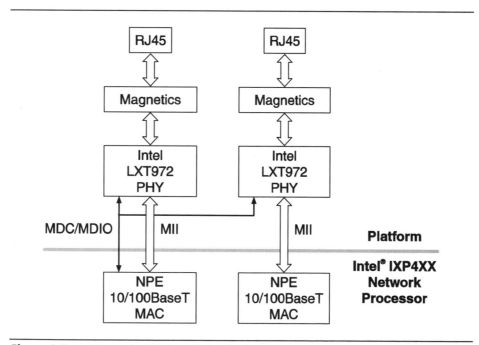

Figure 3.5   Example MAC to PHY Block Diagram

Figure 3.5 shows two separate PHYs to simplify the diagram. Intel also produces the LXT973 dual PHY, which is ideal for an application that requires both Ethernet ports. The LXT973 PHY provides a very useful feature known as MDI/MDIX. This mechanism auto detects whether the attached cable is a crossover or straight and configures the PHY to operate correctly. So no more searching the lab for the right kind of cable!

Next, Figure 3.6 shows a very common configuration used for residential gateways. One Ethernet port is connected to an ADSL or cable modem that connects to the Internet, and four local Ethernet ports are bridged together and form a local LAN.

Although not shown in the diagram, residential gateway platforms would usually contain one or more wireless (802.11a,b/g) cards connected via PCI. Traffic from the 4-port Ethernet switch is bridged in software through the network processor to the wireless interfaces.

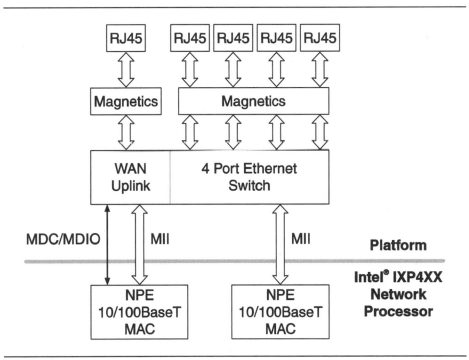

Figure 3.6   Example Residential Gateway Configuration

A couple of points about the configuration above have caused some trouble in the past. The first thing to note is that the configuration actually has five separate PHYs, each of which can be configured individually via the MDC/MDIO bus. Most Ethernet device drivers have a one-to-one relationship between the PHY and the MAC. So, to support the multiple PHYs attached to the device, the Ethernet device driver must be modified to support the concept of multiple PHYs per MAC. Second, we mentioned before that the configuration of the MII interface from the MAC should match that of the attached PHY. That is okay for the WAN uplink, but what about the MII interface connected to the switch? It needs to be configured to match the switch vendor's specifications, most likely 100-megabit full duplex.

One final note: this configuration shows an unmanaged switch. You can also use managed switches that provide proprietary VLAN header extensions that allow you to create special demilitarized zone (DMZ) ports on the switch. You can use a DMZ port to make a specific LAN Ethernet port on the managed switch accessible from the Internet, while protecting the other LAN ports.

UTOPIA

UTOPIA is an interface defined by The ATM Forum. It is designed to carry ATM cells between devices. The IXP4XX network processor conforms to the UTOPIA Level 2 Specification (The ATM Forum 1995). The bus consists of an 8-bit data bus, address lines, flow-control signals, and transmit and receive clocks. The bus can operate up to 33 megahertz.

The UTOPIA interface is incorporated within one of the NPEs. The NPE microcode and associated Intel XScale core software provide AAL5 (ATM adaptation layer 5) and AAL0 (raw ATM cell transmit/receive) interfaces. The NPE performs all segmentation and reassembly (SAR) functions for AAL5.

Customers primarily use the interface to connect the IXP4XX network processor to xDSL (ADSL, VDSL) PHYs. All DSL variants in use today use ATM to carry the data from the client locations to the central office. The IXDP425 and IXDP465 development platforms supply ADSL daughter cards to demonstrate the UTOPIA interface. Figure 3.7 shows different use cases of the UTOPIA interface.

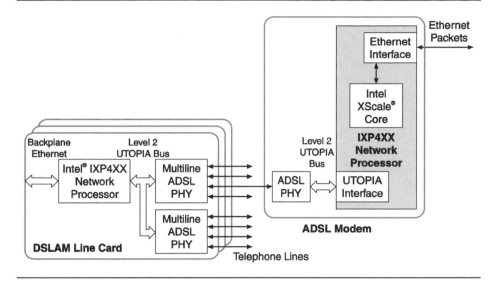

Figure 3.7   UTOPIA Interface Use Case Examples

The Level 2 specification includes a facility to address separate logical and physical devices on the UTOPIA bus. This facility allows you to attach multiple PHYs to the IXP4XX network processors when the UTOPIA interface is configured in Level 2 master mode. This capability is important in digital subscriber line access multiplexer (DSLAM) applications, as it allows the network processors to serve multiple PHYs. The UTOPIA interface may also be configured in single PHY mode where the IXP4XX network processor may be connected to a single UTOPIA master device.

You can also use the UTOPIA interface as a high-speed interface to proprietary FPGA or ASIC designs. The AAL0 API provides a mechanism to send and receive data directly on the UTOPIA interface.

High-Speed Serial

The high-speed serial (HSS) interfaces on IXP4XX network processors provide the capability to interface to time division multiplex (TDM) buses. The IXP4XX product line provides two HSS interfaces. They are electrically identical and designated as HSS 0 and HSS 1. Timeslots within each TDM bus may be configured to support either voice or HLDC frames.

Each HSS interface consists of six pins—transmit data, receive data, transmit frame pulse, receive frame pulse, transmit clock, and receive clock. The serial interfaces can operate at speeds from 512 kilohertz to 8.192 megahertz. The NPE microcode and associated Intel XScale core software control the capabilities of the HSS interface. The NPE microcode can provision such items as frame length, start of frame offset, signal polarity, and channel mappings. Specifically, you can configure the ports to support T1, E1, multi-vendor integration protocol (MVIP) and quad MVIP standards.

Although voice and data can be mapped within a single TDM stream, it is common to allocate a single HSS port for voice traffic coming from standard analog phones via a plain old telephone service (POTS) line. The HSS interface, being a digital Pulse Code Modulation (PCM) in nature, cannot connect directly to POTS lines. It requires the use of a subscriber line interface circuit (SLIC) and compressor/decompressor (CODEC). Intel development platforms use the combined SLIC/CODEC Si3210 by Silicon Laboratories. The SLIC/CODEC converts the voice samples to and from the phone to digital samples. It then interfaces to the TDM interface and writes/reads from the appropriate time slot within the TDM interface. Multiple SLIC/CODECs can be connected to the TDM bus as they transmit on the TDM bus only during the appropriate time slots. Figure 3.8 shows an example configuration using four SLIC/CODECs.

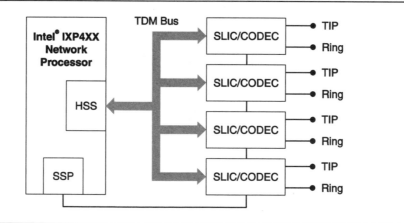

Figure 3.8   Logical Connections of SLIC/CODECs to IXP4XX Network Processor

The configuration above is quite common on an IXP4XX network processor-based VoIP platform. The NPE microcode and Intel XScale core software collect multiple samples—for example 10 milliseconds worth—per channel and place the samples in contiguous locations in DRAM. Voice CODECs process these samples—for example G.729a, available in the Intel IXP400 DSP software. These encoded samples are then processed by an RTP stack on the Intel XScale core, which generates VoIP packets for transmission on the Ethernet interfaces.

Timeslots within an HSS port can be provisioned to carry HDLC packet data. The NPE microcode supports one HDLC channel per E1/T1. A channel is defined as a contiguous set of time slots within a TDM stream. The maximum number of E1/T1s and, hence, channels is eight (two HSS Ports—each in MVIP mode). Each HSS port can be connected directly to up to four T1 or E1 framers (MVIP mode). A framer is a device that takes a sequence of bits that arrive on the line and recovers the receive clock and alignment of the frame. The framer passes the data over the TDM bus to the HSS port in a frame-aligned format, which is much easier to process.

PCI

The PCI interface is a very useful interface as it allows you to connect a large range of commercially available devices to the IXP4XX network processor. Its uses range from 802.11 wireless cards to video displays, PCMCIA controllers, audio cards, and proprietary ASICs. The interface complies with the PCI 2.2 standard. The IXP4XX network processor functions as a four-port PCI host or as a single PCI option. Host mode is the more common mode of operation. In host mode, PCI peripherals such as video controllers, wireless cards, and USB 2.0 host adaptors can be plugged into the PCI slot on the development platform. The IXP4XX network processor is the main CPU controller in this configuration.

The single-option mode is used when the IXP4XX network processor is slave to another master card. An example of this situation is when the IXP4XX network processor is placed on a PCI card for insertion into a standard PC.

Figure 3.9 shows the layout on the development platform.

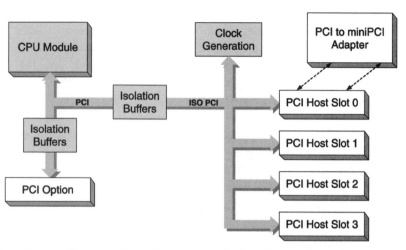

Note: You must have isolation buffers to support both host and option mode on the same platform. Your board may not need these buffers if you support only one mode.

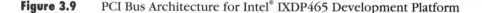

Figure 3.9   PCI Bus Architecture for Intel® IXDP465 Development Platform

Figure 3.9 shows the use of a PCI to mini-PCI adaptor. In applications such as wireless routers, the mini-PCI connector is typically mounted directly on the board. In some cases, the actual wireless chip sets are placed on the motherboard to reduce the costs of the board.

All PCI buses need an arbiter function. The IXP4XX network processors provide a 4-device arbiter function. The internal arbiter can be disabled and replaced with an external arbiter if support for additional devices is required.

PCI interrupts (INTA, INTB, INTC, INTD) should be connected to the GPIO pins. You should configure the GPIO pins to generate an interrupt when the interrupt line is active.

The IXP4XX network processors provide a memory-mapped window from the Intel XScale core to the PCI Memory space on the PCI bus. The addresses are mapped as four separate 16-megabyte windows, although the BSP typically maps the four separate regions as one 64-megabyte contiguous window. Similarly, the PCI devices have four 16-megabyte windows that provide visibility from PCI devices into the Intel XScale core memory space. The PCI to Intel XScale core windows are mapped to the bottom 64 megabytes of DRAM memory.

The PCI controller does not provide any Intel XScale core memory window translation to PCI I/O space. All PCI I/O space can be accessed via PCI controller registers on the IXP4XX network processor; APIs are provided in each BSP. Although PCI I/O memory typically is not used in modern devices, a large number of devices require access to PCI I/O space. Frequently, the drivers for these devices assume that PCI I/O space is available through a processor memory-mapped window. This assumption can cause issues when porting legacy drivers from other platforms that do provide PCI I/O space processor mapped window.

One final note: if you do not need to use the PCI interface, you should not access the PCI controller from your BSP at all. All access to the PCI controller will hang if you have not provided the PCI clock to the IXP4XX network processor.

Universal Serial Bus—Device

The IXP4XX network processors provide a USB device 1.1 interface (USB Implementers Forum 1998). USB is an asymmetric protocol with the endpoints designated as either host or device. The host controller is the master and is what you have in your PC. The device controllers are usually the peripherals connected to your PC, such as a camera or ADSL modem.

The USB signals on the wire are differential analog in nature, and therefore, you need some analog components between the USB bus and the IXP4XX network processor. You must also provide a USB cable presence indication via a GPIO pin.

The IXDP425 and IXDP465 development platforms provide a remote NDIS (RNDIS) target device driver for operation with a Windows-based PC. Windows XP already comes with an RNDIS host driver. The RNDIS drivers allow the USB port to act as a network interface to carry Ethernet packets.

The USB standard has a provision to power the devices attached to the bus. The development platforms consume far too much power to allow them to be powered directly by the USB bus, but a few customer designs are powered directly from the USB bus.

The USB device supports all the defined endpoint types—control, interrupt, bulk, and isochronous. It has 16 endpoints in total.

Universal Serial Bus—Host

In addition to USB device support, the IXP45X and IXP46X network processors introduce a USB host controller. A common approach is to provide an EHCI and OHCI controller. The OHCI operates with USB 1.1 devices, and the EHCI controller operates with USB 2.0 devices. The host-mode support on the IXP45X and IXP46X is a little confusing as there is a USB 2.0 EHCI controller on the device, but due to manufacturing considerations, the high-speed mode as defined in the USB 2.0 specification is not supported. So the USB host controller can operate at a maximum speed of 12 megabits per second. USB class drivers define the support for attached devices, such as hard drives, mouse, and keyboards. These drivers are supplied with the operating system. The IXDP465 development platform provides a standard host USB connector to demonstrate the use of the interface. At the time of writing, software support of the USB host function has not been released.

IEEE 1588 Time Synchronization

The IXP45X and IXP46X network processors have introduced a feature to assist in network time synchronization. In a distributed control system containing multiple clocks, the individual clocks tend to drift apart. Some kind of correction mechanism is necessary to synchronize the individual clocks to maintain the concept of global time, which is accurate to some requisite clock resolution on all nodes. For this purpose, you can use the IEEE 1588 standard (IEEE 2002a), which defines a precision clock synchronization protocol for networked measurement and control systems. The IEEE standard defines several messages that are used to exchange timing information. The hardware assist unit on the IXP45X and IXP46X network processors captures these messages and provides information to the Intel XScale core that is then used to maintain synchronization with the global time.

The IEEE 1588 hardware assist block actually monitors the Ethernet traffic on the MII (SMII) interfaces and, under software control, maintains a copy of the system time within the required resolution. The IXP400 software contains a device driver for this hardware block.

Synchronous Serial Port

The IXP45X and IXP46X network processors have introduced a synchronous serial port (SSP). The SSP is a full-duplex synchronous serial interface. It can be used to connect to a variety of external analog-to-digital (A/D) converters, audio and telecom CODECs, and many other devices that use serial protocols for transferring data. It supports National Microwire, Texas Instruments-defined synchronous serial protocol, and Motorola-defined serial peripheral interface (SPI) protocol.

I²C Inter-Integrated Circuit Port

The IXP45X and IXP46X network processors have introduced an inter-integrated circuit (I²C) bus controller. The I²C bus controller allows the IXP46X network processor to serve as a master and slave device residing on the I²C bus. The I²C bus is a serial bus developed by Phillips Corporation consisting of a 2-pin interface. Serial Data/Address (SDA) is the data pin for input and output functions, and Serial Clock Line (SCL) is the clock pin for reference and control of the I²C bus. On the IXP42X network processors, the I²C bus function is provided by software control of two GPIO pins.

Operating System Board Support Packages

Three primary operating systems are available for the Intel® IXP4XX network processors: Linux[†], VxWorks[†], and Windows[†] CE. Using the board support package (BSP) for one of these operating systems, you can adapt the necessary code sections for your specific hardware design. This chapter is not a complete description of the operating system or BSP, but it should guide you through the task of porting the BSP to your platform.

Platform-Specific Updates

To minimize the changes required to the BSP, you should base your design on the appropriate Intel development platform, the IXDP425 for IXP4XX network processor-based designs or the IXDP465 for IXP46X and IXP45X network processor-based designs. As the network processors provide a significant number of integrated peripherals, you should not have to make extensive changes to the board support package to accommodate changes in your platform. Customers usually need to change the following items:

- *General-purpose pin mappings*. The IXP4XX network processors provide 16 general-purpose input/output (GPIO) pins. GPIO pins are used for a wide range of functions, such as generating interrupts to the processor, detecting the state of a device, and providing visual indications on the platform.

∎ *PCI interface.* The PCI interface uses up to six GPIO pins. The pins provide PCI clock generation, PCI reset bus control, and collection of PCI interrupts INTA, INTB, INTC, and INTD.

∎ *DRAM.* The amount and configuration of memory are the most likely changes that you will need to make to your platform. The amount of memory in your system can range from 8 megabytes to 1 gigabyte depending on the IXP4XX network processor. The BSPs require updates to support the memory device configuration and the specific memory map of the operating system.

∎ *Flash memory.* The operating system uses flash memory to provide nonvolatile storage. You need to configure the device drivers used for the flash file system to manage the flash devices on your platform.

∎ *Debug display.* Intel development platforms provide a debug display. Boot loaders and BSPs that indicate the boot-up progress use the display. The display attaches to the expansion bus on chip select 2. If you do not have anything connected to the chip select, you should remove this code.

∎ *Serial console.* The IXP4XX network processors provide two UARTS. You may frequently find that your system requires only one port. You must configure the BSP to define which UART is used for the default console output.

∎ *Ethernet PHY device.* The Intel platforms use the LXT972 Ethernet PHY devices. Provisioning the PHY is managed using the *ethMii* component within the Intel IXP400 software. It is quite common that you will have to replace at least one PHY with an Ethernet switch. The currently supported PHY devices are the Intel LXT971, LXT972, LXT973, and the Kendin KS8995 4-port Ethernet switch. You must update the `<CSR_DIR>/src/ethMii/IxEthMii.c` file to manage the Ethernet PHY on your platform.

∎ *Expansion bus devices.* If you want additional hardware on the expansion bus, you must map the physical memory to an appropriate virtual memory range. For example, on Linux, mapping may be done either statically or by making an `ioremap()` request to the operating system. Alternatively, you could use the operating system abstraction layer in the IXP400 software to map the expansion bus memory in an operating system agnostic fashion.

Linux[†]

All embedded Linux systems consist of three main components: the operating system, a Linux support package, and a file system. The operating system is available on the Linux kernel source Web site, listed in "References." The two major kernel versions in use at the time of writing are 2.4 and 2.6. Most current IXP4XX network processor-based products are using the 2.4-based kernel, although some customers are transitioning their products to the 2.6-based kernel. On the SourceForge Web site, listed in "References," you can find extensive documentation on the key differences between the kernels and patches to update the Intel IXP400 software. The main 2.4 kernel code base does not actually support the Intel® XScale microarchitecture; you must patch the kernel with the Intel XScale core patches. These patches are available at Montavista's ftp site. The Intel XScale architecture is fully supported in the 2.6 code base.

The Linux support package (LSP) provides all low-level device drivers needed to support the operating system. As the name suggests, the LSP is specific to each board. Most changes needed for your platform are typically limited to the LSP.

All Linux systems require a file system. On desktop Linux systems, this file system is usually on the PC's hard disk. On embedded Linux systems, the initial file system is typically a compressed RAM-based disk (cramfs), known as a ram disk. The ram disk is usually compressed and loaded by the boot loader into memory, where the kernel code subsequently decompresses and mounts the file system during system boot up. The file system contains the user-level programs needed. It typically contains items such as a command shell, initialization scripts, Web servers, and kernel modules. Although you can make changes to the ram disk file system while the system is operational, all changes are lost if the system is restarted. Typically, platforms also need some form of persistent storage, which is provided by a flash-based file system. The most common flash-based file system is known as Journaling Flash File System version 2 (JFFS2). To assist development, the root file system can instead be mounted from a network drive using the Network File System (NFS) protocol, which allows you to make easy updates from your workstation.

To compile and build the kernel, you need an Intel XScale core tool chain. Each major kernel version is typically tied to a particular version of the GCC cross-compiler that the kernel has been tested and validated with. The 2.4 kernel tree uses GCC version 2.95.3, whereas the 2.6 kernel uses version 3.x. The cross-compiler allows you to compile code on a different processor architecture than the one on which the code will execute. The tool chain is much more than just the cross-compiler; you also need binary utilities and user level libraries, such as glibc.

All of the items discussed thus far are generic items needed for embedded Linux kernels. The specific items needed for IXP4XX network processor-based platforms are the Intel software library and the device drivers. Both of them can be downloaded from the Intel Developer Web site, listed in "References."

To summarize, you need the following items to operate an embedded Linux system on an IXP4XX network processor-based platform:

■ A cross-compiler and tool chain compatible with Intel XScale core technology

■ A Linux kernel and the associated LSP

■ An initial root file system

■ The Intel software library

■ Device drivers specific to IXP4XX network processors

The next question is where to get all the required components. You have a number of options:

■ *Montavista Linux Professional Edition.* This product is sold by Montavista. It is fully supported and provides the kernel, LSP, file system, and tool chain. Montavista validates all the components supplied and provides support should you need help. They also provide a preview kit that you can download from their Web site, listed in "References." Intel developers use this product when developing the Intel access library and device drivers.

■ *SourceForge Open Source with unsupported distribution.* This option does not require significant effort as most items needed have been built by others and uploaded to the SourceForge Web site, listed in "References." One consideration with this option is the lack of any formal support; you must rely on the goodwill of others to help you should you have issues. At the time of writing, the Web site contained all the required items to develop an IXP4XX network processor-based Linux platform. The actual distribution on SourceForge was provided by SnapGear. For more information on the SnapGear distribution, see the SnapGear home page (SnapGear 2005).

■ *On your own entirely.* Do everything yourself from available open source code. Although all the required components needed are open source, this option requires the most time, effort, and considerable expertise on your part.

Embedded Linux platforms are constantly evolving, and the trend is to move as much of the low-level board initialization as possible into the boot loader.

Most customers use a 2.4-based kernel. The Linux support code associated with Intel platforms can be found in 2.4_kernel_source/ arch/arm/mach-ixp425 directory. The Linux build system uses configuration scripts to define the features and target platform included in the kernel. The SDRAM initialization, expansion bus setup, and other low-level board initializations are the responsibility of the boot loader, which in this case is RedBoot.

Platform Configuration

You can find initial default configuration scripts for the IXDP425 and IXDP465 platforms in ../arch/arm/def-configs/ixdp425 and ../arch/arm/def-configs/ixdp465. The following platform-related definitions are defined in the configuration files. You should not edit the files directly as they have been automatically generated. To change the configuration files do a make menuconfig.

File:
../arch/arm/def-configs/ixdp465

```
256   /* GPL License */
257
258   CONFIG_ARCH_IXP4XX=y
259   CONFIG_ARCH_IXDP465=y
260   CONFIG_ARCH_IXP465=y
261
```

Line 258

Configure the system as an Intel IXP4XX network processor-based platform.

Line 259

Configure the system as the Intel IXDP465 development platform.

Line 260

Configure the system as an Intel IXP465 network processor-based platform.

GPIO Settings

The assignment of a GPIO pin function is typically defined in the device driver that makes use of the GPIO pin. The following example shows a segment from the I²C device driver for the IXDP425 development platform.

File:

```
./drivers/i2c/i2c-adap-ixp425.c
262    /* GPL License */
263    if(machine_is_ixdp425()) {
264        gpio_data.scl_line = IXP425_GPIO_PIN_6;
265        gpio_data.sda_line = IXP425_GPIO_PIN_7;
266    }
```

Line 263

This code is a run-time check to identify if the code is running on an IXDP425 platform. In general, you should keep run-time checks such as this to a minimum.

Line 264

Set the I²C driver to use GPIO pin 6 for the I²C clock line.

Line 265

Set the I²C driver to use GPIO pin 7 for the I²C data line.

PCI Bus Configuration

The PCI bus requires a number of GPIO pins to assist in the operation of the PCI bus. The functions required are PCI clock, PCI reset pin, and four GPIO pins for the PCI bus interrupts INTA, INTB, INTC, and INTD. The code sequence below shows the GPIO pins allocated to these functions. Sharing the PCI bus configuration between the boot loader and the kernel does not occur, so you must update the PCI sections for the hardware pin assignments in the LSP and boot loader. The allocation of GPIO pins is identical on both the IXDP425 and IXDP465 platforms.

File:

`./arch/arm/mach-ixp425/ixdp425-pci.c`

```
267    /* GPL License */
268    #define INTA_PIN            IXP425_GPIO_PIN_11
269    #define INTB_PIN            IXP425_GPIO_PIN_10
270    #define INTC_PIN            IXP425_GPIO_PIN_9
271    #define INTD_PIN            IXP425_GPIO_PIN_8
272
273    #define IXP425_PCI_RESET_GPIO    IXP425_GPIO_PIN_13
274    #define IXP425_PCI_CLK_PIN       IXP425_GPIO_CLK_0
275    #define IXP425_PCI_CLK_ENABLE    IXP425_GPIO_CLK0_ENABLE
```

Lines 268–271

Assign the GPIO pins for each PCI interrupt.

Line 273

Assign the PCI reset signal to GPIO pin 13.

Lines 274–275

Assign the PCI clock signal to GPIO pin 14, which is also defined as CLK 0.

All of the Intel reference platforms provide four PCI slots. Many embedded applications do not require all four PCI slots to be provided. The following section shows an example of a two mini-PCI slots-based platform.

File:

`./arch/arm/mach-ixp425/ixdpg425-pci.c`

```
276    /* GPL License */
277    void __init ixdpg425_pci_init(void *sysdata)
278    {
279        gpio_line_config(IXP425_GPIO_PIN_7,
280                         IXP425_GPIO_IN |
281                         IXP425_GPIO_ACTIVE_LOW);
282        gpio_line_config(IXP425_GPIO_PIN_6,
283                         IXP425_GPIO_IN |
284                         IXP425_GPIO_ACTIVE_LOW);
285
286        gpio_line_isr_clear(IXP425_GPIO_PIN_7);
287        gpio_line_isr_clear(IXP425_GPIO_PIN_6);
288
289        ixp425_pci_init(sysdata);
290    }
291
```

```
292     static int __init ixdpg425_map_irq(struct pci_dev *dev,
        u8 slot, u8 pin)
293     {
294             if(slot == 12)
295                     return IRQ_IXP4XX_GPIO7;
296             else if(slot == 13)
297                     return IRQ_IXP4XX_GPIO6;
298             else return -1;
299     }
```

Line 277

This line is the PCI initialization function called by the kernel.

Lines 279–287

Set up GPIO pins 6 and 7 as interrupt pins and clears any pending interrupt.

Line 289

Call the IXP425 function that performs the initialization of the PCI controller. The function also triggers the scanning of the bus for PCI devices.

Line 292

This function maps the interrupt associated with a particular PCI slot to an interrupt. Note that the PCI slots are defined by the address select line (ADSEL) to decode it.

Line 294

For the PCI slot defined by ADSEL line 13, allocate GPIO pin 7 as the interrupt line.

Line 296

For the PCI slot defined by ADSEL line 12, allocate GPIO pin 6 as the interrupt line.

Flash Storage

Journaling Flash File System version 2 (JFFS2) is the default flash file system used on the IXDP425 and IXDP465 development platforms. JFFS2 is a robust file system supporting power failure without having to perform extensive file system checks (fsck) after reboot. This file system relies on an underlying flash driver layer, known as memory technology devices (MTDs). Most of the information required by the MTD device driver is obtained automatically by probing the flash devices. The platform specific details are set up in the following file.

File:

```
./drivers/mtd/maps/ixp425.c
```

```
300   /* GPL License */
301   if (machine_is_ixdp465()) {
302           ixp425_map.size = 0x02000000;
303   } else {
304           ixp425_map.size = 0x01000000;
305   }
```

Lines 301–302

If this code is executing on the IXDP465 platform, indicate to the MTD layer that there are 32 megabytes of flash.

Lines 303–304

For all other IXP4XX network processor-based platforms, assume that there are 16 megabytes of flash on board.

Information on the MTD block mapping can be obtained by performing the following command at the user shell:

```
> cat /proc/mtd

root@10.243.18.139:~# cat /proc/mtd

dev:    size    erasesize   name

mtd0: 00400000 00020000 "image"

mtd0: 01bc0000 00020000 "user"
```

You can then create and mount JFFS2 using the MTD block device. The MTD block should be erased before using this command for the first time.

```
>mount -t jffs2 /dev/mtdblock0 /mnt/jffs2
```

You can find further details in the Linux MTD, JFFS how-to (Malik 2001).

Serial Console

Both UARTS are enabled by default on the Intel development platforms. You select which console device to use in the Linux command line. The Linux command line is set when RedBoot loads the kernel. The following is an example from RedBoot to transfer control from RedBoot to a kernel previously loaded into memory.

```
> exec 0x01080000 -c "console=ttyS1,115200 root=/dev/ram
initrd=0x02000000,13M ramdisk_size=12288"
```

Among other things, this command sets the console device as UART 1 with a baud rate of 115,200 baud. Something to watch out for, RedBoot provides a console on both UARTs. It is a common mistake to start the kernel on the opposite serial port to the one you issued the command on and then wonder if the board has crashed!

RedBoot

RedBoot is the primary boot loader used to boot the Linux operating system on IXP4XX network processor-based platforms. RedBoot is based on eCos and is maintained by Red Hat, Inc. For more information visit the Red Hat Web site, listed in "References." RedBoot is a very generic boot loader and is not limited to launching the Linux operating system; it can also be used to load standalone customer code or VxWorks images. The boot loader initializes the IXP4XX network processor and platform to a sufficient extent to load the Linux kernel image. The kernel image may be loaded from a basic flash-file system through a serial port or downloaded from the network via the NPE Ethernet interfaces.

The first step in platform porting is to identify the hardware abstraction layer (HAL) most appropriate to your platform. In this case, you should select either the IXDP425 or IXDP465 platforms as your initial starting point. You should copy the initial HAL into your own platform directory, following the same directory pattern as the one for the HAL provided by Intel. Change all instances of the Intel platform name to your platform name. Names that need changing include file names, package definitions, and names within the code itself. You must then update the ecos.db file to include your board definition. At this point, you should rebuild RedBoot for the new platform and verify that it is still operational on the Intel development platform before you make any specific platform changes. The following section identifies the code fragments that may require modification to port RedBoot to your platform. Additional details on porting RedBoot are discussed in the eCos software development book (Massa 2002).

GPIO Configuration

The GPIO pins are configured in the `plf_hardware_init()` function during RedBoot startup. The GPIO pins may be configured as input, output clock generating, or processor interrupts pins. By default, all GPIO pins are configured as input pins.

File:

`redboot/packages/hal/arm/xscale/ixdp425/current/src/ixdp425_misc.c`

```
306   /* ECOS License */
307   void
308   plf_hardware_init(void)
309   {
310     // GPIO (15) used for ENET clock
311     HAL_GPIO_OUTPUT_ENABLE(15);
312     *IXP425_GPCLKR |= GPCLKR_CLK1_ENABLE;
313     *IXP425_GPCLKR |= GPCLKR_CLK1_PCLK2;
314
315     HAL_GPIO_OUTPUT_SET(GPIO_EEPROM_SCL);
316     HAL_GPIO_OUTPUT_ENABLE(GPIO_EEPROM_SCL);
317
318     HAL_GPIO_OUTPUT_SET(GPIO_EEPROM_SDA);
319     HAL_GPIO_OUTPUT_ENABLE(GPIO_EEPROM_SDA);
320
321     // ENET-0 IRQ line
322     HAL_GPIO_OUTPUT_DISABLE(GPIO_ENET0_INT_N);
323     HAL_INTERRUPT_CONFIGURE(CYGNUM_HAL_INTERRUPT_ETH0,1,0);
324
325     // ENET-1 IRQ line
326     HAL_GPIO_OUTPUT_DISABLE(GPIO_ENET1_INT_N);
327     HAL_INTERRUPT_CONFIGURE(CYGNUM_HAL_INTERRUPT_ETH1,1,0);
328
329     /* remaining platform setup */
```

Let's look at what is going on in this code:

Line 308

> This RedBoot function is called to set up the hardware on the platform. It is called very early in the initialization sequence.

Line 311

> Select the GPIO pin as an output pin.

Lines 312–313

> Set the GPIO pin 15 to generate a clock. Only a subset of the GPIO pins can generate a clock.

Line 315

> Set the I²C EEPROM clock line to a logical one on the pin. For this platform, the GPIO pin 6 is used as an EEPROM clock line. Pin 6 is defined in the platform header file `ixdp425.h`.

Line 316

> Configure the I²C EEPROM clock pin as an output pin. The IXP4XX network processors do not contain an I²C controller. The I²C bus protocol is emulated through software manipulation of the GPIO pins.

Lines 318–319

> Set the I²C EEPROM data pin to a logical one on the pin and configure the pin as an output.

Line 322

> Configure the Ethernet PHY interrupt pin as an input. This pin is used to interrupt the processor when there is an Ethernet event such as loss of signal. This interrupt is not currently used by the Ethernet device drivers. They currently poll the PHY to check for changes in link state or configuration.

Line 323

> Configure the GPIO pin as an interrupt pin. Specifically, it is an active low-level triggered interrupt, which means the GPIO gives an interrupt indication to the Intel XScale core whenever the GPIO pin is at a logical zero value. The GPIO pins support active high-level, active low-level, rising-edge, falling-edge, and both-edge triggered-interrupt configurations.

Lines 326–327

Configure the interrupt line of the Ethernet PHY for port one as an active low interrupt source.

In summary, if your platform makes alternate use of the GPIO pins, you must make the appropriate changes in the `plf_hardare_init()` function and the appropriate platform header definition file.

SDRAM Initialization

The DRAM configuration has two main parts. The first is the actual low-level initialization of the memory controller before the memory can be used. The second is the configuration of the memory map for differing amounts of DRAM on the system. As the DRAM is not yet available, the code must be written in Intel XScale core assembly language and forms part of the first code sequence to be executed after the chip is reset. You cannot use C code, as it requires the DRAM to store the function call stack. We do not intend to show the full initialization sequence in the code sequences below. Only the segments that you are likely to change due to differing memory device configuration are shown.

The IXDP425 platform file:

```
redboot/packages/hal/arm/xscale/ixdp425/current/include/ixdp425.h
```

```
256   /* ECOS License */
257   #define IXP425_SDRAM_CONFIG_INIT
258             (SDRAM_CONFIG_CAS_3 | SDRAM_CONFIG_4x32Mx16)
259   #define IXP425_SDRAM_REFRESH_CNT   0x081
260   #define IXP425_SDRAM_SET_MODE_CMD SDRAM_IR_MODE_SET_CAS3
261
```

Lines 257–258

These lines define initialization values for the SDRAM controller. The value shown is for a total 256-megabyte SDRAM. The configuration consists of four separate devices, each device providing 64 megabytes via a 16-bit data bus. The devices have a common address strobe (CAS) latency of 3. The definitions are used in the low–level SDRAM controller initialization code found in the following file:

```
.../xscale/ixdp425/current/include/hal_platform_setup.h.
```

Line 259

Depending on the amount and configuration, you may need to change the definition of the refresh count.

The IXDP465 platform file:

```
redboot/packages/hal/arm/xscale/ixdp465/current/include/i
xdp465.h
```

```
262   /* ECOS License */
263   #define BMP_SDCR0_INIT        (0x52220106)
264   #define BMP_SDCR1_INIT        (0x2560f084)
265   #define BMP_SDRAM_REFRESH_CNT 0x410
266   #define BMP_SBR0_INIT         (0x80000002)
267   #define BMP_SBR1_INIT         (0x80000004)
268
```

Lines 263–264

These lines write the initialization values to the DDR memory controller. To identify the appropriate values for the DRAM on the platform, you must consult the appropriate developer manual listed in "References." The low-level DDR SDRAM controller initialization can be found in the following file:

```
/xscale/ixdp465/current/include/hal_platform_setup.h
```

Line 265

Define the DRAM refresh counter. This value may need to be updated for differing amounts of SDRAM.

Lines 266–267

These lines write the initialization values in the SDRAM boundary registers 0 and 1. Specifically, they configure each bank with a 256-megabit device connected by a 16-bit data interface. The total amount of memory defined in this case is 128 megabytes. You must change these values if the platform has a different amount of memory.

SDRAM Footprint

The previous section provided details on changes you must make to allow the SDRAM controller to operate with the attached memory. The macro SDRAM_SIZE defines the actual footprint.

The IXDP425 platform file:

```
redboot/packages/hal/arm/xscale/ixdp425/current/include/i
xdp425.h
```

```
269    /* ECOS License */
270    #define SDRAM_SIZE    0x10000000    // 256MB
```

Line 270

This code defines the total amount of SDRAM on the platform. The memory map and MMU tables are set up based on this definition. The amount of SDRAM in the system is transferred from the boot loader to the Linux operating system using ATAGs.

PCI Configuration

The PCI bus requires a number of GPIO pins to assist in the operation of the PCI bus. The functions required are PCI clock, PCI reset pin, and four GPIO pins for the PCI bus interrupts INTA, INTB, INTC, and INTD. The code sequence below shows how the GPIO pins were allocated to these functions. The implementation for the IXDP425 and IXDP465 platforms is very similar. The PCI setup is performed by the function hal_plf_pci_init().

File:

```
redboot/packages/hal/arm/xscale/ixdp425/current/src/
ixdp425_pci.c
```

```
271    /* ECOS License */
272    // PCI pin mappings
273    #define PCI_CLK_GPIO      14   // CLK0
274    #define PCI_RESET_GPIO    13
275    #define PCI_INTA_GPIO     11
276    #define PCI_INTB_GPIO     10
277    #define PCI_INTC_GPIO     9
278    #define PCI_INTD_GPIO     8
279
280    #define INTA      CYGNUM_HAL_INTERRUPT_GPIO11
```

```
281    #define INTB    CYGNUM_HAL_INTERRUPT_GPIO10
282    #define INTC    CYGNUM_HAL_INTERRUPT_GPIO9
283    #define INTD    CYGNUM_HAL_INTERRUPT_GPIO8
284
285    static const int
       pci_irq_table[IXP425_PCI_MAX_DEV][IXP425_PCI_IRQ_LINES] =
       {
286        {INTA, INTB, INTC, INTD},
287        {INTB, INTC, INTD, INTA},
288        {INTC, INTD, INTA, INTB},
289        {INTD, INTA, INTB, INTC}
290    };
291
```

Line 273

Define GPIO pin 14 as the PCI clock. The code configures this pin to generate the PCI bus clock. If you provide the PCI clock directly on your board, remove the code related to the generation of the PCI clock from the GPIO pin.

Line 274

The PCI bus contains a reset signal that must be driven low for at least 1 millisecond before the PCI bus can be enumerated. The PCI initialization code performs this reset function.

Lines 275–283

Allocate the PCI INT signals to GPIO pins.

Lines 285–290

The IXP4XX development platforms contain four PCI slots. The table defines how the interrupts are allocated to each slot. The function cyg_hal_plf_pci_translate_interrupt() uses this table to identify the correct interrupt assignment for a particular PCI slot. If you have fewer PCI slots, change the table to map to your hardware implementation. Address select lines used to decode the actual physical connector define the slot used in this function.

Expansion Bus Configuration

During RedBoot startup, the expansion bus chip selects are initialized in the `plf_hardware_init()` function. The following code segment sets up the detailed chip select timing chip select 4. The chip selects have a large number of configuration options. Your board designer should provide the low-level details of the devices connected to the chip selects.

File:
`redboot/packages/hal/arm/xscale/ixdp425/current/src/ixdp425_misc.c`

```
292    /* ECOS License */
293    void
294    plf_hardware_init(void)
295    {
296      /* Code removed */
297
298        *IXP425_EXP_CS4 = (EXP_ADDR_T(3)   |
299                           EXP_SETUP_T(3)  |
300                           EXP_STROBE_T(15) |
301                           EXP_HOLD_T(3)   |
302                           EXP_RECOVERY_T(15) |
303                           EXP_SZ_512 |
304                           EXP_WR_EN | EXP_CS_EN);
305
306      /* code removed */
```

Lines 298–302

Configure the detailed timing of the expansion bus interface. For further details please consult the appropriate developer manual listed in "References."

Line 303

Each chip select can support devices up to a maximum of 16 or 32 megabytes in size, depending on the IXP4XX network processor. The expansion bus can be configured to limit the memory size of attached devices. In this case, the maximum size of the device attached is 512 bytes. Therefore, if your program attempts to access memory outside this range, the access will fail.

Line 304

Enable the chip select for both reading and writing.

Prior to accessing any additional hardware attached to the expansion bus, you must configure the particular expansion bus chip select with the appropriate options.

Debug Display

Both development platforms provide a debug display. The display is attached to the expansion bus chip select 2. The initialization of the chip select is controlled by the macro `IXP425_EXP_CS2_INIT`. The display is written to via either of two function calls. The `DISPLAY` macro may be called from the Intel XScale core assembler, and `DISPLAY_HEX()` may be called from C code. If you do not provide a debug display on your platform, you should remove the initialization of the chip select and the contents of the display functions.

Flash Storage

The Intel reference platforms use Intel StrataFlash® memory. RedBoot configures the particular flash device driver to use by including the appropriate flash support package. For example, the `packages/devs/flash/arm/ixdp425/current/cdl/flash_ixdp425.cdl` defines the inclusion of the Intel StrataFlash chip driver. If you select different flash devices for your platform, you must also identify a new flash driver that supports it.

Serial Console

Both UARTS are enabled by default on the Intel development platforms. They are enabled in the appropriate file component description file. The example below shows the component description file for the IXDP425 platform.

File:

.../hal/arm/xscale/ixdp425/current/cdl/hal_arm_xscale_ixdp4
25.cdl

```
307   /* ECOS License */
308       cdl_option CYGSEM_HAL_IXP425_PLF_USES_UART1 {
309           display      "IXDP425 uses IXP425 high-speed UART"
310           flavor       bool
311           default_value 1
312           description  "
313               Enable this option if the IXP425 high-speed
314               UART is used as a virtual vector
315               communications channel."
316       }
317
318       cdl_option CYGSEM_HAL_IXP425_PLF_USES_UART2 {
319           display      "IXDP425 uses IXP425 console UART"
320           flavor       bool
321           default_value 1
322           description  "
323               Enable this option if the IXP425 console UART
324               is to be used as a virtual vector
325               communications channel."
326       }
327   /* code removed */
```

Lines 311 & 321

The default is to enable both UART ports by setting the default value to 1. You should change the value to zero if you do not wish RedBoot to configure the UART port.

VxWorks

VxWorks is a real-time operating system provided by Wind River Systems. The Intel reference platform BSPs are fully supported Wind River products and are available for download from their Web site, listed in "References." The IXP4XX network processors are supported by the General Purpose Platform, VxWorks edition, and the market-specific Platform for Network Equipment (PNE), VxWorks edition. The PNE edition provides a highly optimized set of networking components and offers substantially higher IP networking performance. As with all development environ-ments, you must also install the latest release of the Intel IXP400 software after you have installed the BSP. The following four BSPs are provided by Wind River Systems:

■ *IXDP425* supports all IXP42X network processor variants with the Intel XScale core configured to run in big-endian mode.

■ *IXDP425_LE* supports all IXP42X network processor variants with the Intel XScale core configured to run in little-endian mode.

■ *IXDP465* supports all IXP45X and IXP46X network processor variants with the Intel XScale core configured to run in big-endian mode.

■ *IXDP465_LE* supports all IXP45X and IXP46X network processor variants with the Intel XScale core configured to run in little-endian mode.

All of the BSPs provide the following set of core features:

■ Core processor initialization, MMU setup, interrupt controller, and operating system timer tick.

■ Both serial ports are enabled; one is used to provide the console input/output.

■ Nonvolatile storage for VxWorks configuration items such as the "bootline" and NPE Ethernet MAC address storage. The BSP sup-ports the storage of nonvolatile data in a serial EEPROM or in the main flash device.

■ The PCI bus is fully supported. The BSP enumerates the bus and starts the appropriate drivers on startup.

■ Intel 8255X Ethernet network interface cards (NICs) are sup-ported via the PCI interface.

■ The NPE-based Ethernet interfaces are supported via an enhanced network driver (END).

■ Debug output on the debug display.

The following section outlines the code segments that you are most likely to modify in porting a BSP to your platform.

GPIO Pin Definitions

The GPIO pin definitions are distributed throughout the BSP. The easiest way to identify all of the GPIO pins being used in the BSP is to search the BSP subdirectory for instances of the function `ixp400GPIOLineConfig()`. The current platforms use GPIO pins for PCI, I²C, and optional modules. All GPIO pins are routed through an FPGA on the IXDP465 platform. The routing of the GPIO pins is set up during platform initialization. It is not likely that you require an FPGA on your own reference platform; in this case, you should remove the code to set up the FPGA.

File:

`../target/config/ixdp465/sysLib.c`

```
328    /* Wind River License */
329
330    /* code removed */
331
332    /* connect GPIO pin 8 to PCI_D interrupt line */
333    ixdp400FpgaIOConfig(FPGA_IO_GPIO_8,
334                        FPGA_IO_DIR_INPUT,
335                        FPGA_IO_ATTACH_PCI_INTD_N,
336                        &fpgaIoError);
337
338    /* code removed */
```

Line 333

Set up the FPGA to connect the interrupt from the PCI INTD to GPIO pin 8. The PCI driver then sets up GPIO8 as the INTD interrupt. If you remove the FPGA from your design, you must remove all instances of this code from the BSP.

Line 334

Configure the connection as an input to the IXP4XX network processor.

SDRAM Initialization

This section covers the code you are most likely to change if you use a different memory configuration to that found on the Intel reference platforms. As the memory controller is different on each platform, so is the code that sets up the controller.

The IXDP425 platform file:

.../target/config/ixdp425/romInit.s

```
339    /* Wind River License */
340    /* code removed */
341
342    /* Program SDRAM Bank0 Boundary  register to 256MB */
343
344        ldr    r0, L$LSDRAM_CONFIG_256MEG
345        ldr    r9, L$LIXP425_SDRAM_CONFIG
346        str    r0, [r9, #0]
347    /* Code removed */
```

Line 344

Load the Intel XScale core register 0 with the value needed for 256 megabytes using a 4-chip configuration. There are also definitions for 32, 64, and 128 megabytes in romInit.s.

Line 345

Load the Intel XScale core register 9 with the address of the SDRAM configuration register.

Line 346

Write the configuration value into the SDRAM register.

The current BSP defines the memory type in the BSP makefile. The IXDP465 platform also supports DDR memory with error correcting code (ECC) support. The BSP enables this default feature in ../target/config/ixdp465/xdp400DdrRam.s.

```
348    /* Wind River License */
349
350        ldr r2, =IXP400_DDR_ECCR
351        ldr r1, =(DDR_ECC_ENABLE |
352                  DDR_ECC_ONE_BIT_CORRECT |
353                  DDR_ECC_MULTI_BIT_REPORT |
354                  DDR_ECC_ONE_BIT_REPORT)
355        str    r1, [r2]
```

Line 350

Load the Intel XScale core register 2 with the address of the memory controller ECC register.

Lines 351–354

Load the Intel XScale core register with the value to be written into the memory controller register. The value enables the ECC function within the controller. It automatically corrects any single bit errors that occur in the memory, and it reports both single and multiple bit errors that the controller detects. When the ECC feature is enabled, all the memory must be written to with a known value. This procedure is known as memory scrubbing and is carried out by the BSP.

Line 355

Store the value in Intel XScale core register 1 into the memory location pointed to by the Intel XScale core register 2.

SDRAM Footprint

The previous section provided details on changes you must make to allow the SDRAM controller to operate with the attached memory. Changing the footprint for VxWorks platforms requires several changes to the `config.h` and makefile. The IDXP425 platform is populated with 256 megabytes SDRAM, and the IXDP465 platform is populated with 128 megabytes of SDRAM. For further details on the configuration of VxWorks memory map, please refer to the Tornado BSP developer's kit available from Wind River Systems.

```
File:

../target/config/ixdp465/config.h
356  /* Wind River License */
357
358  #define LOCAL_MEM_SIZE          (0x08000000)
359  #define RAM_HIGH_ADRS           (0x04000000)
360
```

Line 358

The LOCAL_MEM_SIZE defines the total amount of SDRAM on your system. In this case it is defined as 128 megabytes. The BSP memory map and runtime MMU tables are updated automatically based on this definition.

Line 359

The RAM_HIGH_ADRS defines location in RAM where the bootcode executes. We usually set this value to half of the total memory. This value is also defined in the BSP makefile. Both values must always be the same.

PCI Configuration

The PCI bus requires a number of GPIO pins to assist in the operation of the PCI bus. The functions required are PCI clock, PCI reset pin, and four GPIO pins for the PCI bus interrupts INTA, INTB, INTC, and INTD. The code sequence below shows how the GPIO pins were allocated to these functions. The implementation for the IXDP425 and IXDP465 platforms is very similar. The PCI setup is carried out in the function `sysPci-Init()`.

File:

`../target/config/ixdp465/ixp400Pci.h`

```
361   /* Wind River License */
362
363   /*define the GPIO pins used for the 4 PCI interrupts*/
364   #define PCI_INT_LVL0   28
365   #define PCI_INT_VEC0   28
366   #define PCI_INT_LVL1   27
367   #define PCI_INT_VEC1   27
368   #define PCI_INT_LVL2   26
369   #define PCI_INT_VEC2   26
370   #define PCI_INT_LVL3   25
371   #define PCI_INT_VEC3   25
372
373   #define IXP425_PCI_INTA_PIN IXP425_GPIO_PIN_11
374   #define IXP425_PCI_INTB_PIN IXP425_GPIO_PIN_10
375   #define IXP425_PCI_INTC_PIN IXP425_GPIO_PIN_9
376   #define IXP425_PCI_INTD_PIN IXP425_GPIO_PIN_8
377
378   #define IXP400_PCI_CLK_PIN   IXP400_GPIO_CLK_0
379   #define IXP400_PCI_GPIO_CLOCK_ON
380
381   #define IXP400_PCI_RESET_GPIO IXP400_GPIO_PIN_13
382
383   /* code removed */
```

Lines 364–365

Define the processor interrupt vectors associated with the INTA pin to GPIO pin 11.

Lines 366–367

Define the processor interrupt vectors associated with the INTB pin to GPIO pin 10.

Lines 367–368

Define the processor interrupt vectors associated with the INTC pin to GPIO pin 9.

Lines 369–370

Define the processor interrupt vectors associated with the INTD pin to GPIO pin 8.

Lines 373–376

These definitions map each INT pin to the appropriate GPIO pin.

Line 378

Define the PCI clock output pin as GPIO 0.

Line 379

Turn on the PCI clock generation on the GPIO pin.

Line 381

Define the PCI reset pin as GPIO pin 13.

Expansion Bus Configuration

The BSP enables only chip select 2 by default. This chip select is used for the debug display on each development platform.

File:

```
../target/config/ixdp465/romInit.s
384    /* Wind River License */
385          ldr     r0, L$CS2_REG
386          ldr     r1, L$CS2_VAL
387          str     r1, [r0]
388
389    /* code removed */
```

Lines 385–387

This code segment initializes the chip select 2 configuration register.

Debug Display

Both development platforms provide a debug display. The display is attached to the expansion bus chip select 2. On the IXDP425 platform you can use the SevenSegDisplay() function or DEBUG_OUT_VAL() macro to display a hex number on the display. On the IXDP465 platform you can use the sysBrdDispOut() function or BRD_DISP_OUT() macro to provide debug output on the LCD display.

Nonvolatile Storage

The Intel reference platforms use Intel StrataFlash memory. The support of the flash devices is enabled in config.h by defining INCLUDE_FLASH. The VxWorks BSP requires a location to store the bootline configuration. The BSPs support the storage of the bootline in a small serial EEPROM or a designated flash section in the flash device. The selection of which device is used for storage is shown below.

File:

../target/config/ixdp465/config.h

```
390    /* Wind River License */
391    #define USE_EEPROM_STORAGE
392    #undef USE_FLASH_STORAGE
393
```

Line 391

This define selects the I²C-based EEPROM to be the storage location for the BSP nonvolatile data. This define should be undefined to use the Intel flash for this purpose.

Line 392

This undefine de-selects the flash device for the storage location for the BSP nonvolatile data. This define should be defined to use the Intel flash for this purpose.

Serial Console

Both UARTS are enabled in the BSPs. One port is defined as the console port. The other port is available to applications, but there is no output on the serial port during the boot up sequence.

File:

../target/config/ixdp465/config.h

```
394    /* Wind River License */
395    #define N_UARTS            2
396    #define NUM_TTY            N_UARTS
397    #define CONSOLE_TTY        1
398    /* code removed */
```

Line 395

Defines the number of UARTS on the IXP4XX network processors.

Line 396

Enables the serial port device drivers on both ports.

Line 397

Set up UART0 on the IXP4XX network processor as the VxWorks console port. The Wind River bootrom and WindSH operates on the console port.

Microsoft Windows CE

Windows CE is a highly configurable operating system with many built-in features. Intel provides a BSP and associated Intel IXP400 software for the IXDP425 platform. At press time, the BSP for the IXDP465 platform is in the beta release stage. Windows CE supports two different types of application: those that are display based, known as headed configurations, and those that do not provide any display function, known as headless configurations. The Windows CE integrated development environment is known as Platform Builder. When creating a new platform using Platform Builder, a range of platform configuration items is presented. Platform Builder provides extensive documentation through its Help menu options.

Headless Configurations

The primary headless configuration for the IXDP425 platform is a *gateway*. A gateway enables the IXDP425 platform to perform all the functions needed in a home IP router. It provides firewall features, network address translation, universal plug and play (UPnP), and a Web server with example configuration Web pages. The NDIS Ethernet drivers have undergone considerable optimization to ensure the highest possible network performance is achieved.

Headed Configurations

Windows CE provides a much larger number of headed configurations, which makes sense given the sophisticated user interface it provides. The *Internet Appliance* configuration available in Platform Builder is a good starting point for a browser-based consumer Internet device with a fixed display such as LCD or CRT keyboard and mouse input. The IXDP425 platform itself does not provide any built in peripheral devices to support a display or keyboard/mouse natively. Intel provides these functions through PCI cards. The Windows CE kit for the IXDP425 platform consists of a Silicon Motion VoyagerGX PCI graphics card, a USB 2.0 host card, mouse, and keyboard. The Internet Appliance provides a stand-alone display based Web terminal with Web browser, and you can even include Windows Media Player.

Eboot

Eboot is the Windows CE Ethernet boot loader. The IXDP425 platform supports Eboot. You should program your flash device with an Eboot image before beginning development on Windows CE. The Eboot boot loader provides a mechanism to download your Windows CE kernel images over an Ethernet interface. It also provides a mechanism to save kernel images into flash and automatically start the kernel image on power up.

Platform Porting

The following sections describe the changes you are most likely to make in porting Windows CE to your platform. The BSP for the IXDP425 platform is located in c:\WINCE500\PLATFORM\INTEL_IXDP425. A significant portion of the platform configurability is controlled in either c:\WINCE500\PLATFORM\INTEL_IXDP425\INTEL_IXDP425.BAT or the platform-specific registry file c:\WINCE500\PLATFORM\INTEL_IXDP425\FILES\platform.reg.

SDRAM Configuration

The SDRAM controller is initialized in the Eboot startup code. The code segment in the following file is where this initialization occurs.

File:

c:\WINCE500\PLATFORM\INTEL_IXDP42\KERNEL\HAL\ARM\
startup_ixp4xx.s

```
399
400    init_dram:
401     set register r9 equal to L_LIXP425_SDRAM_CONFIG_BASE
402     set register r0 equal to L_LSDRAM_CONFIG_64MEG
403     write the value from r0 to address r9
404
405    /* code removed */
406
407      set register r9 equal to L_LIXP425_SDRAM_REFRESH
408      set register r0 equal to
409                 L_LIXDP425_SDRAM_CONFIG_REFRESH_CNT
410      Write the valie from r0 to address r9
```

Line 400

This line is a label indicating the start of the code segment that initializes the SDRAM. The `startup_ixp4xx.s` file is included in both the kernel and Eboot builds. The SDRAM is initialized only during the Eboot phase.

Line 401

Load the Intel XScale core register 9 with the address of the SDRAM configuration register. This address is the physical address of the register as the memory management unit is not active at this point of the boot sequence.

Line 402

Load the Intel XScale core register 0 with the SDRAM configuration value. There are configurations defined for 32, 64, 128, and 256 megabytes of SDRAM. You should verify that the definition matches your exact memory configuration, as there are a number of different chip configurations that can be used for each particular memory footprint.

Line 403

Write the configuration value into the SDRAM configuration register.

Line 408

The SDRAM controller performs the refresh cycles for the SDRAM. The SDRAM chip defines the frequency at which the SDRAM must be refreshed. SDRAM is usually described in terms of a matrix of rows and columns. The refresh cycle refreshes an entire row each time it executes. The SDRAM specification usually indicates how frequent each device must be refreshed. If your SDRAM configuration or footprint changes, check this value to ensure it is still accurate.

SDRAM Footprint

The footprint defines the amount of SDRAM in the system. It controls the memory map and not the actual configuration of the SDRAM controller. The default configuration is 64 megabytes.

File:

c:\WINCE500\PLATFORM\INTEL_IXDP425\intel_ixdp425.bat

```
411
412    set the BSP environment variable BSP_32
413    set the BSP environment variable BSP_64 to one
414    set the BSP environment variable BSP_128
415    set the BSP environment variable BSP_256
416
417    /* code removed */
```

Lines 412-415

These lines are the environmental variables used to control the memory footprint. Only one of them should be set equal to 1 at any time.

Nonvolatile Storage

The nonvolatile storage is provided by the main flash device. The BSP supports two flash-based file system types, namely binary file system (BINFS) and transaction FAT (TFAT). Eboot stores the kernel image (NK.BIN) in a BINFS partition. This partition can be made visible to the application to facilitate the upgrade of the kernel image. The BINFS partition is only large enough to accommodate the kernel image; the remainder of the flash is configured as a TFAT partition. The TFAT partition system shows up as a folder that can be accessed just like any other Windows folder. The contents are persistent across a platform restart.

File:

c:\WINCE500\PLATFORM\INTEL_IXDP425\intel_ixdp425.bat

```
418
419    REM Strata Flash driver.
420    set the BSP variable BSP_IXP4XX_STRATAFMD to one
421    set the BSP varialbe SYSGEN_TFAT to one
422    /* code removed */
```

Lines 420-421

Enable the Intel StrataFlash memory media driver for IXP4XX network processors and enables the Microsoft transaction FAT file system.

Along with the settings in the batch file shown above, the registry contains settings to enable the flash drivers and file system.

File:

c:\WINCE500\PLATFORM\INTEL_IXDP425\DRIVERS\BLOCK\MSFLASHF
MD\STRATA\Dll\ixp4xx_stratad.reg

```
423
424    Under the StorageManager\Profiles\MSFlash key
425       Set "Name" equal to "MSFLASH for STRATAFLASH"
426       Set "DefaultFileSystem" equal to "FATFS"
427       Set "Folder" equal to "NOR Flash"
428       Set "PartitionDriver" equal to "mspart.dll"
429       Set "AutoMount" equal to 1
430       Set "AutoPart" equal to 1
431       Set "AutoFormat" equal to 1
432       Set "MountFlags" equal to 2
433
434    Under the StorageManager\Profiles\MSFlash\FATFS key
435       Set "Dll" equal to "fatfsd.dll"
436       Set "Flags" equal to hex:0100024
437       Set "Util" equal to "fatutil.dll"
438       Set "Paging" equal to 1
439       Set "EnableCache" equal to 1
440       Set "CacheSize" equal to 0
441       Set "CacheDll" equal to "diskcache.dll"
442       Set "FormatTfat" equal to 1
```

The interesting details are covered here; for all other register values see the Platform Builder Help.

Line 427

This line is the folder name under which the TFAT partition is accessible.

Line 442

This line explicitly enables the transaction features. Transaction flash file systems are much more resilient than other file systems during power cycles of the platform.

PCI Configuration

The PCI bus requires a number of GPIO pins to assist in the operation of the PCI bus. The functions required are PCI clock, PCI reset pin, and four GPIO pins for the PCI bus interrupts INTA, INTB, INTC, and INTD. The code sequence below shows how the GPIO pins were allocated to these functions. The PCI interrupts are allocated using the Windows CE installable interrupt service routines component (GIISR).

```
File:

c:\WINCE500\PLATFORM\INTEL_IXDP425\inc\ixdp425.h
443
444
445   Set IXP425_PCI_INTA_PIN to IXP425_GPIO_PIN_11
446   Set IXP425_PCI_INTB_PIN to IXP425_GPIO_PIN_10
447   Set IXP425_PCI_INTC_PIN to IXP425_GPIO_PIN_9
448   Set IXP425_PCI_INTD_PIN to IXP425_GPIO_PIN_8
449
450   set IXP425_PCI_CLK_PIN to IXP425_GPIO_CLK_0
451   set IXP425_PCI_RESET_GPIO to IXP425_GPIO_PIN_13
452   /* code removed */
```

Lines 445-448

Allocate the GPIO pins 8 to 11 for the PCU interrupts.

Line 450

Allocate the GPIO pin 14 for the PCI clock.

Line 451

Allocate GPIO pin 13 as the PCI bus reset pin.

Serial Port

Both serial ports are available to the application. They can be assessed as COM0 and COM1. They are explicitly enabled in the platform registry file and the platform batch file.

```
File:

c:\WINCE500\PLATFORM\INTEL_IXDP425\intel_ixdp425.bat
453
454    set BSP_variable for UART1 equal to 1
455    set BSP_variable for UART2 equal to 1
456
```

Lines 454-455

Both UARTs are enabled by default. To disable a UART you must set the appropriate variables.

Chapter 5

Software Toolkit Architecture

There are two ways of constructing a software design. One way is to make it so simple that there are obviously no deficiencies. The other way is to make it so complicated that there are no obvious deficiencies.

—Sir Tony Hoare

The Intel® IXP400 software serves as the software toolkit for the Intel® IXP4XX Network Processor. This toolkit is partitioned into a set of components or software libraries that closely corresponds to the hardware interfaces on the IXP4XX network processor. The design of each of these components follows some common principles. In this chapter, we outline these principles and describe the components at a high level. We also show you how the Intel IXP400 software can fit within the architecture of your own application.

What is Software Architecture?

First, a short digression on software architecture—what it is and why it is important. *Software architecture* is the overall map of the software system, sometimes called the high-level design. An architecture can provide the designer with significant help during the construction of a system.

> *"… the quality of the architecture determines the conceptual integrity of the system. That in turn determines the ultimate quality of the system. Good architecture makes construction easy."*
>
> —Steve McConnell (McConnell 1993)

Every system has an architecture whether you identify it or not. This book has an architecture, an outline, that helped us stay on course during the writing of it. Some systems have evolved without any documented architecture, but they still have an architecture.

Identifying an architecture for your system is an important consideration. As a designer, you must decide whether you want to make the architecture explicit or implicit. For small systems, creating an intricate, detailed architecture can be a waste of valuable development time. For medium- to large-sized systems, an implicit, unconscious architecture can turn your system into quite literally a "big ball of mud" (Foote and Yoder 1997).

Software architectures vary in size. Some methodologists advocate keeping the documentation of the architecture short, specifying the system's characteristics at a very general level, serving as a system metaphor (Beck 1999). Some architectures require specifications hundreds of pages long.

Krutchen (1995) describes five different types of architectural views of a system. These can be represented as Unified Modeling Language (UML) diagrams. These diagrams can in turn be classified as one of three types of models, which are particularly useful in describing the kinds of systems in which you might use the IXP4XX network processor.

- The static model stresses components, libraries, or modules and their dependencies.

- The dynamic model focuses on the main scenarios that the system performs. In a networking application, this model would focus on the reception, processing, and transmission of packets.

- The deployment model focuses on the allocation of processing to processors and threads.

The Software Engineering Institute (SEI) has an excellent Web site, listed in "References," on software architecture. It contains references to many useful books, papers, and Web sites.

The Intel IXP400 Software in Your System Architecture

In this section, the three architecture models are discussed.

Static Model

You should know where the static model of the software for the IXP4XX network processors fits in the bigger picture of the architecture of the full system you are designing. Typically, an embedded networking/communications system has a static model similar to the one shown in Figure 5.1.

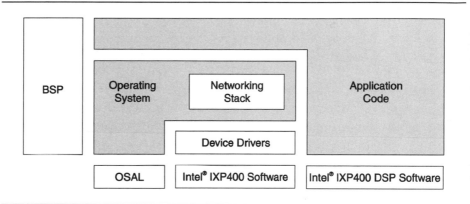

Figure 5.1   Typical Communications System Static Architecture

The Intel IXP400 software component in the diagram signifies the collection of software components for the IXP4XX network processor. Above them, you typically see a component that implements operating system (OS)-specific device drivers. The Intel IXP400 software contains some of these drivers. For example, it contains an Ethernet device driver that implements the Linux device driver model using calls to the Intel IXP400 software Ethernet API. You might have to implement OS-specific device drivers if Intel or your OS vendor does not supply the ones you need.

Intel IXP400 software also makes use of some services such as semaphores, interrupt control, and timers in the OS you have selected. Intel IXP400 software contains a component called an OS abstraction layer (OSAL), which is an adapter for these services. All OS-specific code for the Intel IXP400 software is isolated into this one component. The RTOS is your "real-time operating system." Again, Intel provides implementations of OSAL for three RTOSs: Linux[†], VxWorks[†], and Windows[†] CE. If you use another RTOS, your vendor might supply an implementation of OSAL for the IXP4XX network processor. If the vendor does not supply an implementation or you have your own internal operating system, you need to implement OSAL using your chosen operating system. You can also use the implementation of OSAL to make your application-specific code RTOS independent.

A large number of RTOSs are available for the IXP4XX network processors. The RTOS provides a framework for your application. It might include a networking stack as shown in Figure 5.1.

The Intel IXP400 DSP software provides a framework and optimized algorithms for voice-processing applications.

Intel created the Intel IXP400 software to abstract the in-silicon features of the IXP4XX network processors and contain code common to all RTOSs and stacks. A device driver then makes a bridge between a specific networking stack or RTOS and the Intel IXP400 software.

Device drivers are available for the three supported RTOSs. For example, the Intel IXP400 software contains a Linux Ethernet device driver. Wind River supplies an Ethernet END driver as part of their BSP for IXP4XX network processors. Microsoft provides an Ethernet NDIS driver for Windows CE as part of their BSP. If you need to write a device driver to connect another RTOS to Intel IXP400 software and an IXP4XX network processor, look at one of these drivers as an example.

The board support package (BSP) implements the connection between your RTOS and the board on which you are going to run your application. For a detailed explanation of BSPs, refer to Chapter 4.

The final component is your application. This component can also consist of a number of libraries or components. Your application can connect directly to Intel IXP400 software transmitting/receiving packets on the interfaces, or it can connect through the RTOS or network stack. Your application is typically the part of the system that connects or glues all the other components together. The other components are generic, common denominators across a number of types of products. Your application is the value-added software, the unique combination that makes a distinct product.

Dynamic Model

In the dynamic model, packets arrive at the interfaces on the IXP4XX network processor. This scenario looks at the case where a packet comes through an interface connected to an NPE. The NPE stores the packet in main memory and sends a descriptor for the packet to the Intel IXP400 software running on the Intel XScale core. The NPE sends the packet via a hardware queue. The Intel XScale processor receives an interrupt for which Intel IXP400 software has registered a handler. Intel IXP400 software delivers the packets to a registered callback function usually to a device driver, which then forwards the packets to the networking stack. Some packets could be control packets that are specific to your application. The networking stack forwards them to your component rather than another interface. Figure 5.2 shows a sequence diagram in UML notation showing this type of scenario.

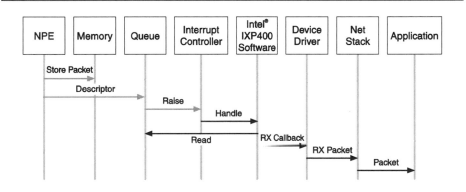

Figure 5.2   Receiving an Application-Specific Control Packet

You can also diagram scenarios using UML collaboration diagrams. Figures 2.7 and 2.8 are examples of this notation.

Deployment Model

Finally, in the deployment view or model, you describe the allocation of processing to processors and threads within those processors. Figure 5.3 shows an example of a deployment model that includes the four processing elements inside the IXP4XX network processor itself, three NPE processors, and the Intel XScale core.

Your application, which may consist of a number of threads, runs on the Intel XScale core. Your design may use other devices for which you develop code, in this example a wireless LAN (WLAN) card. The deployment view can show the interconnection of those devices to the IXP4XX network processor.

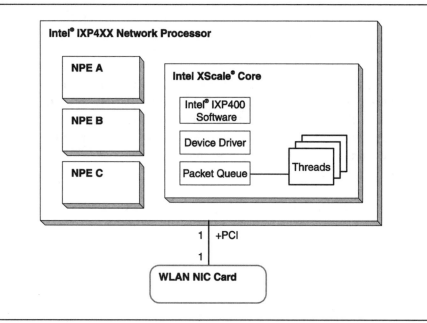

Figure 5.3   An Application-Specific Deployment Model

The Components in Intel IXP400 Software

Internally, Intel IXP400 software consists of a number of components or libraries. These components fall into a number of categories. Each component name begins with "Ix." Some component names end with "Acc," which is an abbreviation for access. For example, the name of the Ethernet component is IxEthAcc.

A number of components correspond to interfaces on the device: IxEthAcc, IxAtmdAcc, and IxHssAcc.

Other components provide hardware acceleration or they offload features that the silicon or NPEs support; for example, IxCryptoAcc.

Finally, a number of utility components provide interfaces to manage the NPEs: IxQmgr, IxNpeDl, and IxNpeMh.

You can find the source code for each of these components in the src/{ComponentName} directory. You can find the interfaces in the header files in the src/include directory. Each header file contains significant documentation for each of the functions in the API. Chapter 9 describes each of these components in some detail.

If you do not need to use some of the components, you can exclude them when creating linked executables of your application. Excluding them will minimize the storage and memory used for instructions.

C-API Advantages

The Intel IXP400 software provides a C-API to abstract the underlying hardware features and accelerators. Three main reasons for this abstraction are simplified development, static checking by the compiler, and insulating your code from the underlying hardware.

The C-API simplifies the development of software that uses the underlying hardware features. The C-API provides a strongly typed interface, which means the compiler can catch a number of error conditions. For example, if your code, which calls an Intel IXP400 software API, uses the wrong type of parameter—a long integer instead of a short, for instance—the compiler generates a warning when you compile the code.

Contrast this with one alternative to the API: putting a value into a register. If you are lucky, resizing the integer does not matter. If you are unlucky, the resizing sends the wrong half-word into the register. The underlying hardware or microcode would need to recognize this register's content as an invalid value at run time and notify your code somehow. In addition, you would have to write code to check for this error condition, and you would have to notice this error condition when the system runs. If you are really unlucky, the underlying hardware would not detect the invalid half-word and your software would seem to run correctly.

The C-API allows the compiler to perform static checks for numerous kinds of programming errors that, if left until run time, you might not detect during testing. In general, it is better to cause a failure as early in the development cycle as possible. Meyers (1997) states compiler errors are more noticeable than warnings, which are preferable to link-errors, which are preferable to assertions, which are preferable to run-time errors.

When the C-API removes this category of error, the underlying microcode or hardware no longer needs to check these error conditions. In the case of microcode, this simplification of the code means fewer checks in potentially critical performance paths. Less microcode means less control store memory for the network processing engines, reducing the amount of die-size used to store microcode and reducing the cost and power consumption of the processor.

The C-API also handles the efficient caching of descriptors and, in most cases, the translation of virtual addresses to physical addresses, which the NPEs require.

Finally, the C-API has one other important advantage. It insulates the customer's code from the underlying hardware and microcode. This abstraction simplifies the customer's code and can make it more portable across the IXP4XX product line. As a result, changes in the underlying hardware should not require you to rework code that uses the C-API, easing maintenance. Don't just take our word for it. The Linley Group, an independent network systems design analyst, describes the C-API abstraction as follows:

> *Intel has taken pains to abstract the capabilities of the IXP425's packet engines. The benefit of this approach is that Intel can easily upgrade the capabilities of the packet engine without requiring that applications be rewritten.*
>
> —Iyer 2004

Without a C-API, your code must do a significant amount of "register-bit-banging," stuffing bits into structures or implementing shift operations to move the values to particular bit positions. This kind of code is error-prone and difficult to maintain.

Ideally, your code should use endian conversion macros for data that the core processor shares with another processor. The C-API implementation that Intel provides handles endian conversion for the hardware interfaces and the underlying NPEs, which relieves a significant burden from the developer.

Common Principles

The components that make up the Intel IXP400 software share some common design principles. It is important you know these principles before looking at individual components. These design principles include:

- Standard functions for each component

- Message buffer management

- Managing cache coherency of packet data

The following sections describe each of these principles in more detail.

Standard Functions

For the Intel IXP400 software components that represent a network interface, the API provides a number of function types.

- *Port Initialization.* This function initializes the port.

- *Register packet/frame receive callback function.* A callback function is a function that the Intel IXP400 software component calls when an event occurs. In this case, Intel IXP400 software calls the callback function whenever a packet, voice sample, or frame arrives on the interface. At initialization time, your code must register the callback for received packets/frames.

- *Packet/frame transmit function.* This function submits a packet/frame for transmission on an interface. Your code passes the packet/frame as a parameter to the transmit function. Where a software component abstracts multiple ports or interface instances, your code needs to specify a port or interface using a parameter to the transmit function.

- *Register transmit done callback function.* Typically, the packets do not transmit immediately, or synchronously, on an interface. They can be queued. The calling code must wait until the packet actually has left on the interface, before it attempts to recycle the storage used for the transmitted packet. The calling code can register a "transmit done" callback function, which Intel IXP400 software calls when packet transmission is complete.

■ *Provide packet descriptor for received packets.* The underlying microcode needs a memory location to store a packet that it received on an interface. Your code must provide this memory by calling a function, which typically ends in `FreeReplenish`. When the access layer software runs out of memory for received packets, it drops packets from the interface. This activity allows the calling code to limit the flow of received packets by limiting the supply of free buffers to the access component.

■ *Show Function.* Each component implements one or more "show" functions, which print statistics. You can use these functions to track buffers and calls to the component APIs and they may help you when debugging your application.

To summarize, the typical sequence of calls to initialize an Intel IXP400 software API is:

1. Initialize the interface.

2. Register callback functions for packet receive and transmit done.

3. Replenish the interface with buffers to store received packets.

4. Enable the interface.

When a packet arrives at an interface, one typical high-level sequence is:

1. Intel IXP400 software calls the receive callback function that is typically located in a device driver.

2. The device driver passes the packet into the networking stack.

3. The networking stack might decide to route the packet to another interface. It might modify the packet removing or adding encapsulation. The stack then calls the transmit function on a device driver.

4. The device driver calls the transmit function on the Intel IXP400 software interface.

5. When the packet transmission is complete, Intel IXP400 software calls the transmit done callback function you registered, which then typically replenishes the packet memory into a system pool or directly back to the interface where the packet came from in step one above.

Message Buffers

Message buffers are parameters on many of the Intel IXP400 software API functions. Message buffers or packet descriptors are structures that reference packets in memory and represent the packets sent to and received from the interfaces on the IXP4XX network processor. You can use message buffers to chain a number of segments of memory together to form a single packet. You can also add encapsulation at the start or append other data at the end of the packet without copying the packet data into another memory buffer.

Intel IXP400 software uses a message buffer structure (IX_OSAL_MBUF) that is similar to the one from BSD. All networking stacks use something like a message buffer. For example, Linux uses a structure called sk_buff and a Linux device driver needs to convert sk_buffs to Intel IXP400 software message buffers. The Linux Ethernet driver contains some good example code where it performs this conversion with "zero-copies" of packet data. The function mbuf_swap_skb in the driver interlinks IX_OSAL_MBUF with Linux sk_buff. IX_OSAL_MBUFs can overlay BSD or VxWorks IPv4 message buffers with minimum descriptor or message buffer conversions.

Intel IXP400 software releases before version 1.5 called the message buffer IX_MBUF. Releases after 1.5 include typedefs and #defines to translate to the new structure names and macros. Therefore, any code you wrote before the 1.5 release will still compile and work.

While the message buffer is a C-struct, Intel IXP400 software provides #defines to allow your code to access the fields of the structure. These #defines insulate your code from changes in the underlying C-struct for the message buffer with no performance penalty. Table 5.1 describes each of the macros for accessing the features of the IX_OSAL_MBUF.

Table 5.1   Macros for Accessing IX_OSAL_MBUF

Macro	Purpose
IX_OSAL_MBUF_NEXT_BUFFER_IN_PKT_PTR	This field is a pointer to the next buffer in the packet. This pointer is NULL if the buffer is the last buffer in the packet.
IX_OSAL_MBUF_NEXT_PKT_IN_CHAIN_PTR	This field allows external code to store packets in a linked list chain. Intel IXP400 software can overwrite this field.
IX_OSAL_MBUF_MDATA	This macro returns a pointer to the data in the buffer, typically the packet data.
IX_OSAL_MBUF_MLEN	The length of the data in this buffer
IX_OSAL_MBUF_TYPE	A type field, component dependent
IX_OSAL_MBUF_FLAGS	A flags field, component dependent
IX_OSAL_MBUF_NET_POOL	A pointer to a pool from which the buffer was allocated
IX_OSAL_MBUF_PKT_LEN	The length of the full packet when all of the buffers are added together

Buffer Allocation

The Intel IXP400 software libraries do not allocate any of the packet buffers. Intel IXP400 software expects your code or an OS-specific device driver to allocate the buffers and provide them to Intel IXP400 software by calling the `transmit` and `replenish` functions mentioned in the Standard Functions section above. The design goal of Intel IXP400 software is to be general purpose and provide abstraction for the underlying silicon without adding a significant amount of overhead.

The Intel IXP400 software library provides comprehensive OS-abstracted buffer management via OSAL. Alternatively, you can use OS-specific buffer allocation and provide translations for the buffers.

Cache Coherency of Packet Data

When you use Intel IXP400 software, you need to be aware of the interactions between packet buffers and descriptors and the cache on the Intel XScale core. The IXP4XX network processor is a multiprocessor system (the Intel XScale core and NPEs), and all of these processors can read and write to main memory independently. Secondly, the Intel XScale core contains an L1 cache, and the IXP4XX network processor does not manage cache coherency automatically in hardware. Hennessy and Patterson (2003) give more information on caches and coherency. When hardware does not manage coherency, the software developer must write code to maintain it.

To understand the need for coherency, consider the following example. Code running on the Intel XScale core updates a packet header. The packet header is in the cache and, as a result, the cached copy is newer than the copy in main memory. The Intel XScale core code then forwards the frame to Intel IXP400 software, which then sends it to the NPE for transmission. When the NPE reads the packet data from the main memory, it reads an out-of-date copy of the data. In this case, the Intel XScale core should have flushed the data to main memory before the NPE read the data.

When the NPE receives a packet on an interface, it stores the packet and a buffer descriptor in main memory. When reading the packet and descriptor, you must make sure you are not reading stale data from the Intel XScale core data cache instead of the data written to memory by the NPE. To avoid this possibility, you must invalidate the memory location in the data cache.

Cache coherency is a complex area and worthy of significant consideration on your part. Stale and unflushed caches can be the cause of bugs that are difficult to diagnose.

Intel IXP400 software handles the flush/invalidate of the message buffer descriptor for you. On transmit, the descriptor is flushed, and on receive, the descriptor is invalidated. However, your code must manage the flush/invalidate of the payload or packet data. Intel IXP400 software does not flush the packet data for two reasons: it is an expensive operation to perform, and it is not always necessary. Consider the case where your application software or IP stack updates a single field in a packet. The stack could simply flush the required number of bytes with minimal impact on system performance. If Intel IXP400 software flushed the entire packet, it would waste unnecessary clock cycles and bus bandwidth.

The OSAL library provides macros that you can use to flush and invalidate cacheable memory.

If you do not store the message buffer descriptors in cacheable memory, you can remove the flush/invalidate operations from the Intel IXP400 software. We recommend that you do so by undefining these operations in OSAL. The OSAL section of Chapter 9 explains how to remove them.

Receive Path

When you replenish a buffer to the Intel IXP400 software library, you are handing over the ownership of that buffer until you receive it again through the callback function.

When you replenish the buffer, Intel IXP400 software invalidates the descriptor. In fact, Intel IXP400 software makes some changes to the descriptor to prepare it for the NPE. Intel IXP400 software then flushes the descriptor and invalidates it. Before Intel IXP400 software calls your receive callback, these changes are reversed.

You need to manage the packet data yourself. You need to invalidate at least the portions of packet data that you intend to read in the receive code you are running. If you are writing a general-purpose driver and passing the packet to a stack, you might not know which parts of the packet are going to be read. In this case, it might be safer to invalidate all of the packet data when you replenish the packet to Intel IXP400 software or receive it in the callback.

You should not access the descriptor in any way between replenishing the descriptor and receiving it again in the callback. Between these calls, the descriptor might contain modified values, and if it is cacheable and your code even reads the descriptor, the Intel XScale core pulls it into the cache. If this erroneous access happens and the NPE then writes to the descriptor, you receive stale descriptor data from the cache.

Transmit Path

Intel IXP400 software flushes the buffer descriptor when it transmits a buffer. It also modifies the descriptor temporarily and undoes these modifications before returning it in the txDone callback. You should not access the descriptor in any way between transmitting the descriptor and receiving it again in the transmit-done callback.

Again, you need to manage the coherency of the packet data yourself. If you allocated the packet data in cacheable-write-back memory and you've written to a portion of a packet, you must flush at least that part of the packet before submitting it for transmission. The NPE transmits the data from main memory. If you are writing a general-purpose driver, you might need to flush the whole packet.

Packet-Processing Mechanisms

When you design a real-time communications system, an important early decision you make is the processing mechanism you use to handle packets. At a high level, you have two choices: polling or event-driven processing. In reality, you can devise a number of hybrids of these two mechanisms. The IXP4XX network processor and Intel IXP400 software support both mechanisms.

Your choice of packet processing mechanism might already be constrained by the RTOS you are using to build your system. If you do have a choice, you need to make a tradeoff decision between the two mechanisms.

Polling

A polling-based system generally contains a loop that regularly polls the network interfaces for traffic.

Polling can be more efficient when a system is in overload. If packets are arriving at a rate faster than it takes to process them, the system will go into overload. When overload happens, a loop polling the interfaces does not incur the overhead of dispatching an event, which in some typical implementations might correspond to the overhead in an interrupt handler.

Event-driven

An event-driven system is driven when an event of interest occurs, for example, when a packet arrives on an interface. It then processes one or more packets in the event handler, or passes them on to another thread or task. A system based on interrupt handlers is a form of event-driven system.

Event-driven systems have an advantage at low data rates. They minimize the latency between the arrival of a packet and its processing. Polling based on a timer could delay a packet for the interval of the timer.

Using the Queue Manager

You can control the packet-handling mechanism using a component called the queue manager and specifically a function called:

`ixQMgrDispatcherLoopRun`

To implement an event-driven system, you can register the function `ixQMgrDispatcherLoopRun` as an interrupt service routine (ISR) for the queue manager interrupts. When the NPE inserts the descriptor pointer for a received packet into the appropriate queue, the queue manager generates an interrupt, which calls the `ixQMgrDispatcherLoopRun` function. It then calls the appropriate access layer, which calls the receive callback function that you had registered.

Figure 5.4 describes an alternative design—a polling-based system where your code calls `ixQMgrDispatcherLoopRun` in a loop. This function calls your receive callback function when traffic arrives on an interface. Some RTOSs might require you to put explicit processor yields or sleep calls into the loop to provide explicit preemption points.

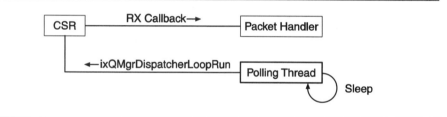

Figure 5.4   A Dynamic Model of Timer-Based Polling for Ethernet Frames

Alternatively, some interfaces and Intel IXP400 software components provide functions that you can call to poll the interface without going through the queue manager.

The only function you should use from the queue manager API is this `ixQMgrDispatcherLoopRun` function. The Intel IXP400 software components use other functions in the queue manager to communicate with the NPEs. You should not use the queue manager to read or write entries directly to a queue.

The system calls your callback functions in the same context as `ixQMgrDispatcherLoopRun`, the polling loop, or an interrupt handler.

The packet-handling mechanism you choose has a global effect for all interfaces. You cannot handle one interface with interrupts and another in a polling loop.

You have two options when triggering the dispatcher explicitly. You can use `ixQMgrDispatcherLoopRun`, which actually is a macro that calls a silicon-specific dispatcher function. If you are using an IXP45X or IXP46X network processor, you can rcdcfine this macro to use a dispatcher that takes full advantage of features in the network processor. Alternatively, you can call the `ixQMgrDispatcherLoopGet` function to get a pointer to a "loop run" function, which you can then register as an ISR, or call in a polled loop.

Hybrid Implementations

You can design a hybrid system that receives an interrupt when a packet arrives, then masks or disables interrupts while processing the packets using the polled access functions. When the interrupt handler runs for a particular period, it can then re-enable interrupts and return.

As an alternative, you could design the system to operate from a hardware timer-interrupt supported by the IXP4XX network processor. In this case, the timer interrupt handler then polls the network interfaces using Intel IXP400 software. Event polling based on handling a regular timing interrupt, which handles many packets per interrupt, can be more efficient and incur less overhead than a system that receives interrupts when a packet is available on an interface.

If you are using a polled system, you need to be careful to ensure you replenish enough receive buffers to buffer the required number of packets during the poll or timer interrupt period. For example, if your timer interrupt runs every millisecond and you want to handle 10,000 packets per second, you must replenish receive buffers at a rate of at least 10 per millisecond.

Further Reading

Ball (2002), Douglass (1999), and Pont (2001) have written good descriptions of the general issues in designing real-time systems using interrupts, events, and polling. Your RTOS programmer's guide contains valuable information specific to the RTOS you are using.

Port-Interface Prioritization

You might need to consider the priority you put on handling traffic on the interfaces you use in your application.

Ideally, you want to avoid dropping packets that traveled across the Internet through 20 routers to arrive at your Ethernet interface only to be discarded because your application is spending its core cycles on handling a lower-priority interface. Similarly, you don't want to process data frames at the expense of voice packets that are more sensitive to delay and packet loss. Finally, when your system goes into overload, receiving a flood of packets, you need to ensure the user interface is not locked up without cycles to run. In general, we recommend you concentrate on the overload scenarios when designing the system.

If you use the polling mechanism, you can handle at least a portion of the traffic from high-priority sources before the lower-priority ones.

A Simple Application Using Ethernet Transmit/Receive

So that you can see first hand how to use the Ethernet APIs and buffer management, this chapter takes you through all of the steps involved in implementing a simple half-bridge application. This example demonstrates the general principles from a Linux[†] perspective. Later in the chapter, you have a summary version of the same example from Windows[†] CE and VxWorks[†] perspectives.

Component Overview

Each physical interface provided on the Intel® IXP4XX network processors has an associated access component. When developing an Ethernet reference example, you can concentrate on three Ethernet access components: `ethAcc`, `ethMii`, and `ethDB`. The underlying principle in the development of the Ethernet access components was to create a series of APIs that abstract Ethernet-related hardware on the IXP4XX network processor. The Ethernet components cover the following areas:

- Ethernet port control
- Data plane for transmission and reception of IEEE 802[†].3 Ethernet frames, hereafter simply called "Ethernet frames"
- Statistics
- Ethernet PHY management
- MAC address database management

The Ethernet access interfaces are defined in the following public header files:

- IxEthAcc.h
- IxEthMii.h
- IxEthDB.h

Figure 6.1 shows the relationship between each subcomponent within the Ethernet component and the associated mapping to the IXP4XX network processor and board-level components. For simplicity, the diagram does not show the support components such as IxQMgr, IxNpeMh, or IxNpeDl.

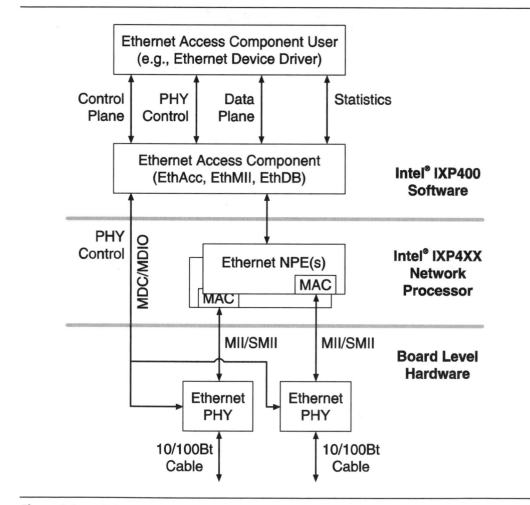

Figure 6.1   Ethernet Access Overview

Ethernet Terminology (NPE, MAC, PHY)

The IEEE Ethernet Standards 802.3/802.1 define separate layers. This chapter deals only with the MAC and PHY layers. The Ethernet NPEs contain an Ethernet MAC block. Designs using Intel IXP4XX Network Processors require an external Physical layer adapter (PHY) to connect to an Ethernet cable or medium.

Ethernet Access Control API

The control API covers a large range of APIs within the component. Typically, these APIs are called infrequently, and they are associated with a change to the control behavior of the component. They are not functions that are called for each Ethernet frame. Enabling and disabling ports, setting up the port's MAC address, and joining/leaving multicast groups are all examples of the control APIs that are provided.

Ethernet PHY Control

This chapter is dual-purpose in that it not only shows a general example of how to use Intel IXP400 software components, but also is a source of details on the Ethernet component. You can skip the following section on PHY control if you want only a general understanding of an Intel IXP400 software component usage.

The IXP4XX network processors require an external Ethernet PHY to connect to an Ethernet cable. PHYs are connected to the IXP4XX network processor via an interface known as media-independent interface (MII). The interface handles the data and control between the MAC and PHY.

The control portion of the interface is simple, consisting of a clock and a data line. The clock and data lines are called MDC and MDIO, respectively. The board designer routes this bus to all PHYs on the board. Each PHY must have a unique address on the bus. Specific hardware pins on the device configure the PHY address. Each PHY has a register map that is accessible through the MDC/MDIO interface. Although no standard register map is defined, most PHY device register maps are similar in function.

The Ethernet MII (`ethMii`) component provides an API to set up and control a number of specific Ethernet PHY components, including the Intel LXT971, LXT972, LXT973 Fast Ethernet PHY Transceivers and the Kendin KS8995 4-port Ethernet switch. The API allows you to set the mode of the PHY. For example, you could set the PHY in 100-megabit full duplex, or set the port in the more frequently used auto-negotiation mode. The API also allows you to query the current link state and mode.

The link mode query API is particularly important if the link has been configured as auto-negotiating because the MAC MII interface must be provisioned in the same mode that has been negotiated by the PHY—for example, full duplex/half duplex. It is a common practice to create a process or thread that polls the PHY every second for its link state/mode. This process or thread must provision the duplex mode of the MAC via ixEthAccPortDuplexModeSet() to match the PHY at all times.

Ethernet Access Data Plane API

The data plane APIs are involved in transmission and reception of the Ethernet frames on an Ethernet interface. The data plane APIs have been optimized for performance because they execute much more frequently than other APIs. The API covers four areas:

■ Ethernet frame submission—for transmission on a port

■ Ethernet frame reception callback

■ Recovery of transmit frame buffers once frame transmission has occurred

■ Provision of receive Ethernet frame buffers

Ethernet Frame Transmission

The Ethernet frame transmit APIs provide a mechanism to submit a frame with a specific priority to an Ethernet port. The frame submit call is non-blocking. This call attempts to place the frame descriptor onto a hardware queue for transmission. Under certain circumstances, the descriptor might be placed in a software queue internally in the Ethernet access component. Once the hardware resource becomes available, the component moves entries from its internal software queues to the appropriate hardware queues.

Once the NPE has successfully transmitted a frame, the ethAcc component must have a mechanism to return the buffer to the users of the component. This return of the buffer is done via a callback. The Intel IXP400 software library provides an API to register a transmit-done callback for each Ethernet port. You must register the callback before the port is enabled; otherwise, you have no mechanism to return the buffers back to you.

Ethernet Frame Reception

To receive Ethernet frames from a port, the `ethAcc` service requires receive buffers. The component itself does not allocate any internal space for receive buffers, so you must replenish each port with buffers to facilitate Ethernet frame reception. The address of the buffers is virtual; the Ethernet access layer converts it to a physical address before it is passed to the NPE. If you do not provide sufficient buffers, the incoming frames are dropped and counted by the NPE. Receive buffers are provided on a per-port basis, thereby providing a mechanism to prevent a port from dominating the processor simply by reducing the number of receive buffers provided to the port in question.

To receive Ethernet frames, a frame-receive callback function must be registered with the `ethAcc` component. Once a receive frame arrives on the wire, it must pass several filters or checks before it is provided to you. The MAC within the NPE performs the first series of checks. The NPE microcode performs subsequent filtering.

MAC Filtering

The MAC hardware block performs Ethernet frame integrity tests. The integrity tests consist of a number of checks that are applied to the frame. Example checks are whether the frame exceeds maximum length, causes a collision on the network, and that the cyclic redundancy check (CRC) is valid. The MAC drops frames that do not pass these initial tests, and it updates appropriate error counts. In addition, the MAC also performs Ethernet frame destination MAC address filtering. An Ethernet MAC address is a 48-bit number. All Ethernet frames contain both a source and destination MAC address. The three different forms of destination MAC address are:

■ *Unicast*. This form is a network-wide or more typically, a globally unique address. The IEEE assigns global addresses, and blocks are available for purchase. A list of current block assignments is available at the IEEE Registration Authority whose Web site is listed in "References." The IXP4XX product line does not come with pre-assigned MAC addresses.

■ *Group Address*. The common name for IEEE group address is "multicast address." Multicast addresses can deliver the same packet to multiple stations. A station that accepts specific multicast packets is said to be a member of that multicast group. To join a multicast group, you must add the group address to the

MAC. Once you add the multicast group entry to it, the MAC can pass traffic with that specific destination MAC address. If a station joins a number of multicast groups, the MAC may pass traffic with a destination MAC address for which it is not specifically a member. The non-precise filtering is due to the use of a hardware hashing function. This hardware implementation is quite common, and typically, the higher software layers subsequently drop the frame/packet.

■ *Broadcast*. This special case of the group address form means all stations. All Ethernet interfaces accept broadcast frames regardless of their unicast address or group membership.

You may provision the Ethernet MAC(s) on the IXP4XX network processors in either promiscuous or non-promiscuous mode. In promiscuous mode, the MAC receives all valid frames and passes them on to the NPE. In non-promiscuous mode, unicast frames must match the provisioned MAC address, for multicast frames the device must be a member of the group, and, of course, broadcast frames are always accepted.

NPE Filtering-Destination MAC address

All Ethernet frames are handled by the NPE microcode. Intel has developed NPE microcode to provide filtering capabilities. A key function of this filtering is to prevent the Intel XScale core from processing Ethernet frames that it is not going to forward. The NPE filtering function drops Ethernet frames that are intended for stations on the same LAN segment as the NPE port. The NPE identifies if the frame is destined for the same LAN segment by snooping the traffic and recording the source MAC address for all frames it receives. A database of source MAC addresses and their associated ports is maintained by both the NPE and the Ethernet database component (ethDB). If a frame contains a destination MAC address that is equal to a source MAC address previously seen on the port, the frame must be intended for a different station on this LAN segment. If the frame is destined for a different station on the LAN segment, the NPE drops the frame. This type of filtering is a standard feature in layer 2 Ethernet switches. This filtering can be performed at line rate, which is defined as the maximum number of frames on an interface at a particular frame size. Usually, the minimum frame size is specified: 64 bytes for Ethernet.

NPE Filtering-Source MAC address

The NPE microcode can be provisioned to compare the source MAC address in the Ethernet header to a list of MAC addresses. The source MAC address of the frame is compared to the list, and the frame is either explicitly dropped (filtered) or explicitly allowed, based on the comparison.

IEEE 802.1Q VLAN Filtering

The Intel IXP400 software version 1.5 introduced the capability to filter packets based on the VLAN tag within the frame. The filtering is performed by the NPE and provisioned by the IXP400 ethDB software component. The following features are provided:

- Acceptable frame type filtering for each ingress NPE Ethernet port

- VLAN tagging and tag removal for each ingress and egress NPE Ethernet port

- VLAN membership filtering for each NPE Ethernet port

- Control of VLAN tagging and tag removal control on a per-Ethernet frame basis

- Support for a maximum of 4095 VLAN groups

You can find further details on the VLAN feature in the Intel IXP400 software programmer's guide (Intel 2004c).

IEEE 802.1D Spanning Tree Filtering

The IxEthDB component provides an interface that can configure each NPE Ethernet port to act in a "spanning tree port blocking state."

Spanning-Tree Protocol (STP), defined in the IEEE 802.1D specification, is a link-management protocol that provides path redundancy while preventing undesirable loops in the network. The STP includes two special frame payload types that bridges use to help close loops in an Ethernet network. These frames are called a configuration bridge protocol data unit (BPDU) and a topology change notification BPDU. The NPE tests each received frame to determine whether it is a BPDU. If an NPE Ethernet port is configured to operate in an STP blocking state, using ixEthDBSpanningTreeBlockingStateSet(), all frames except STP BPDUs are dropped by the NPE. A statistic counter is maintained to track the number of frames dropped while in this state.

Receive Buffer Replenishment

A frequent question arises: how many receive buffers should be provided to the Ethernet receive services prior to the port being enabled? It is difficult to give an exact number because the ideal value depends on the driver model that is using the Ethernet access component. An understanding of the component can help assess the "best" number. The NPE requires a receive buffer in order to receive a frame and pass it up to the Intel XScale core. When you replenish a port with buffers, a pointer to the receive buffer is written into a hardware queue in the queue manager block. If the hardware queue is full, the buffer is saved in a software queue. Once the hardware queue becomes empty, the component draws down buffers from the software queue and places them in the hardware queue.

As you can see, the core must execute substantially more code if the hardware queue is depleted and the application must resort to the software queue. You can choose one of two replenishment strategies. The first is to replenish a buffer as the core receives each frame. The second is to process N packets then replenish N buffers, where N should be less than 128. The block replenishment strategy is a little more complex but usually results in higher performance. So where does the number 128 mentioned above come from? The current hardware queue depth is 128 entries; therefore, the optimal number of buffers you should provide to the Ethernet access receive service is 128. As a rule, it is not advisable to rely on such magic numbers as the configuration may change in the future. Don't take this number literally, as you must tune this value to the needs of your particular application.

Cache Coherency

The Intel XScale core contains a 32-kilobyte instruction cache, a 32-kilobyte data cache, and a 2-kilobyte mini-data cache. The frames and buffer descriptors are located in SDRAM, and they are shared between the NPEs and the core. As in any multiprocessor system with caching, the application developer must consider maintaining consistency between the data in the cache and the contents of the main memory, the DRAM in this case.

Consider the example where the core has updated a packet header. The packet header is in the cache and, as a result, the cached copy is newer than the copy in main memory. The core then forwards the frame to the NPE to be transmitted by the MAC. When the NPE reads the packet data from the main memory, it reads an out-of-date copy of the data. In this case, the core should have flushed the data to main memory before the NPE read the data. This inherent cache coherency problem manifests on platforms that do not automatically maintain cache coherence in hardware. The point to remember is the Intel XScale core does not maintain cache coherence with SDRAM.

All Intel IXP400 software components explicitly manage the cache coherence of buffer descriptors that are supplied to the component. Intel IXP400 software does not manage the coherence of the payload associated with the buffer descriptors. Therefore, in the previously cited case, the Ethernet access component flushes the buffer descriptor to main memory before a message is sent to the NPE to transmit the frame, but it does not flush the payload. The application must flush the payload before the frame-submit call is made.

The component does not flush for two reasons: it is an expensive operation to perform, and it is not always necessary. Consider the case where the stack has updated a single field in a packet. The stack could simply flush the required number of bytes with minimal impact on system performance. To flush the entire packet is considerably more expensive and wasteful. You may also consider mapping transmit data to memory that is mapped as a write-through coalesced by the MMU. In that case, the transmit data is always coherent with main memory, and no explicit flush is necessary.

It is very important that you do not read or write to buffers that have been submitted to an Intel IXP400 software component. Doing so can have an effect on the cache coherence that is being managed by the software.

You may allocate packet buffers to the Intel XScale core mini-cache using your BSP. It should result in higher network performance. The Intel IXP400 OSAL software component uses macros to manage the cache coherency of memory. If you make changes to the cache attributes of the memory buffers, you should update the appropriate macros.

Ethernet Port Disable

Using the `ixEthAccPortDisable()` call, you can disable the Ethernet ports at any time. When a port disable is initiated, all buffers submitted to the Ethernet service are returned to the user. Buffers submitted to the transmit service are returned via the transmit-done callback, even if the frame was not actually transmitted on the port. Buffers that were submitted to the receive path are returned via the receive frame callback, even though they do not contain valid data. You should take care not to pass received buffers to the IP stack when a port shutdown is in progress, as they do not contain valid data.

Ethernet Statistics

The NPE maintains statistics such as Ethernet errors and the number of frames filtered by the NPE. The API to retrieve the counts is `ixEthAccMibIIStatsGet()`. You must provide a DRAM buffer for the statistics. The NPE writes the statistics into the provided buffer in DRAM. The Ethernet access component maintains the coherence of this memory. The NPEs do not maintain counters that you can easily maintain, such as transmitted frames.

Developing the Code

We want to create a simple representative application that uses the Ethernet component APIs. The example we have chosen is to develop a simple MAC layer bridge. We use the term "bridge," but we are in no way creating a fully compliant IEEE 802.1D MAC layer bridge. The example provides frame transport between both Ethernet ports and MAC source address learning/destination filtering. This example does not perform any topology discovery of the network. The topology of a network is established by running a topology discovery protocol, such as spanning tree (Perlman 1992).

The code described in the following sections is a considerably simplified version of the Ethernet access codelet, the source for which can be found in the Intel IXP400 software at `src/codelets/ethAcc`.

Initialization

The following shows the initialization sequence needed to use the Ethernet NPEs. The initialization is broken into two specific portions. A core component initialization sequence is the initialization code required by almost all data path components. The component specific initialization is also covered for the Ethernet component itself.

Core Component Initialization

```
254    #include "IxOsal.h "
255    #include "IxEthAcc.h"
256    #include "IxEthDB.h"
257    #include "IxQMgr.h"
258    #include "IxNpeDl.h"
259    #include "IxNpeMh.h"
260
261    #define ETH_NPEB_IMAGEID IX_NPEDL_NPEIMAGE_NPEB_ETH
262    #define ETH_NPEC_IMAGEID IX_NPEDL_NPEIMAGE_NPEC_ETH
263
264    IX_STATUS ixEthAccExampleInit()
265    {
266      ixQMgrDispatcherFuncPtr ixEthAccExampleDispatcherFunc;
267
268        /* Initialise Queue Manager */
269
270        if (ixQMgrInit() != IX_SUCCESS)
271        {
272            printf("Error initializing queue manager!\n");
273            return (IX_FAIL);
274        }
275
276        ixQMgrDispatcherLoopGet(
277                        &ixEthAccExampleDispatcherFunc);
278
279        if (ixOsalIrqBind (IXP425_INT_LVL_QM1,
280            (IxVoidFnVoidPtr)(ixEthAccExampleDispatcherFunc),
281            (void *)IX_QMGR_QUELOW_GROUP) != IX_SUCCESS)
282        {
283          /* Failed to bind to QM1 interrupt */
284          return (IX_FAIL);
285        }
286
287        if ( ixNpeDlNpeInitAndStart(ETH_NPEB_IMAGEID) !=
288            IX_SUCCESS)
289        {
290            /* Error initializing and starting NPE B */
291            return (IX_FAIL);
```

```
292          }
293
294          if ( ixNpeDlNpeInitAndStart(ETH_NPEC_IMAGEID) !=
295              IX_SUCCESS)
296          {
297              /* Error initializing and starting NPE C */
298              return (IX_FAIL);
299          }
300
301          if(ixNpeMhInitialize(IX_NPEMH_NPEINTERRUPTS_YES) !=
302              IX_SUCCESS)
303          {
304              /* Error initializing NPE Message handler */
305              return (IX_FAIL);
306          }
307
308      }
309
```

Lines 254–259

Include all the required header files for this example.

Lines 261 & 262

Create definitions for the microcode image tag to use later in the example. The microcode images are stored in the IxNpeMicrocode.h file.

Line 270

All data path components require the queue manager component. It is responsible for signaling specific hardware queue events and the appropriate data path components. You must initialize the queue manager component only once.

Line 276

The queue manager component provides several different dispatch loops. The appropriate one to use depends on the silicon version and revision. You must call the function ixQMgrDispatcherLoopGet() to get a function pointer to the appropriate queue manager dispatch loop.

Line 279

You must provide an execution context for the queue manager dispatch loop to execute. The different options for dispatch loop execution contexts are described in more detail in Chapter 5. In this design, the dispatcher loop is executed directly from the queue manager interrupt.

The hardware queue block has two separate groups of queues. All queues required by the Ethernet components have been mapped to the lower set of queues. As a result, we specifically bind to the interrupt for the lower queues (IXP425_INT_LVL_QM1). The ixOsalIrqBind binds the callback function to the appropriate hardware interrupt. Each OS supported by the Intel IXP400 software has a specific implementation of ixOsalIrqBind, which calls the appropriate OS service call to bind to the interrupt.

Lines 287–299

These lines download the NPEs with the appropriate microcode image and start execution of that microcode. The microcode is released as initialized data structures in the IxNpeMicrocode.c file and as a binary data file. A list of NPE images and their features is available in the Intel IXP400 software programmer's guide (Intel 2004c).

The NPE download component provides the API to download the NPE and start program execution. The Ethernet service is available on NPE B and NPE C. To operate both ports, download and start each NPE individually.

Line 301

The final step of the core component initialization is initializing the message-handling component. This step is required for the Ethernet access component to communicate to and from the NPEs. Specifically, the component is used internally by the IXP400 software to send control messages, such as MAC address learning events and statistics queries. The message handler is not involved in the data path.

You should not use any other message handler APIs directly. You should configure the message handler to use interrupts, as in the example code segment shown.

Ethernet Component Initialization

```
310
311    …
312    IxEthAccMacAddr npeMacAddr1 =
313                   {{0x2, 0x0, 0x0, 0x0, 0x0, 0x1}};
314    IxEthAccMacAddr npeMacAddr2 =
315                   {{0x2, 0x0, 0x0, 0x0, 0x0, 0x2}};
316
317    if (ixEthAccPortInit(IX_ETH_PORT_1)!= IX_ETH_ACC_SUCCESS)
318    {
319        /* Error initializing Ethernet port 1 */
320        return (IX_FAIL);
321    }
322    if (ixEthAccPortInit(IX_ETH_PORT_2)!= IX_ETH_ACC_SUCCESS)
323    {
324        /* Error initializing Ethernet port 2 */
325        return (IX_FAIL);
326    }
327    /* Initialize the PHY */
328    ixEthAccCodeletPhyInit();
329
330    if(ixEthAccPortUnicastMacAddressSet(IX_ETH_PORT_1,
331           &npeMacAddr1) != IX_ETH_ACC_SUCCESS)
332    {
333        return (IX_FAIL);
334    }
335
336    if(ixEthAccPortUnicastMacAddressSet(IX_ETH_PORT_2,
337           &npeMacAddr2) != IX_ETH_ACC_SUCCESS)
338    {
339        return (IX_FAIL);
340    }
```

Lines 312–315

The IXP4XX network processors do not come with MAC addresses pre-provisioned. These lines contain sample MAC addresses. You can get these addresses from some form of nonvolatile storage available on your platform, such as an area in flash or serial prom.

Lines 317–326

This code initializes the Ethernet ports. At this point, the ports are initialized but not enabled for traffic.

Line 328

> The Ethernet PHYs must be initialized at startup. The function to do initialization is available in the Intel IXP400 software `EthAcc` codelet (`src/codelets/ethAcc`).

Lines 330–340

> These lines provision each NPE with a unique MAC address, which is required before the NPEs are enabled.

Ethernet Access Database Initialization

> The Ethernet access database (`ethDB`) function is closely integrated with the Ethernet access component. All initialization required for the NPE ports is performed automatically by the Ethernet access component (`ethAcc`).
>
> The Ethernet MAC database performs automatic aging of MAC address entries. Aging is the removal of database entries for MAC addresses that have not been seen in a certain period. By default, MAC addresses older than 15 minutes are removed. To keep track of time, the `ixEthDBDatabaseMaintenance()` function must be called if the MAC source learning feature is required, as is the case for our sample application.

Ethernet Access Database Initialization

> You must create an operating system thread or task in which the following code section executes.

```
341
342    while (1)
343    {
344       /* The database maintenance function must be
345          called at a period of approximately
346          IX_ETH_ACC_MAINTENANCE_TIME seconds regardless
347          of whether learning is enabled or not.
348
349       */
350       ixOsalSleep (IX_ETH_DB_MAINTENANCE_TIME * 1000);
351       ixEthDBDatabaseMaintenance();
352    }
353
```

Line 342

This line is the start of an infinite loop that calls the database maintenance functions. You must create a thread/process and execute this code within the thread context.

Line 350

Use the operating system abstraction layer sleep function to pause the process.

Line 351

This call is to the `ethDB` maintenance function. It provides time keeping to the `ethDB` service. The function will age out unused entries and keep the internal databases in an optimal (fastest search) configuration.

In addition, the `ethDB` component can manage the MAC learning database function for other ports such as PCI-based NICs. This functionality, however, is not automatic. You must call the `ethDB` APIs explicitly.

Data Path Initialization

To provide transmit and receive capabilities you must register the appropriate callbacks with the Ethernet access service.

```
354  ...
355  if(ixEthAccPortRxCallbackRegister(IX_ETH_PORT_1,
356                                 ethPortReceiveCallBack,
357              IX_ETH_PORT_1) != IX_ETH_ACC_SUCCESS )
358  {
359      /* Failed to register Rx callback for port 1 */
360      return (IX_FAIL);
361  }
362  if(ixEthAccPortRxCallbackRegister(IX_ETH_PORT_2,
363                                 ethPortReceiveCallBack,
364              IX_ETH_PORT_2) != IX_ETH_ACC_SUCCESS )
365  {
366      /* Failed to register Rx callback for port 2 */
367      return(IX_FAIL);
368  }
369  if (ixEthAccPortTxDoneCallbackRegister(IX_ETH_PORT_1,
370                                 ethPortTxDoneCallback,
371              IX_ETH_PORT_1) != IX_ETH_ACC_SUCCESS)
372  {
373      /* Failed to register Tx done callback for port 1 */
374      return (IX_FAIL);
```

```
375     }
376
377     if (ixEthAccPortTxDoneCallbackRegister(IX_ETH_PORT_2,
378                              ethPortTxDoneCallback,
379                  IX_ETH_PORT_2) != IX_ETH_ACC_SUCCESS)
380     {
381         /* Failed to register Tx done callback for port 2 */
382         return (IX_FAIL);
383     }
384
```

Lines 355–368

Show the registration of the receive callback function for each Ethernet port. The Ethernet access component calls the receive callback when a valid Ethernet frame is received; that is, only if the frame has not already been filtered by the MAC or NPE microcode. You might have noticed that the same callback is used for both Ethernet ports, which is fine because we have also registered a tag with the callback. The tag is passed into the receive callback function when it is called. In this simple case, the port identifier is used as the tag. When developing an OS device driver, the tag is more likely to be used to point to device-driver metadata.

Lines 369–383

Show the registration of the transmit-done callback function for each Ethernet port. The Ethernet access component calls the transmit-done callback once the frame has been successfully transmitted on the media. The transmit-done callback is called with the buffer that has been transmitted and the registered tag.

Receive Buffers

You must provide receive buffers to each Ethernet port before any frames can be received. To simplify the example, statically allocated buffers are supplied to the Ethernet access receive service. In a device-driver implementation, implementing a buffer pool mechanism would be better because you can allocate and free buffers.

```
387     #include "IxOSAL.h"
388     #define NUM_BUFFERS_TO_REPLENISH (128)
389     #define NUM_PORTS (2)
390     #define RX_PKT_SIZE (1536)
391
392     IX_OSAL_MBUF *receiveMbuf;
```

```
393   UINT8    *mbufData;
394
395   IX_OSAL_MBUF *mBufPtr;
396   UINT32 numBufs;
397   UINT32 mBufCacheSize;
398   IxEthAccPortId portId = IX_ETH_PORT_1;
399
400   /* Round up the size of the mbuf to the cache line */
401    mBufCacheSize =
402    ((((sizeof (IX_OSAL_MBUF)) +
403     (IX_OSAL_CACHE_LINE_SIZE - 1)) /
404     IX_OSAL_CACHE_LINE_SIZE) * IX_OSAL_CACHE_LINE_SIZE);
405
406    for   ( portId = IX_ETH_PORT_1 ;
407                  portId <= IX_ETH_PORT_2 ; ++portId )
408    {
409       receiveMbuf =
410            IX_ACC_DRV_DMA_MALLOC(NUM_BUFFERS_TO_REPLENISH
411                                    * mBufCacheSize);
412
413       mbufData =
414            IX_ACC_DRV_DMA_MALLOC(NUM_BUFFERS_TO_REPLENISH
415                                    * RX_PKT_SIZE);
416
417       mBufPtr = receiveMbuf;
418
419       for(numBufs =0;
420            numBufs < (NUM_BUFFERS_TO_REPLENISH);
421            numBufs++)
422       {
423
424         /* Initialize payload */
425         IX_OSAL_MBUF_MDATA(mBufPtr) = (char *)
426             &mbufData[numBufs * RX_PKT_SIZE];
427
428         /* Initialize length */
429         IX_OSAL_MBUF_MLEN(mBufPtr) =
430             IX_OSAL_MBUF_PKT_LEN(mBufPtr) = RX_PKT_SIZE;
431
432         /* No chained receive buffers */
433         IX_OSAL_MBUF_NEXT_BUFFER_IN_PKT_PTR(mBufPtr) = NULL;
434
435         IX_ACC_DATA_CACHE_INVALIDATE(
436                            IX_OSAL_MBUF_MDATA(mBufPtr),
437                            IX_OSAL_MBUF_MLEN(mBufPtr));
438
439         if(ixEthAccPortRxFreeReplenish(portId, mBufPtr)
440                    != IX_SUCCESS)
441         {
```

```
442                return (IX_FAIL);
443            }
444
445        mBufPtr += mBufCacheSize;
446    }
447 }
```

Line 388

Provide this number of receive buffers to each Ethernet port before the port is enabled.

Line 389

This example uses two Ethernet ports.

Line 390

The receive MBUFs do not have any buffer storage themselves. You must attach a payload buffer to each MBUF, which defines the size of the payload buffer for each MBUF. The NPE writes the packet data into the payload buffer. The size of the buffer must be larger than the largest Ethernet frame you will receive, and then the length is rounded up to be an integer multiple of the cache line size on the Intel XScale core.

Lines 393–394

These pointers will be initialized and point to the MBUF memory and payload memory respectively.

Lines 395–398

Here, the local variables needed to initialize the MBUFs are declared.

Lines 401–404

You must allocate MBUFs a way that prevents multiple MBUFs residing in a single Intel XScale core cache line. As the cache coherence is managed at the granularity of the cache line, any cache coherence operations to one MBUF may have an unintended side effect on another MBUF should they both reside within a single cache line. This segment of code rounds up the size of the MBUF to a multiple of the cache line size. When partitioning the MBUF memory, use this value to align each MBUF on the start of a core cache line.

The OSAL component provides a module to manage MBUF buffer pools. If you use this module, it takes care of all the cache alignment issues mentioned above.

Lines 406–407

Iterate through the code for each Ethernet port.

Line 409

Allocate the memory for the MBUFs. This line of code uses a macro that has been defined by the operating system abstraction service supplied in Intel IXP400 software. The macro returns memory for which the cache attributes are known. The memory may be cacheable or uncacheable, depending on the OS used. Intel IXP400 software also provides flush and invalidate macros that should be used with memory allocated in this way. These macros perform the appropriate actions (if any) on the cache, depending on the type of memory allocated by the IX_ACC_DRV_DMA_MALLOC MACRO. The address returned is always aligned on a core cache line boundary. Again, here the MBUFs are explicitly allocated, but you can also avail of the OSAL buffer pool module to allocate the buffer pools.

Lines 413–415

These lines allocate the payload buffer area.

Lines 419–421

These lines contain the general program flow that iterates through all the MBUFs that have been allocated for this port.

Lines 425–426

This code attaches a data payload buffer to the MBUF.

Lines 429–430

An MBUF contains both a buffer and packet length field. This example does not show the use of chained receive MBUFs, so both fields are set to the size of the data buffer attached in line 422.

Line 433

Clear the next packet entry, as chained buffers are not used in this example.

Lines 435–437

The coherency of payload memory is not managed by the Ethernet access component. The MACRO explicitly invalidates any copy of the data that may reside in the core cache.

Lines 439–443

Finally, hand the buffer over to the Ethernet access receive service.

Line 445

Increment the pointer to the next MBUF.

Port Initialization

This section shows the code required to enable each Ethernet port. You should register your transmit-done and receive callbacks as shown later, prior to enabling the ports.

```
448    if(ixEthAccPortEnable(IX_ETH_PORT_1)
449                                        != IX_ETH_ACC_SUCCESS)
450    {
451        printf("Error enabling port 1\n");
452        return (IX_FAIL);
453    }
454
455    if(ixEthAccPortEnable(IX_ETH_PORT_2)
456                                        != IX_ETH_ACC_SUCCESS)
457    {
458            printf("Error enabling port 2\n");
459            return (IX_FAIL);
460    }
```

Line 448

This API enables the port for transmit and receive. It is the last call in the initialization sequence. At this point, the queue manager dispatch loop starts to process frames as required.

Lines 449–453

Perform basic error checking on the return code from the Ethernet access API.

Lines 455–460

Do the same again but for the second Ethernet port this time.

Ethernet Receive Callback

All the frames received on one Ethernet port are transmitted on the opposite Ethernet port. In a typical application, the Ethernet receive callback forwards the packet to an IP protocol stack.

```
461
462    static void ethPortReceiveCallBack(
463                                        UINT32 cbTag,
464                                        IX_OSAL_MBUF* mBufPtr,
465                                        IxEthAccPortId resrv)
466    {
467        /* Transmit the buffer on the opposite port */
468        if(cbTag == IX_ETH_PORT_1)
469        {
470            ixEthAccPortTxFrameSubmit(
471                        IX_ETH_PORT_2,
472                        mBufPtr,
473                        IX_ETH_ACC_TX_DEFAULT_PRIORITY
474                        );
475        }
476        else if(cbTag == IX_ETH_PORT_2)
477        {
478            if(ixEthAccPortTxFrameSubmit(
479                        IX_ETH_PORT_1,
480                        mBufPtr,
481                        IX_ETH_ACC_TX_DEFAULT_PRIORITY
482                        );
483        }
484    }
```

Line 462

Here is the entry point for the receive callback function that is registered with the Ethernet access component.

Line 463

Callback tag (cbTag) is the parameter that is registered with the receive callback.

Line 464

The receive Ethernet frame buffer (mBufPtr) is a pointer to an MBUF structure, which contains a valid Ethernet receive frame.

Line 465

The resrv parameter is provided for future expansion of the interface.

Lines 468 & 476

In this example bridge application, the receive port is identified via the callback tag. Here the tag value is tested to decide on which port to transmit the received Ethernet frame.

Line 470

The API to transmit an Ethernet frame on a specific interface. The function returns asynchronously; that is, the function does not wait for the frame to be transmitted on the interface before returning.

Line 471

This argument specifies the port that the frame is to be transmitted on.

Line 472

The mBufPtr is the buffer to the frame that is to be transmitted. No modification is needed, as the buffer is the same format that was received.

Line 473

The transmit priority of the frame is indicated here. This argument is ignored in the example case because the default transmit scheduling discipline, FIFO, is used. The NPE transmits all Ethernet frames submitted to the Ethernet access component in order.

Lines 476–484

This sequence of code forwards frames from port two to port one.

Transmit-Done Callback

The transmit-done callback returns the buffer to the original receive port. Error check code has been removed to simplify the example.

```
486    void ethPortTxDoneCallback (UINT32 cbTag,
487                                IX_OSAL_MBUF* mBufPtr)
488    {
489      IX_OSAL_MBUF_MLEN(mBufPtr)    = RX_PKT_SIZE;
```

```
490        IX_OSAL_MBUF_PKT_LEN(mBufPtr) = RX_PKT_SIZE;
491
492        if(cbTag == IX_ETH_PORT_1 )
493        {
494           ixEthAccPortRxFreeReplenish(IX_ETH_PORT_2, mBufPtr);
495        }
496        else
497        {
498           ixEthAccPortRxFreeReplenish(IX_ETH_PORT_1, mBufPtr);
499        }
500
501   }
```

Line 486

This transmit-done callback function entry point is registered with the Ethernet access component.

Lines 489–490

You must restore the length fields of the MBUF to initialization values as the NPE updated the length with the length of the packet received.

Line 494

Replenish Ethernet receive port two with this MBUF.

Line 498

Replenish Ethernet receive port one with this MBUF.

Cache Coherence of Packet Data

The Intel IXP400 software does not maintain the cache coherence of the payload within the MBUFs. The device driver must perform this responsibility. Two separate cases arise, data being transmitted to the NPEs and data being received from the NPEs. For data being transmitted to the NPE you can use any of the following:

■ *Un-cached data.* In this case you use the MMU to map the transmit data buffers to uncached memory. Uncached memory is always coherent. In this case you do not have to do anything special with the payload data before submitting it to the transmit function.

■ *Cached data, write-back.* In this case you must explicitly flush the contents of your payload data to main memory before calling the transmit function. This operation can be expensive if the packet is large.

■ *Cached data, write through.* In this case, every time the packet is updated, it is written to main memory. Although the data is not waiting in the cache, it may still be pending in the Intel XScale core write buffers. You must drain the write buffers to make sure the data is in main memory before calling the transmit function.

For packets received from the NPE, you have to make sure that the Intel XScale core reads from main memory and not a stale copy of data left in the data cache.

■ *Uncached data.* In this case, you use the MMU to map the received data buffers to uncached memory. As in the transmit case, you do not have to perform any special behavior in dealing with receive packet.

■ *Cached data (write-back and write through).* The receive-data buffer must be invalidated before your application reads it. The data can be invalidated before the buffer is submitted to the receive-replenish or in the receive-callback function. For receive-data payload, the MMU attribute of copyback or write through is irrelevant.

Using the Tool Chains

The next step is to compile the example code into a form that can be loaded onto the reference platform. We have chosen Linux as the target operating system to illustrate our example. The code is compiled on a computer, such as a PC, and executed on the IXP4XX network processor platform. The IXP4XX network processor-based board is known as the target, and the machine you run the tools on is called the host. The process of compiling code on a host to execute on a different target is known as cross-compiling. Although Linux is the target and the tool's operating system, the process is still cross-compiling, as the processor architectures are different.

The first thing you need is a tool chain for your chosen target operating system. For Linux target systems, it is best to select the same compiler used to compile the Linux kernel that executes on the target to avoid any compatibility issues. At the time of publication, the Intel IXP400 software supports the Montavista[†] Linux Professional Edition Version 3.1. The Montavista release provides a modified version of the 2.4.20 Linux kernel that supports the IXDP425 development platform, GCC compiler version 3.3.1, and other tools such as GNU assembler and linker. You can purchase the Montavista BSP and tool chain or, alternatively, you can build your own BSP and tool chain. All of the required tools and kernel patches are also available in the open-source community.

Intel IXP400 software components are designed to run in kernel mode under the Linux operating system. The Intel IXP400 software build system allows you to link a number of the Intel IXP400 software components into a Linux loadable module. Linux provides the ability to load modules into the kernel from a user space command. To run the example described, you must first create a Linux module with all of the dependent components. Once you have installed Intel IXP400 software and the required tool chain the following command creates a Linux module that includes all of the Intel IXP400 software access components:

```
make ixp400.o
```

Our example requires `ethAcc`, `ethDB`, `ethMii`, `qmgr`, `npeMh`, `npeDl`, `osal`, and `featureCtrle` components. However, for simplicity, use the `ixp400.o` module, which includes all the access components.

The code described so far has no operating-system dependencies. At this point, we have to develop the Linux-specific code to create a Linux module and load it into the system. The Linux operating system has a well-defined mechanism to create and load modules into the kernel at run time.

Ethernet Example Linux Module

The following code creates a Linux loadable module and starts the Ethernet bridge application.

```
502
503    #include <linux/config.h>
504    #include <linux/kernel.h>
505    #include <linux/module.h>
506    #include <linux/init.h>
507    #include <linux/sched.h>
508
```

```
509    static int startExample(void *unused)
510    {
511        ixEthAccExampleInit();
512        return 0;
513    }
514
515    static int __init ethAccExample_init_module(void)
516    {
517        printk ("Load IXP4XX Ethernet example\n");
518        kernel_thread(startExample, NULL, CLONE_SIGHAND);
519        return 0;
520    }
521
522    static void __exit ethAccExample_cleanup_module(void)
523    {
524        /* Detailed shutdown available in ixp400_eth.c  */
525        printk("Unloading Module, C\n");
526    }
527
528    module_init(ethAccExample_init_module);
529    module_exit(ethAccExample_cleanup_module);
530
```

Lines 503–508

The minimum set of includes needed to create a Linux module.

Lines 509–513

This function is a simple wrapper that calls the `ixEthAccExampleInit()`. This procedure allows the initialization code to run in the context of a separate kernel thread.

Line 515

Here is the entry point to the module. It executes when the module is loaded into the kernel. The __init keyword is a GCC extension, which Linux uses to identify the entry points into the module.

Line 517

`Printk` is the mechanism provided by the kernel to log output. When the module is loaded, the string will be displayed.

Line 518

This code spawns a kernel thread with the entry point of `startExample`. The kernel will schedule the `startExample` function to run at a later point.

Line 519

Return from the module initialization code indicating it was successful.

Line 522

This function is executed when the module is unloaded from the system. For simplicity, this example does not fully support unloading. Unloading typically returns all allocated memory, frees up resources, and disconnects from interrupt services before returning.

Lines 524–525

When unloading, display a message. The Intel IXP400 software Ethernet driver supplied with Linux fully supports unloading the kernel module.

Line 528

This code exports the module initialization code to the kernel loader.

Line 529

This code exports the module termination/exit code to the kernel loader.

To create the module, place all the code above into a file and compile it. In this example, all the code is placed in a file called `IxEthAccExample.c`.

To compile the code and produce a Linux loadable module called `IxEthAccExample.o`, run the following command on your build platform:

```
xscale_be-gcc -mbig-endian -D__KERNEL__ -
I<kernel_install>/include -Wall -Wno-trigraphs -fno-
common -pipe -mapcs-32 -mshort-load-bytes -msoft-float -
DMODULE -I<Intel IXP400 software _install>/src/include -
D__linux -DCPU=33 -DXSCALE=33 -D__LINUX_ARM_ARCH__=5 -
mcpu=xscale -mtune=xscale -O2 -DNDEBUG -DEXPORT_SYMTAB
IxEthAccExample.c -c -o IxEthAccExample.o
```

Downloading the Code

You must follow the release notes for your target OS and the appropriate IXDP425 or IXDP465 platform. Start the Linux kernel running on the platform and transfer the `ixp400.o` and `IxEthAccExample.o` to the target. Once both modules are available on the target, they must be loaded into the kernel. The command to load modules into the kernel is `insmod`.

```
> insmod ixp400.o

> insmod IxEthAccExample.o
```

Once the `IxEthAccExample` has been loaded, the bridge is active. Ethernet frames transmitted to either port are forwarded to the opposite Ethernet port. The bridge operates at line rate; that is, it forwards all packets between ports. If you have configured your operating system with an NPE-based Ethernet device driver, you will not be able to execute the example bridge application because the hardware resources are already in use. It is also important to note that Linux is a constantly changing environment, and details we have provided here may be out of date by the time you try them.

Other Operating Systems

Intel IXP400 software supports three operating systems: Linux, Wind River VxWorks, and Microsoft Windows CE .NET. A significant portion of the example is operating system agnostic. The operating system-specific portion is related to the module-loading mechanism. Each operating system provides a different mechanism to load a module into the system.

For VxWorks: The Tornado[†] environment provides a shell (WindSh) that allows standard elf format object files to be loaded. In this case, the bridge example code can be linked into a single object. No additional operating system specific code is required. The example is started by calling the `ixEthAccExampleInit()` from the shell.

For Windows CE .NET: The easiest way to load the example code into the Windows CE platform is to create an executable.

```
531    #include "pkfuncs.h"
532    #include "oalintr.h"
533
534    int wmain(int argc, WCHAR **argv)
535    {
536        ixEthAccExampleInit();
537    }
538
```

You must update your Windows CE build system to create the executable with this code. You can find an example in the INTEL_IXDP425\ACCESSLIBRARY\codelets\ethAcc\sources file supplied with the Windows CE BSP. The Windows CE build creates an executable that can be transferred to the target and then run.

Chapter 7

Some Example Networking Applications

If your eyes are blinded with your worries, you cannot see the beauty of the sunset.

— Jiddu Krishnamurti

The Intel® IXP4XX Network Processor is a versatile device, combining a high-performance core processor with connectivity to a large number of networking and communications interfaces. You can utilize this network processor in a wide range of applications. This chapter describes a few of the many possible networking applications, such as:

- SOHO routers and residential gateways

- Security appliance

- Enterprise wireless access points

- Network-addressed storage

- Embedded/industrial control

Each application is described in the overall network context, identifying specific products that can utilize an IXP4XX network processor. Possible board or system designs are outlined for each product. Finally, each description contains the software architecture for that application, focusing on the components you need to construct or modify.

You may not find an exact match for the product you want to build, but you should find building blocks and ideas you can apply to your own design. The Intel Developer Web site, listed in "References," contains a number of system reference designs that you can use as a starting point for your system or platform design.

From a software perspective, you typically construct a product from the following components:

■ *Intel IXP400 software.* The Intel IXP400 software includes the hardware access libraries and some device drivers.

■ *Operating system and networking stack.* You might use an in-house operating system and networking stack or purchase one from an independent software vendor (ISV).

■ *Application toolkits.* You can optionally decide to purchase an application-specific toolkit from an ISV, which contains at least a significant subset of the functionality your product requires.

■ *Build the remaining components yourself.* You can do all the remaining development from the ground up or reuse and modify components you have already developed for other products.

SOHO Routers and Gateways

A *gateway* is a networking product that is typically deployed as the demarcation point between a private local area network (LAN) and the public wide area network (WAN). A residential or small-office-home-office (SOHO) gateway typically contains router and firewall functionality.

A *router* is a networking product that contains more than one communications interface. It receives packets from those interfaces and makes a decision to forward the packet to another interface based on the IP protocol information in the packet. A router might also include features to tunnel or translate IPv4 protocols to IPv6.

Routers come in all shapes and sizes, from routers in the core network with fiber-optic interfaces that forward tens of millions of packets per second, to work group routers that contain a number of 10/100 Ethernet interfaces and forward hundreds of thousands of packets per second. Core network routers typically contain ASICs or high-end network processors, such as the Intel IXP2800 Network Processor (Johnson and Kunze 2003). The IXP4XX network processors are more applicable to entry-level and work group routers, which are sometimes called small-medium enterprise (SME), small-medium business (SMB), or SOHO routers.

The network diagram in Figure 7.1 shows a gateway/router in the context of other networking equipment.

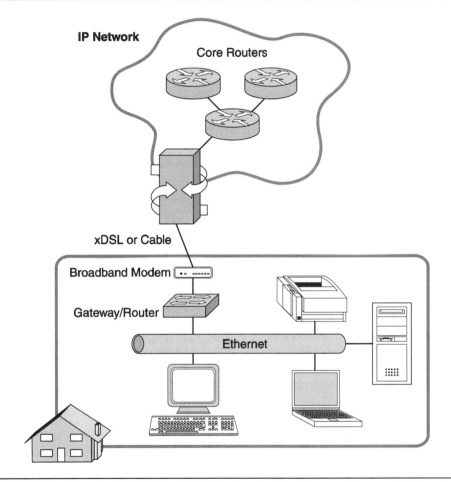

Figure 7.1   SMB Router/Gateway Network Diagram

Besides routing, a gateway also contains firewall functionality. A *firewall* protects the networked devices inside the home or small office from external Internet attacks. It detects attacks by analyzing incoming packets and filtering the offending packets. Running a firewall on the entry point to your network means you can concentrate security efforts in one place. It means you do not need to run individual firewall applications on all of the PCs inside the gateway.

New gateway products are integrating features, such as virtual private networking (VPN) and wireless interfaces. Security and wireless features are covered in later sections of this chapter. This section concentrates on the router with basic gateway and firewall functions.

System Design

An SMB router/gateway connects to a number of pieces of equipment on the local (LAN) side, such as servers, PCs, and printers. On the WAN side, the router/gateway connects to a broadband modem, such as a DSL or cable modem. Some SMB router/gateways integrate both the gateway function and the broadband modem in a single product. Internally, such a product looks something like the diagram in Figure 7.2.

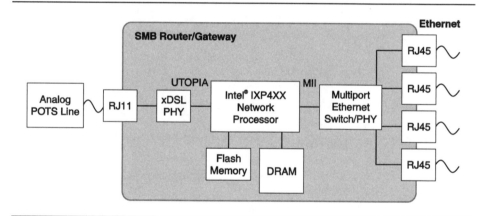

Figure 7.2   SMB Router/Gateway System Design

On the LAN side, the IXP4XX network processor connects to an Ethernet switch/PHY device through its MII interface.

In this design, the broadband WAN interface is xDSL. An xDSL PHY chip on the board connects to the IXP4XX network processor over the UTOPIA interface.

If this product had no integrated broadband capability, it might use Ethernet to connect to a dedicated broadband modem in a separate box. To provide this interface, you need an Ethernet PHY device connected to the other MII interface on the IXP4XX network processor.

Routers/gateways might also have the capability to interface with legacy WAN technologies, such as T1/E1 links. The high-speed serial (HSS) interface on the IXP4XX network processor can connect to a framer device for these kinds of applications.

Software Architecture

Figure 7.3 shows the software architecture of a router application with integrated broadband access. The Intel components are shaded. You would then choose an OS and networking stack. Some OSs may include higher-level applications, such as firewalls or NAT. If the OS you have selected does not, you need to implement those applications.

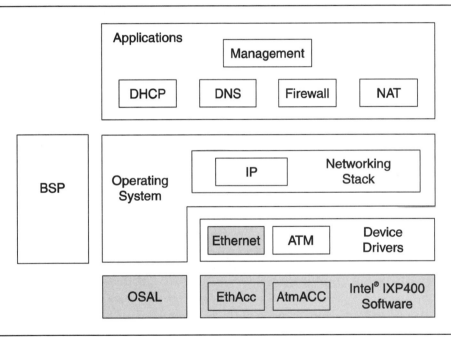

Figure 7.3   Software Architecture of a Router/Gateway

Starting at the lowest level, the device drivers are OS-specific bridges between the Intel IXP400 software and the networking stack. The RTOS or networking stack you have selected typically contains an Ethernet device driver. The Intel IXP400 software package includes a Linux Ethernet device driver.

Asynchronous transfer mode (ATM) is used to transport data over the DSL/UTOPIA interface. The ATM access components of the Intel IXP400 software deliver packets in the form of AAL5 to the ATM driver. The ATM driver is an OS-specific bridge between Intel IXP400 software and the networking stack you have selected. For a Linux networking stack and OS, you can download an ATM device driver from SourceForge, whose Web site address is listed in "References." Other OS and networking stack products might supply an ATM device driver, which uses the ATM access components. If not, you will need to create one. From a network perspective, an encapsulation is used to transport Ethernet frames over ATM.

The IP networking stack receives packets from both the LAN and WAN. The stack looks up the IP address to decide the port on which to retransmit the packet, decrements the time-to-live (TTL) value in the packet header, and forwards the packet on the appropriate port. The stack also supports a facility to allow higher-level applications to hook into the packet flow and inspect the packet in more detail. In Linux, this facility is called `netfilter` and can be configured from user-level programs such as `iptables` to implement a firewall or network-address translation (NAT). Similar facilities exist in other RTOSs.

NAT is an application that modifies the source IP address of packets sent from the LAN destined for the WAN. NAT substitutes the IP address of the gateway and changes the port ID. When a response comes back from the WAN, the feature then reverses the NAT process, inspecting the port destination in the packet header, translating it into the internal IP address, and modifying the header before retransmitting the packet to the LAN side of the gateway. NAT allows you to have a small number of publicly visible IP addresses and conceals the internal IP addresses from the public Internet.

A gateway might also include functionality such as domain name service (DNS) and dynamic host configuration protocol (DHCP). DNS maps a domain name such as `developer.intel.com` to an IP address. If it doesn't have a local translation, it forwards the DNS request. DHCP allows you to allocate dynamic IP addresses to network nodes inside your LAN.

The gateway should include some management facility. This facility might be a mini-web server, which allows the user to configure the router using a Web browser. Again, this server might be part of the RTOS or residential gateway toolkit you select.

Finally, a number of third-party application toolkits are available that contain implementations of a number of the gateway functions and applications. Some of the third-party companies that produce these toolkits are:

■ FuturcSoft

■ Intoto

■ IP Fusion

■ Jungo

■ Wipro

This partial list was created at the time of writing. The Intel Communications Alliance Web site, listed in "References," contains more information on Intel's partners and third-party software vendors. These vendors can supply software components for many applications.

Security Appliance

The previous section described a gateway with basic firewall features for intrusion prevention. This section covers two enterprise applications: virtual private network (VPN) and intrusion detection system (IDS).

A VPN product allows you to run a virtual private network over the Internet. It is a typical feature of an SME gateway product. You would use a VPN gateway to connect a small branch office with a larger enterprise office over the Internet. The gateway encrypts all data traffic between the branch and the main office to secure it as it passes over the Internet. Bulk cryptographic and authentication algorithms are computationally complex, and the silicon support in the IXP4XX network processor frees the Intel XScale core cycles for your application code. The independent Tolly Group (Tolly 2004) has shown the IXP4XX network processor implements the highest performance VPN gateways in this class of product.

The network diagram in Figure 7.4 shows enterprise VPN and IDS products in the context of other networking equipment.

An IDS monitors packets traveling on a network. Its Ethernet interfaces run in promiscuous mode, which means it receives all Ethernet frames, not just those addressed to its MAC address. It then inspects those packets, looking for suspicious data or patterns. When it finds something suspicious, it might store a copy of the packet or notify another system to trigger human intervention.

Packet inspection in an IDS can involve significant processing, which means an IDS system can usually inspect only a sample of the passing traffic. A high performance core, such as the Intel XScale core, can maximize the amount of traffic inspected.

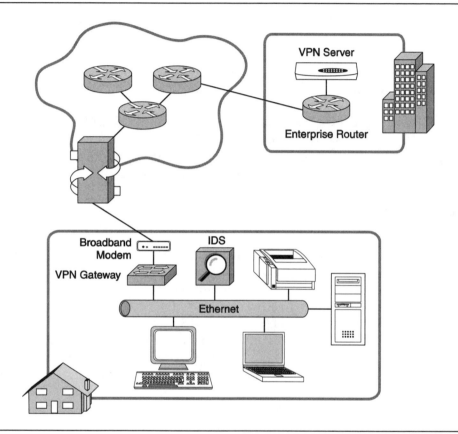

Figure 7.4   VPN Gateway and IDS Network Diagram

System Design

Figure 7.5 shows the system design for a VPN gateway. In this design, the Ethernet uplink connects to an external broadband modem. The uplink Ethernet PHY connects to the IXP4XX network processor through MII. It provides multiple Ethernet interfaces to the LAN just like the SOHO gateway in the previous section.

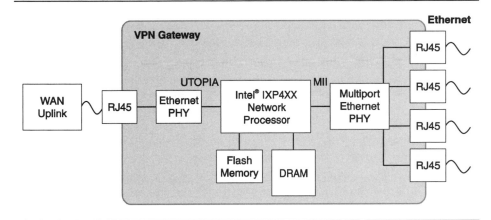

Figure 7.5   VPN Gateway System Design

The IDS system design is typically much simpler. It usually contains two Ethernet interfaces, one of which connects to the LAN segment under observation. The other connects to management systems for configuration and notifications.

Software Architecture

Figure 7.6 shows the typical software architecture of a VPN gateway. Intel IXP400 software provides low-level drivers for the Ethernet and cryptographic silicon features. The IP security (IPsec) application handles the setup of the VPN tunnels, which involves key exchange for the bulk cryptographic algorithms. When the VPN gateway sets up a tunnel to a VPN server in the enterprise, the gateway encrypts all traffic routed to that tunnel when transmitted towards the enterprise. The VPN gateway decrypts received data. The IPsec software interfaces with the IP networking stack to intercept packets destined for a VPN tunnel. It uses the CryptoAcc functionality to offload cryptographic processing from the Intel XScale core.

One such IPsec application for Linux is FreeS/WAN. Intel has modified and published patches to a version of FreeS/WAN to take advantage of CryptoAcc. For more information on this patch, refer to the Intel Developer Web site listed in "References."

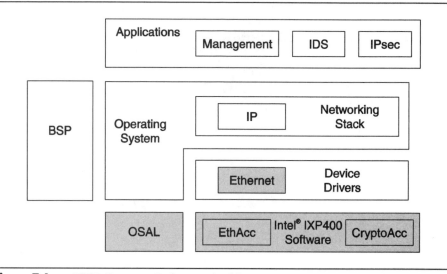

Figure 7.6 VPN Gateway Software Architecture

IDS is a separate application. It uses an Ethernet interface configured in promiscuous mode as an event generator. It analyzes the data on the LAN segment for intrusions such as port scans and buffer overflow attacks. Snort is a well-known IDS implementation for Linux systems. For more information refer to the Snort Web site listed in "References."

If you don't want to develop your own IPsec or IDS application, many of the third-party software vendors already mentioned also provide development suites for VPN gateways and IDS. For the list, refer to the SOHO Routers and Gateways section in this chapter.

Wireless Access Points

A *wireless access point* manages communication in an 802.11 network. If a node, or *station* in 802.11 terminology, wants to communicate with another station in the same service area, the access point relays the frames between the nodes. If frames are destined for a wired network, or distribution system in 802.11 terminology, the access point converts the wireless frames from 802.11 to 802.3 (Ethernet) frames for transmission on an Ethernet network. The access point acts as a bridge between the wireless and wired networks. An access point might also integrate router functionality. Conversely, SOHO gateway products might also integrate a wireless interface. Figure 7.7 shows a wireless access point in a network context.

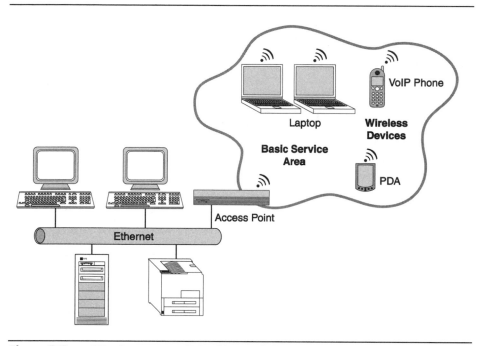

Figure 7.7   Wireless Access Point Network Diagram

The access point can also store and buffer frames for stations that have gone into power-save modes. When a station's wireless interface is first enabled, it tries to associate with the access point. The access point makes a decision on the station's association request based on local data or a backend interaction with an authentication server in the distribution system. Access points also support encryption of the wireless frames transmitted over the air. A number of forms of encryption exist: wired equivalent privacy (WEP), WiFi protected access, and 802.11i. You can use silicon-based offloads in the IXP4XX network processor to offload wireless encryption algorithms from the Intel XScale core, saving processor cycles for your own application code.

Finally, the access point controls the level of access the stations have to the wireless medium, thus providing quality of service (QoS) to the wireless medium. QoS ensures that when a high-bandwidth data transfer between stations occurs and saturates the bandwidth available in the basic service area, the latency sensitive data stream, such as voice traffic from a wireless VoIP phone, is not adversely affected.

System Design

Figure 7.8 shows a possible design for a dual-band wireless access point. On the left of the diagram, you can see two Personal Computer Memory Card International Association (PCMCIA) cards. These cards contain an antenna connector, an analog front end, and a wireless MAC device. The access point uses PCMCIA cards to allow the user to change or upgrade the wireless interfaces in the future. This design contains two cards that allow the system to act as both an 802.11a and 802.11g access point at the same time. The PCMCIA cards connect to a PCI-to-PCMCIA bridge device on the board. This bridge then connects to the PCI bus on the processor. Alternatively, you can use a mini-PCI wireless card or put the wireless devices directly on the board connected to the IXP4XX network processor through the PCI bus.

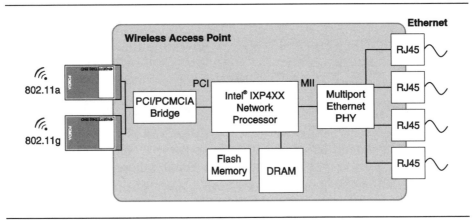

Figure 7.8   System Design of a Wireless Access Point

The access point connects to the distribution system through the standard Ethernet interfaces similar to the ones shown in earlier designs.

Software Architecture

Figure 7.9 shows the software architecture of a wireless access point. Each wireless PCMCIA adapter has a device driver that implements a bridge between the hardware on the PCMCIA board and the networking stack running on the host processor. This device driver should be available from your wireless adapter vendor. It converts frames destined for the distribution system from 802.11-frame format into Ethernet 802.3 frames. Intel IXP400 software contains some functionality that accelerates the conversion of 802.11 frames to Ethernet, thus offloading the core processor. To optimize the device driver, you can use this acceleration. Likewise, the wireless drivers can use the CryptoAcc features of Intel IXP400 software to accelerate the AES-CCM and RC4 bulk cryptographic algorithms.

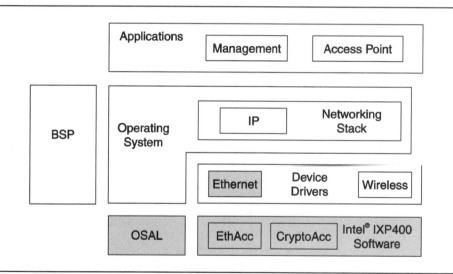

Figure 7.9   Software Architecture of a Wireless Access Point

Some wireless device drivers make the wireless card seem like another Ethernet device. Other drivers, such as Host AP for Prism wireless cards, contain access point features. The open source driver for Atheros wireless cards is called Multiband Atheros Driver for WiFi (MADWifi).

You then need to build an access point application with some kind of management interface. The access point application manages association, power-save, and station-to-station traffic. It might also run a radio-resource-control algorithm to manage the stations in the basic service area of the access point and dynamically tune their 802.11e parameters to enable wireless QoS.

Again, many third-party software vendors provide application-specific software development toolkits. Many of the vendors already mentioned support some wireless applications. Instant802 has an application framework and specific feature packs for many wireless applications.

The Intel/Linksys Case Study (Intel 2003) contains more information on a real-world application of the IXP422 network processor in a wireless access point.

Network-attached Storage

A *network-attached storage* (NAS) device is a network file server that contains or attaches to one or more disks and provides access to them over a network. The IXP4XX product line is applicable in SOHO/SME NAS applications, and a number of such products are currently commercially available. The IXP4XX network processor provides sufficient processing power when dedicated to a file-serving application to provide a compelling low-cost NAS solution. Figure 7.10 shows a network diagram containing a NAS device.

The NAS contains storage and is shared and accessible to all of the devices in the network. In the past, you might have used a dedicated PC for serving files to the network. A NAS device provides a lower-cost solution and consumes less power. You can even share the NAS disks with wireless clients if you have a wireless access point on the wired network. Some products are now emerging that integrate NAS with wireless and gateway functionality.

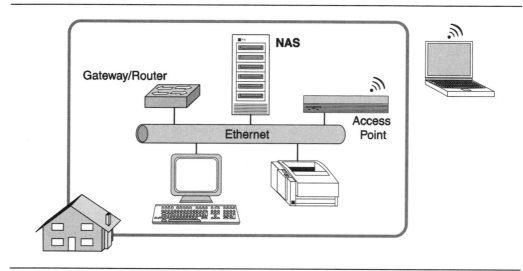

NAS

Gateway/Router

Ethernet

Access
Point

Figure 7.10   NAS Network Diagram

System Design

From a system design perspective, you have two main options for connecting the disk to the product. Figure 7.11 illustrates a system design that uses both options.

The first option connects an Integrated Drive Electronics (IDE) controller device to an IDE hard disk mounted on the board. The IDE controller connects to the processor over the PCI bus. Alternatively, you can use a serial advanced technology attachment (SATA) controller and hard disk.

The second option connects to one or more external hard disks or pen-drives with a universal serial bus (USB) interface. A customer can replace or upgrade an external hard disk more easily than an internal one. While the IXP45X and IXP46X network processors contain a USB 1.1 host interface, this interface can be a bottleneck for disk applications. USB 2.0 has sufficient bandwidth for NAS. This design adds a controller device to provide USB 2.0 connectivity. The device connects to the IXP4XX network processor through its PCI interface.

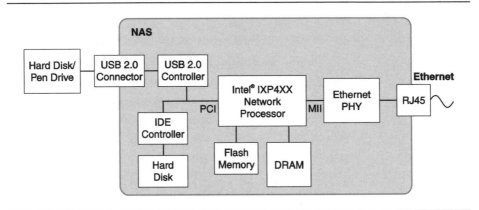

Figure 7.11 System Design of an NAS Product

The product connects to the network over an Ethernet interface. A single Ethernet PHY device connects to the IXP4XX network processor through its MII interface.

Software Architecture

Figure 7.12 shows the software architecture of both variants of the system design. For the internal hard disk product, you need a device driver for the IDE controller you select. The device driver provides the low-level interface the operating system expects to read and write to IDE disks attached to the controller.

For the USB/external hard-drive variant, you need a device driver for your USB controller device along with a USB mass-storage class driver. USB host controllers support standard interfaces, such as Enhanced Host Controller Interface Specification (EHCI).

From an application software perspective, you need a file server application that implements protocols, such as the server message block (SMB) or the Sun network file system (NFS). The file server application authenticates access and supports multiple connected clients. On Linux, the Samba application provides SMB protocol support to allow Microsoft Windows[†] clients to connect to the NAS device. Most UNIX[†] systems contain support for NFS clients.

Finally, many NAS products contain utilities for backup, formatting, and checking the integrity of the file systems on the disk.

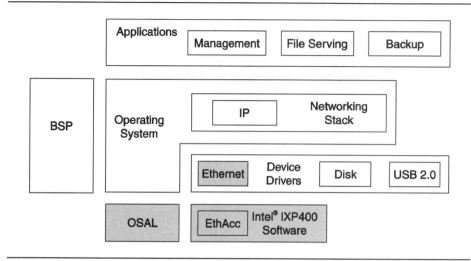

Figure 7.12   NAS Software Architecture

If you are developing an NAS application and need very high performance, you should investigate one performance characteristic of ARM-based processors. The Intel XScale core is based on the ARM 5 architecture. ARM 5 contains a virtually addressed, virtually tagged L1 cache. As such, you must flush and invalidate the L1 cache and TLB when context switching in an operating system where each process has its own address space. Linux is one such operating system. Unfortunately, many network file applications, such as Samba and NFS, create a separate process for each client. Separate processes help simplify these applications, but, in a Linux-based NAS product running on an ARM 5-based processor, separate processes will context switch frequently, causing the loss of many CPU cycles, clearing the cache, and stalling when the cache is cold.

To optimize such applications, a group of researchers at the University of New South Wales, Australia and Snapgear have come up with a technique called fast address space switching (FASS). The technique uses ARM domain technology and fast context switch extensions (FCSE) to postpone L1 cache flush and invalidate until an address collision happens. For more details, go to the FASS Web site, listed in "References."

A good example of a NAS product is the Linksys Network Storage Link for USB 2.0 Disk Drives or NSLU2. A group of enthusiasts has analyzed and developed a number of other applications for this IXP4XX network processor-based product. The NSLU2 Web site, listed in "References," contains significant information on tool-chains, component information, and novel applications for the Linksys product.

Embedded/Industrial Control Applications

The IXP4XX network processor is applicable in a diverse range of embedded and industrial control applications. Typically, these products function in challenging environments, such as the factory floor. Two technologies are redefining embedded/industrial products: the increasing proliferation of Ethernet as a communications technology and the need to connect factory equipment to the IP network. Embedded/industrial covers a wide range of different applications:

- Industrial automation

- Medical equipment

- Military and avionics

- Test and measurement

- Radio Frequency Identification (RFID)

In general, these products require low-power consumption and high general-purpose processor performance. In addition, they need reliability features, like error correction code (ECC), on-memory controllers, and parity checking on internal memories. The IXP46X network processor supports both features. Finally, the integrated nature of the IXP4XX product line minimizes the device count on your platform, increasing the reliability of your solution. Figure 7.13 shows a network diagram containing industrial control applications.

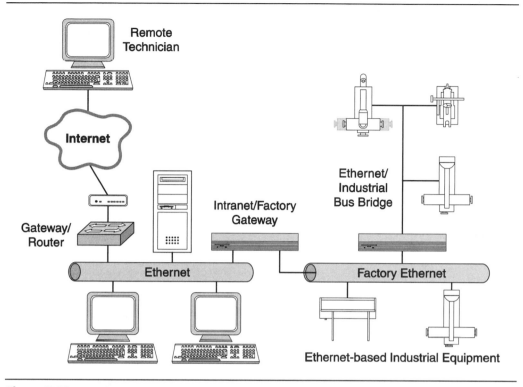

Figure 7.13   Industrial Control Network Diagram

Using Ethernet to connect industrial automation products creates two product opportunities. These networks need a communications bridge between Ethernet and the existing industrial communications technologies. Secondly, Ethernet must be extended to cope with the real-time constraints in industrial applications. The IXP46X network processor supports real-time Ethernet using IEEE 1588 precision clock synchronization protocol.

Adding IP to automation equipment enables two important capabilities. It allows real-time data collection from nodes on the factory floor from applications on the intranet. It also enables remote debug capabilities from equipment vendors potentially from remote sites. Making the factory floor visible to the IP network means you need to secure access between the domains and protect the data when passing through the other domain.

In RFID applications, the IXP4XX network processor is ideally suitable in an RFID reader product. The RFID reader scans RFID tags on products at points in a factory, warehouse, retail shelves, or retail checkout. It communicates with back-end enterprise servers to implement a number of different applications from inventory management to point of sale checkout.

In summary, the IXP4XX network processor is applicable in a number of devices in the embedded/industrial segment. It can function as a control and communications processor in the Ethernet-based industrial equipment and as a communications processor in the Ethernet/industrial bus bridge device. We have already seen its applicability in firewall/VPN applications.

System Design

Figure 7.14 shows the system design for an industrial controller with Ethernet communications interface. This diagram shows just a subset of the control possibilities of the IXP4XX network processor.

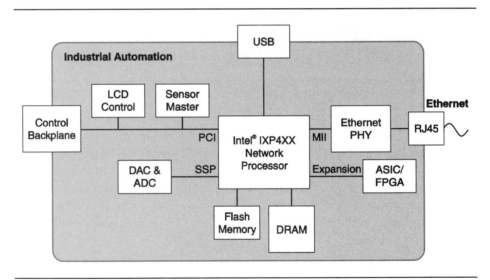

Figure 7.14   Industrial Control System Design

A sensor master device connects to the PCI bus and can manage and interface with other sensors on the board. You can connect an LCD controller through the PCI bus. The LCD provides a simple local user interface for the equipment. The platform itself can connect to a control backplane through the PCI bus.

The platform can also provide analog signal generation and monitoring by connecting the analog-to-digital converters (ADC) and digital-to-analog converters (DAC) through the SSP interface on the IXP46X network processor. You can use the expansion bus to interface to existing ASIC or FPGA devices. Finally, you can use a USB interface to connect to printers and input devices. The IXP45X and IXP46X product lines contain USB host capability.

You can use many of the other interfaces, such as GPIO, I²C, and UTOPIA, on the IXP4XX network processor to connect to devices for embedded industrial applications.

In an RFID design, you can connect the RFID antenna and analog front-end circuitry through a DSP to the expansion bus on the IXP4XX network processor. In the future, you might find devices that implement the RFID air interface and connect to the processor's UTOPIA bus. The IXP4XX network processor provides sufficient performance to run significant portions of the RFID protocol on the core processor.

Software Architecture

The software architecture for embedded industrial products is usually quite different from other segments. As Figure 7.15 indicates, these applications do not use standard real-time operating systems, but in-house operating systems, specialized hard-real-time operating systems, or no operating system at all.

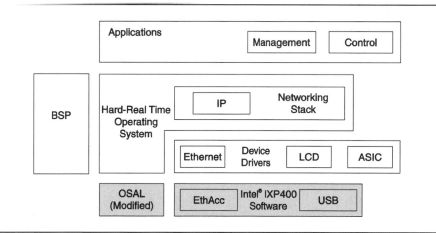

Figure 7.15   Embedded/Industrial Control Software Architecture

If you are using an in-house operating system, you must implement OSAL to provide OS services to the Intel IXP400 software drivers. The Intel IXP400 software drivers should not need significant modification. You might need to implement an Ethernet driver above EthAcc. You should be able to get reference device drivers for the other devices on the platform from the device vendors. These drivers will almost certainly need modification for your environment.

Finally, you must write or port your application to the IXP4XX network processor. Keep in mind, the IXP4XX network processor can run in big-endian or little-endian mode. Select the appropriate endian mode to ease the task of porting the software you are reusing.

A number of third-party software and platform vendors implement subsystems and software toolkits for IXP4XX network processor embedded applications. For RFID, ThingMagic has created a number of solutions with the IXP4XX network processor.

Intel has published a white paper on applying the full range of Intel processors in industrial-control applications (Intel 2004d).

Multimedia Applications

This chapter describes using Intel® IXP4XX Network Processors in multimedia applications. These applications can be grouped into two specific device classes:

- *Voice over IP (VoIP) adapters and gateways.* This class of product uses the DSP capabilities of the IXP4XX network processors to provide VoIP CODEC support.

- *Display-based applications.* This class of product shows the application of the IXP4XX network processor in point-of-sale applications, media-streaming platforms, industrial-controller user interfaces, and IP videophones.

VoIP Applications

Voice traffic has been carried over the IP networks of long-distance voice telephone providers for quite some time. With the massive acceptance of broadband services, VoIP-based services are now available to home and small office users. Broadband access (ADSL, cable modem) is used to provide the access infrastructure from your home to the provider's network. To help you understand the application context in which IXP4XX network processor-based products are deployed, we briefly describe the elements within a VoIP network.

VoIP Network Overview

The VoIP-based network has several main components as shown in Figure 8.1.

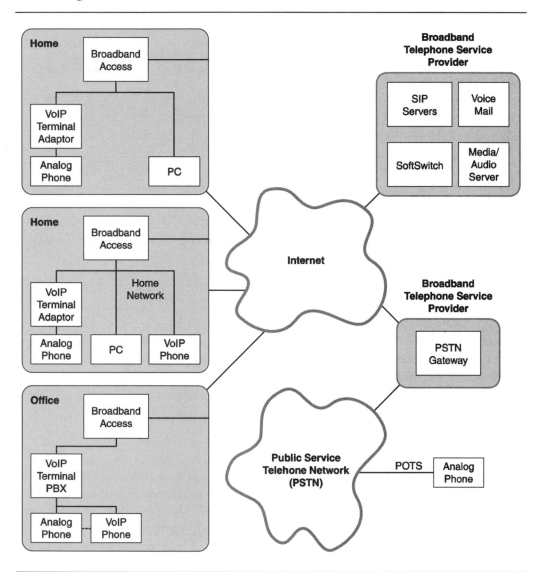

Figure 8.1   VoIP Network Overview

These components are further explained in the following sections.

Voice Adapter Products

An adapter is needed to convert the analog voice signals into a digital form and then package these voice samples into IP packets. Several product classes exist that perform this function.

- *Analog Terminal Adapters.* These adapters convert the signals from a regular analog phone into a stream of VoIP packets on an Ethernet interface. The adapter also registers with a signaling server to assist in making and accepting calls.

- *Voice Residential Gateways.* This product integrates the functions of an analog terminal adapter and a gateway into one product.

- *VoIP Phones.* These products are standalone phones that can connect directly to an IP network instead of the standard analog telephone network. These phones have handsets, dial pad, and displays. They do not provide any analog phone output. A number of these products are also Wi-Fi[†] enabled.

- *VoIP enabled PBXs.* This class of product is used in a business environment where a large number of phones must be adapted to VoIP. It also provides local services such as voice mail.

- *Personal Computers.* A PC can also be used to perform the functions of a VoIP phone with the help of a software-based-IP phone application. These are also known as soft phones.

Infrastructure

The VoIP network needs to manage the voice calls and advanced telephone services such as call forwarding, conferencing facilities, voice mail, and billing services. The main call management protocol currently in use is the session-initiation protocol (SIP). SIP is a standard Internet protocol used in many applications today. For example, several instant-messenger clients use SIP to manage the status or presence of contacts. High-availability servers and specialized telecommunications equipment provide the infrastructure components of a VoIP network. The IXP4XX network processors may be used on line-cards within such a system.

Public Switched Telephone Network Gateway

If you are a subscriber of a broadband voice-service provider, you want the ability to call any phone number in the world, just as you can do with your traditional phone line. To facilitate this, the VoIP provider must have gateways from the IP network to the Public Switched Telephone Network (PSTN). These gateways convert the VoIP-based call to a standard telephone network call. Typically, the provider will have multiple PSTN gateways; for example, one in each main city.

Analog Terminal Adapter Hardware

This section describes the additional components needed to create a VoIP terminal adapter. Figure 8.2 shows an IXP4XX network processor-based terminal adapter.

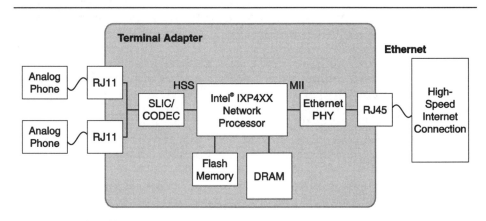

Figure 8.2   A VoIP Terminal Adapter Based on an IXP4XX Network Processor

You can use the IXP4XX network processor in a TA application with very little additional hardware. Only a few external components are required:

■ *Flash Memory* provides the nonvolatile storage for the boot loader, operating system, and configuration details.

■ *Random access memory (DRAM)* is needed to operate all network processors.

■ *SLIC/CODEC* performs all battery, over voltage, ringing, supervision, coding, and hybrid and test (BORSCHT) functions. It converts the analog signal to digital PCM and vice versa. The products predominantly used provide the same audio bandwidth range (300–3300 hertz) as the standard telephone service. Wideband SLIC/CODECs, which increase the audio bandwidth range from 50–7000 hertz, are gaining popularity.

High-Speed Interface

The IXP4XX network processors have a high-speed, digital serial interface. This interface is used to transmit and receive voice samples to the SLIC/CODEC. Details on this interface are provided in Chapter 3.

Medial Independent Interface

The media-independent interface (MII) connects the Ethernet PHY to the IXP4XX network processor. Details on the interconnection between an Ethernet PHY and the IXP4XX network processor are provided in Chapter 3.

The IXP4XX network processor can also interface to ADSL and Wi-Fi chip sets to provide a fully integrated voice-enabled wireless residential gateway.

VoIP Terminal Adapter Software

We have chosen the Linux operating system to illustrate the software architecture of a VoIP terminal adapter, although many of the same components are required for other operating system implementations. Figure 8.3 shows an example software architecture for an IXP4XX network processor-based VoIP terminal adapter.

The following is a description of each software component.

■ *Operating system*—chosen operating system is Linux. We selected Linux to illustrate our application because Linux introduces additional complexities due to the differences between user space and kernel space.

■ *NPE Ethernet device driver*—needed to send and receive Ethernet packets from the operating system IP stack.

■ *EthAcc*—an Intel IXP400 software component that provides access to the NPE Ethernet capabilities.

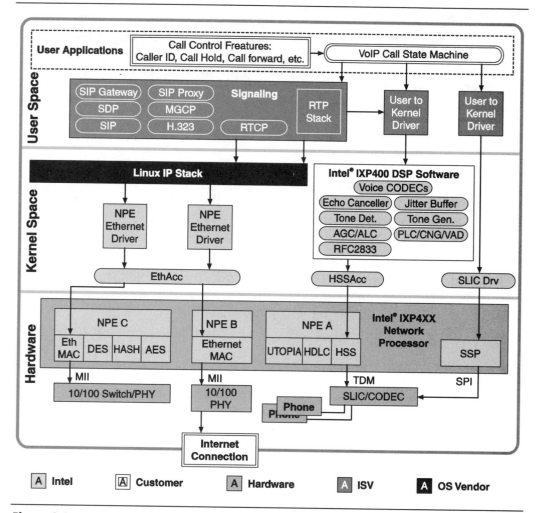

Figure 8.3   Software Overview VoIP Terminal Adapter Based
on an IXP4XX Network Processor

■ *Linux IP Stack*—provides IP services to the adapter. User applications use the IP stack to send and receive packets.

■ *HssAcc*—an Intel IXP400 software component that provides access to the high-speed serial port on the IXP4XX network processor. The component gathers a number of voice samples (usually 10 milliseconds worth) and places them into a buffer. The HssAcc component then calls an application callback with the voice data.

- *SLIC/CODEC device driver*—controls the SLIC/CODEC chip set. The driver provides the capability to ring and detect on-hook off-hook events on the analog phone. The control interface to the SLIC/CODEC is a serial peripheral interface (SPI) bus.

- *Intel IXP400 DSP software*—the DSP software provided by Intel. Further details of the component are provided later in the Intel IXP400 DSP software section.

- *Signaling stacks*—allow the adapter to start new calls and access advanced services such as network voicemail. Session initiation protocol (SIP) is the most prevalent signaling stack in use today. The adapter registers itself with the VoIP provider's SIP server. The server also sends events such as incoming calls to the adapter.

- *Real-time Transport Protocol (RTP) stack*—takes the voice samples and generates an RTP packet. The RTP packet contains the voice payload and timing information needed to replay the voice samples at the destination.

- *Application*—the glue that ties all the software together. It connects all the components so that when you lift a telephone receiver, you can make a call.

- *User to kernel drivers*—for exchanging information. As a portion of the application resides in the Linux user space and the remainder is in the kernel, user-to-kernel drivers are needed to exchange information between the two layers.

You may have noticed above that moving voice traffic from kernel space to user space is not ideal. The problem is that the device driver must run in kernel space, whereas the RTP stack requires access to user level socket APIs, so there is little choice in the decision. Also, the data rate of a compressed voice channel is very low, around 100 packets per second in each direction for an uncompressed voice stream encoded in G.711. To ensure adequate priority of the user thread and *IXP400 DSP software* kernel processes, we recommend that you enable your Linux kernel with real-time scheduler support. In Montavista's kernel, real scheduler support is enabled using CONFIG_RTSCHED in the configuration.

Now that you have an overview of the components, below is the sequence of events needed to make a VoIP call.

1. Turn on the adapter that is connected to the broadband Internet connection.

2. The VoIP adapter registers with your provider's VoIP SIP server.

3. The SLIC/CODEC detects when you lift the phone handset and sends the off-hook event to the VoIP application.

4. The application triggers the Intel IXP400 DSP software component to generate a dial tone back to the phone.

5. You then dial a number of digits. These digits are DTMF tones sent from your phone. Tone detectors within Intel IXP400 DSP software detect the DTMF tones.

6. Once all the digits are detected, a message is sent to the SIP server. The message contains the digits of the dialed party.

7. The provider's server looks up its dialing plan to identify the IP address of the party being called—assuming we are dialing a subscriber with a VoIP phone on the same provider's network.

8. The SIP server sends an incoming call message to the party being called. It also sends an indication back to our adapter to play a ringing tone.

9. The remote phone starts to ring, and the other party answers.

10. The answer message is sent back to the SIP server, which then forwards it back to your voice adapter.

11. Your voice samples are encoded and encapsulated in an RTP packet and sent to the remote adapter. The RTP packets travel directly between the two VoIP adapters across the IP network. Your conversation can now begin.

Two main issues affect the overall quality of the call. The first is the end-to-end delay encountered by the packets, and the second is the delay variation. Delay variation is accommodated by the use of jitter buffers in the terminal adapters. In the IPX4XX network processor-based system, the Intel IXP400 DSP software component has a built-in jitter buffer. When your broadband Internet connection is being shared between the voice terminal adapter and other computers using the connection, significant jitter can be introduced when a VoIP packet is delayed behind a large packet being sent from another computer on your network. For example, a 1,500-byte packet takes almost 50 milliseconds to travel up a 256-kilobits per second DSL line. As a result, it is advisable to select the highest speed broadband connection available if you plan to use a VoIP service.

Intel IXP400 DSP Software

The Intel IXP400 DSP software provides the basic components and media-processing capabilities required for VoIP applications. The features of the Intel IXP400 DSP software v.2.5 are listed below.

- G.711 μ-Law and A-Law CODEC with voice activity detection and comfort noise generation

- G.723 voice CODEC

- G.729ab—G.729a supports voice activity detection and comfort noise generation

- G.722 voice CODEC

- G.726 voice CODEC—with variable encoding rates of 40, 32, 24, and 16 kilobits per second

- Packet loss concealment (PLC)—supported for G.711, G.726, and G.722 CODECs

- Echo cancellation—supporting both narrow and wide band CODECs. The tail length of the cancellation is up to 64 milliseconds.

- Automatic gain and level control—allows manual override and mute control

- DTMF—generation, detection, and clamping

- Fax tone detection (CGG, CED, and V.21 PRE)

- Caller ID—generation and reception of FSK modem signals

- Call progress tone generation

- Dynamic/adaptive jitter buffer

- Audio player—playback of announcements stored in G.711 and G.729 formats

- Audio mixer—supports 3-way calls and conferences of up to five parties

Figure 8.4 shows the internal architecture of the Intel IXP400 DSP software.

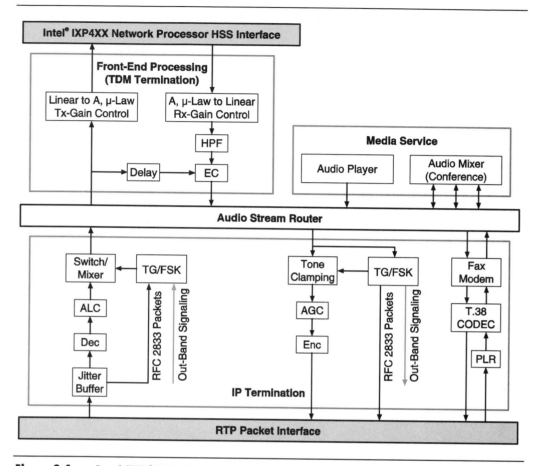

Figure 8.4   Intel IXP400 DSP Software Internal Data Flow

The Intel IXP400 DSP software provides three specific interfaces: the control, PCM data, and the packet interface. A group of media processing resource (MPR) components forms a channel for full duplex media processing. They are the addressable entities that are controlled individually by the application.

The control interface uses a message-passing construct. Messages are submitted to the component using the xMsgSend() function. The application receives events from the Intel IXP400 DSP software component by calling the xMsgReceive() function. Each MPR component within the Intel IXP400 DSP software has its own set of control messages. For example, call the XMSG_CODER_START macro which sends a message to the decode block to start the voice CODEC. The message takes the two parameters: the CODEC type, such as XCODER_TYPE_G711A_10MS, and the number of frames per packet. It is important to recognize that as the compression achieved by the CODEC increases, so too does the CPU usage needed to run the CODEC.

The PCM data interface represents the audio data stream between the Intel IXP400 DSP software and the telephone interface via the TDM data bus. The PCM data interface relies on the HSS hardware integrated in the IXP4XX network processors.

In contrast to the data network interface, such as the Ethernet interface, the HSS interface is an integral part of the Intel IXP400 DSP software. The application must provide configuration information related to the HSS interface by passing parameters into the Intel IXP400 DSP software during initialization. The user application configures the HSS by specifying the signal format to be presented on the TDM bus of the HSS device, including the clock rate, time slots, frame sync, endian, and so on. Such information is organized in two data structures:

■ IxHssAccConfigParams

■ IxHssAccTdmSlotUsage

Using this information, the Intel IXP400 DSP software initializes the HSS interface and starts data transfers.

The Intel IXP400 DSP software supports both narrow and wideband PCM interface over the HSS port. In the narrowband mode, the PCM data format is 8-bit A-law or μ-law compressed data at an 8-kilohertz sampling rate. In the wideband mode, the data format is 16-bit linear data at 16-kilohertz sampling rate. To share the TDM bus of the HSS, a wideband audio channel takes four time slots at the 8-kilohertz frame rate. User applications need to specify how those time slots are located if a channel is configured to wideband mode during the system initialization. Sampling rate conversion (SRC) is applied automatically if a wideband channel is connected to a narrowband media processing resource or vice versa. The superior voice quality of a wideband interface is achieved only when both the interface and the Intel IXP400 DSP software resources operate in the wideband mode.

The packet interface contains two functions and an associated packet format. The Intel IXP400 DSP software defines the packet format and provides the packet receive function. Your application must provide the transmit function.

On the ingress path—packets coming from the IP interface—the IP interface converts each incoming VoIP packet it receives to an Intel IXP400 DSP software data packet and then calls `xPacketReceive()` to deliver it to the Intel IXP400 DSP software. The application decodes the incoming IP packets and forwards the RTP payload and extracted time-stamp to the Intel IXP400 DSP software packet interface. You cannot pass RTP packets directly to Intel IXP400 DSP software. The Intel IXP400 DSP software provides an example, known as a codelet, that demon-strates the transfer of packets to and from the Intel IXP400 software. The details of the packet format are provided in the Intel IXP400 DSP soft-ware programmer's guide (Intel 2004a).

Jitter Buffer

The Intel IXP400 DSP software has an integrated adaptive jitter buffer. A jitter buffer is required as incoming encoded audio packets traverse an IP network where packets may be delayed, arrive out-of-order, are dupli-cated, or are lost without re-transmission. The jitter buffer delays incom-ing packets to allow delayed and out-of-order packets to arrive. The jitter buffer is constantly assessing the IP network conditions by checking the timestamps of the RTP packets. Based on these timestamps and the packet arrival characteristics, the jitter buffer component dynamically ad-justs this delay that it introduces.

Operating System Specifics

The Intel IXP400 DSP software currently supports both VxWorks[†] and embedded Linux operating systems. Figure 8.3 shows a Linux-based solu-tion but does not identify the run-time issues you may encounter while integrating such a system. The three primary performance issues typically encountered are:

■ Performance of the system in Ethernet overload scenarios

■ Network processor scheduling of Intel IXP400 DSP software tasks

■ Variations in delay (jitter) encountered by voice IP packets

Ethernet Overload

Each Ethernet interface operates at up to 100 megabits per second full duplex, which translates to a maximum of 148,809 packets per second in each direction. In a gateway router, these packets typically pass through the Intel IXP400 software access layers, Ethernet device drivers, IP stack, firewall intrusion detection module, and network address translation (NAT) modules. If the device is flooded with Ethernet packets, all of this per-packet processing will fully occupy the CPU, and packets will be dropped.

The application can control the rate at which packets are received on a particular port by controlling the provision of receive buffers to the port. It is important to prioritize traffic coming from the WAN Ethernet port, as it is the primary interface carrying the voice data stream, and any packet loss on this interface may significantly degrade voice quality. The simplest way to achieve port priority is to provide receive buffers to the WAN Ethernet port more frequently than the LAN Ethernet port. When a burst of traffic arrives on a specific Ethernet interface, all of its receive buffers are consumed, which prevents further packets from being processed on that that port until additional receive buffers are provided for use by the interface.

Intel IXP400 DSP Software Scheduling

To ensure optimal voice quality, the Intel IXP400 DSP software component must run frequently enough to perform all voice processing on the RTP packets. For most CODECs, the Intel IXP400 DSP software component must be allowed to run to completion once every 10 milliseconds. The Intel IXP400 DSP software manages the creation and scheduling of all threads required within Intel IXP400 DSP software. Your system design must ensure that nothing prevents the Intel IXP400 DSP software threads from running at the required interval (usually every 10 milliseconds). If the threads do not run, voice quality is adversely affected.

As we discussed above, each packet can lead to a significant amount of processing. To guarantee that Intel IXP400 DSP software gets the required amount of CPU, Intel has introduced a feature known as CPU reservation as in the Intel IXP400 software release. This feature allows the application to defer packet processing on nonvoice-related interfaces. Specifically, this feature allows the application to postpone processing of packets on the Ethernet interface while the Intel IXP400 DSP software media components are running. This feature does not guarantee that the system will be well behaved. You must also ensure that other interfaces, such as wireless, do not prevent the Intel IXP400 DSP software component from obtaining its required share of the XScale core CPU.

Uplink Jitter Control

In the reference example, the WAN uplink is shared between VoIP and non-VoIP traffic. Depending on the speed of the uplink, it is possible that the VoIP traffic is delayed significantly (in VoIP terms). Figure 8.5 shows the differential delay experienced by packets of varying sizes for typical ADSL uplink rates. The max transmission unit (MTU) is the maximum size of a packet on the WAN Ethernet interface. Reducing the MTU results in reducing the maximum amount of delay that is experienced by packets waiting for large packets to be transmitted.

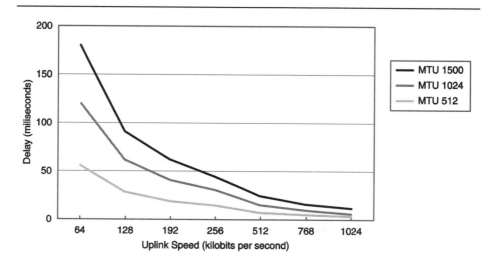

Figure 8.5   Delay Variation Suffered for Different Link MTUs

As you can see, the delay variation can be reduced by altering the size of the MTU on the WAN interface. In Linux you can change the size with the following command:

```
> ifconfig eth0 mtu 512
```

If the MTU is reduced only on this gateway, the IP stack will fragment packets that it receives on other Ethernet ports prior to transmission on the eth0 interface. This fragmentation increases the number of Intel XScale core cycles utilized by the IP stack within the VoIP adapter. Ideally, all devices generating traffic on the LAN also reduce their MTU.

Overview of the Intel XScale Core DSP Instructions

The Intel IXP400 DSP software consists of a range of features such as voice CODECs, tone detectors, and generators that require digital signaling processing. This processing typically relies on the efficient implementation of multiply-and-accumulate operations and saturated arithmetic. The arithmetic logic unit (ALU) of most general-purpose processors does not perform these operations efficiently. To improve the performance of these operations, the Intel XScale core implements ARM's DSP extended instruction set and has also added a multiply and accumulate co-processor. You can find further information on the ARM DSP-enhanced instruction set in the ARM architecture reference manual (Seal 2000).

The Intel XScale core MAC co-processor is known as co-processor zero (CP0) and provides a 40-bit accumulator and eight new instructions. The 40-bit accumulator is referenced by several new instructions that were added to the architecture. MIA, MIAPH, and MIAxy are multiply/accumulate instructions that reference the 40-bit accumulator instead of a register-specified accumulator. MAR and MRA provide the ability to read and write the 40-bit accumulator. Figure 8.6 shows the operations of the MIAPH instruction. The MIAPH instruction performs two 16-bit signed multiplies on packed half-word data and accumulates these to a single 40-bit accumulator.

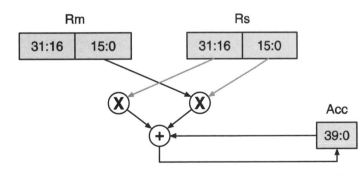

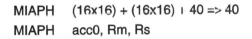

Figure 8.6   Intel XScale Core DSP Multiply-and-Accumulate Extensions

Networked-Multimedia Applications

Due to the high degree of connectivity, the Intel XScale core performance, and low power consumption of the IXP4XX network processor, the IXP4XX network processors have been used in quite a few different applications outside the traditional application area for network processors. Specifically, point-of-sale, industrial-control, and media-processing applications using the IXP4XX network processor are in use today. This section outlines the range of applications other than the traditional network-based bias.

Media Server/Personal Video Recorder (PVR)

Although the IXP4XX network processors do not have sufficient processing power to perform real-time video encode/decode for video CODECs, such as MPEG2 and MPEG4, this capability can be provided easily with the addition of devices to your platform. A large number of video chip sets can be connected over the IXP4XX network processor's PCI interface to encode and decode video. In addition to video conversion, the personal video recorder requires a mechanism to store the video data. This storage is easily accomplished by adding an IDE or SATA controller chip on the PCI bus. The Intel XScale core has more than sufficient processing power to move the data to and from the video subsystem and the mass storage or, alternatively, it can stream the data over one of the network interfaces. Figure 8.7 shows the block diagram for a network enabled PVR.

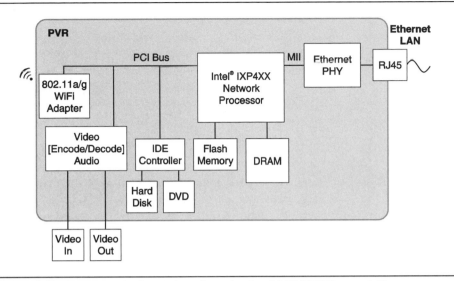

Figure 8.7   Networked PVR Based on the Intel IXP4XX Network Processor

PVR Software

The PVR software consists of a video encode and decode operation, a storage mechanism, and a graphical application. The drivers needed to perform the video encode/decode function are supplied by the video chip-set vendor. Storage of the encoded media is typically on a hard disk. Numerous IDE controllers—for example, the Promise† PDC20275 IDE controller—operate under Linux on the IXP4XX network processors. The application provides the on-screen menus and is controlled via an infrared remote control. A good example of open-source software that currently provides this function is the MythTv application. The infrared remote control interface is connected via a serial port, and software control is provided by the Linux infrared remote control (LIRC) device driver. The Ethernet interface can also be used to stream media to and from other platforms and to connect to the Internet for programming schedule information.

Point-of-Sale/Display Terminal

The IXP4XX network processor can easily perform the role of a simple point-of-sale terminal or multimedia terminal showing advertisements and real-time information updates. The network processor's low power, networking capabilities, and the simple addition of graphics display hardware make it an ideal choice for such an application. A 667-megahertz based IXP460 network processor-based platform can play back multimedia messages encoded using Windows[†] Media 9 CODECs at a frame rate of at least 25 frames per second at a screen resolution of 640 × 480 pixels.

The media can be stored locally or streamed from a media server on the network. The platform supports Windows CE, which, along with Microsoft's Embedded Visual Studio, facilitates the easy development of graphics based applications. The platform even supports the Microsoft Foundation Class (MFC) Libraries. The addition of a compact flash adapter allows the administrator of the system to upgrade the platform with ease. Figure 8.8 shows a point-of-sale/multimedia presentation platform for use in public places such as shows, elevators, and public transport systems.

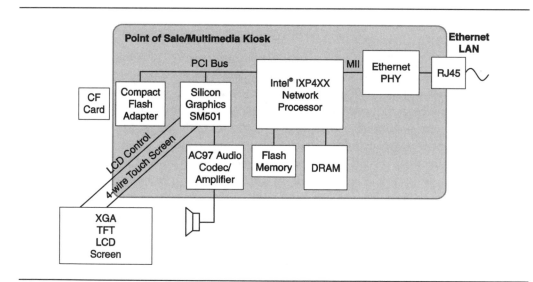

Figure 8.8   Networked Point-of-Sale/Multimedia Presentation Platform Based on the IXP460 Network Processor

Point-of-Sale Application Software

The simplest way to implement the point-of-sale application above is to use the Windows CE operating system. Using the Platform Builder to create the BSP with the required drivers is quite straightforward. The graphics and compact flash drivers are both available from the respective vendors. Intel provides the BSP for the IXP4XX network processor that includes support for the flash, DRAM, PCI interface, and NPE-based Ethernet interfaces. Windows CE provides the operating system, graphics windowing, flash-file system support, and a range of prebuilt example applications. Applications are created using the Embedded Visual Studio application. The number of applications for this platform is endless. Just a few examples include:

■ *Product pricing display with integrated bar code reader.* The application typically displays advertising in a loop until a customer presses on the screen or places a product under the bar code reader. Information about the product is then displayed.

■ *Music store media player.* The user searches a server-based database for the music of choice, or places a copy of the product under the bar code reader. The music source is streamed from the server to the platform. Audio—possibly in the form of MP3—can be played to the speaker/headphones. Meanwhile, information about the album can be displayed on the LCD.

■ *Video rental store.* This application is similar to the one above, with the extension of streaming video in MPEG4/Windows media. The user could watch a trailer for the movie and reserve the movie if it is not available.

Thin Client/Internet Kiosk

IXP4XX network processors are ideally suited to the creation of a thin client/Internet kiosk platform. Typically, a thin client is a very simple compute platform. In our case, we add a touch-sensitive LCD screen, audio, and USB host capabilities. The USB host interface on the IXP45X and IXP46X network processors provides connection to a mouse, keyboard, and additional flash storage/upgrade options to the platform. Figure 8.9 shows an IXP4XX network processor-based thin client.

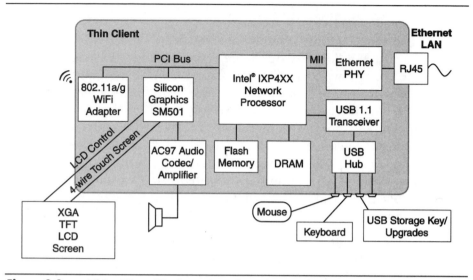

Figure 8.9   Thin Client Platform Based on the IXP4XX Network Processor

The LCD screen is controlled by a graphics chip such as the Silicon Graphics SM501. It also provides an interface to an AC97 audio CODEC. You can use the USB host feature of the IXP45X or IXP46X network processor to provide keyboard and mouse user input. We have also shown a wireless adapter to allow the thin client to operate wirelessly or wired over the Ethernet interface.

Thin Client Software

You can use any of the supported operating systems to develop a thin client. The deciding factor is likely to be the applications available on the target operating system. In the case of a simple Internet kiosk, Windows CE is probably the easiest to get operational because the Microsoft Internet Explorer application comes bundled with it. Windows CE also supports the USB devices such as a mouse, keyboard, and optional USB key support. The USB key interface allows the user to store downloaded data. Figure 8.10 shows the screen shot from a Windows CE platform.

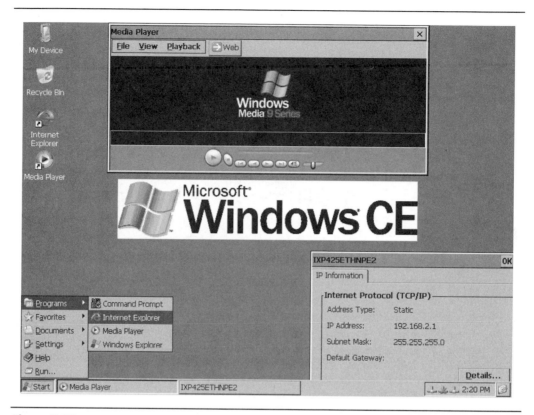

Figure 8.10 Windows CE 5.0 Internet Appliance Screen Capture

IP Videophone

The IP videophone application brings together numerous features described above. The IXP4XX network processor is responsible for all networking aspects, SIP protocol stacks, and application. It also performs software decode of the MPEG2/4 video stream, as the resolution required for this application is quite low (CIF 352 × 288). The picture is captured from the CCD camera and encoded by the MPEG4 video chip set. The Intel IXP400 DSP software performs all audio encoding and decoding.

The IXP4XX network processor's power is adequate to provide such network features as video mail and interoperability with 3G multimedia messaging.

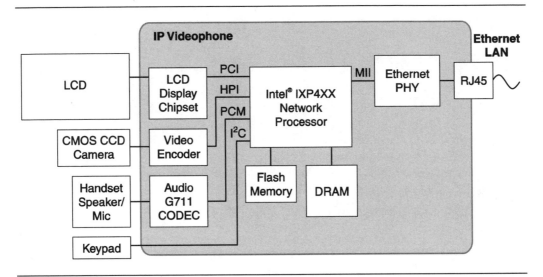

Figure 8.11   IP Videophone

IP Videophone Software

The IP videophone performs video decode and audio encode/decode on the Intel XScale core. The Intel IXP400 DSP software library provides all the features needed for audio. MPEG4 Intel integrated performance primitives (IPPs) are available from Intel for the Windows CE operating system. Numerous vendors provide optimized video CODECs for the Intel XScale core. The video capture subsystem is defined by the chip set chosen. Chip sets from WIS Technologies and Vweb have been incorporated into video capture applications.

Chapter 9

Intel® IXP400 Software API

It's hard to read through a book on the principles of magic without glancing at the cover periodically to make sure it isn't a book on software design.

— Bruce Tognazzini

This chapter describes the APIs that make up the Intel® IXP400 software. In most cases, each API corresponds to an interface on the device and provides a C-language abstraction to control, transmit, and receive data on the interface. The Ethernet interface and access component IxEthAcc has been covered in detail in Chapter 6. The APIs, or components, discussed in this chapter are:

- Cryptography
- ATM/UTOPIA
- HSS/HDLC
- TimeSync
- OSAL
- UART
- USB
- NPE download and message handler
- Queue manager

For each API, you have a description of the functions available on the API and some example code fragments to show you how to use the functions. Complete details of each software API are covered in the software programmer's guide (Intel 2004c).

Cryptography

This section describes `IxCryptoAcc`, the Intel IXP400 software security API. This software component provides support for authentication and encryption/decryption services needed in cryptographic applications, such as IPSec authentication and encryption, secure sockets layer (SSL), and 802.11i wireless LAN security. You can use this API to offload the execution of significant parts of these computationally expensive algorithms, freeing Intel XScale® core cycles for your applications.

For background information on authentication, cryptographic algorithms, and cipher modes, see Applied Cryptography (Schneier 1996).

The `IxCryptoAcc` API supports the following operating modes:

■ Encryption only

■ Decryption only

■ Authentication calculation only

■ Authentication check only

■ Encryption followed by authentication calculation

■ Authentication check followed by decryption

It supports the following cryptographic algorithms:

■ Data encryption standard (DES)

■ Triple DES

■ Advanced encryption standard (AES)

■ ARC4

The API supports the following cipher modes:

■ NULL—for stream ciphers, like ARC4

■ Electronic code book (ECB)

■ Cipher block chaining (CBC)

- Counter (CTR)—for AES algorithm only (RFC 3686)

- Single-Pass AES counter with CBC MAC (AES-CCM)—for 802.11i

The API supports the following authentication algorithms:

- Secure hash algorithm 1 (SHA-1)

- Message digest 5 (MD-5)

- WEP integrity check value (ICV)

Finally, the component supports up to 1,000 simultaneous security associations or tunnels.

You have two choices of implementations of the ARC4 and WEP ICV algorithms. You can use a microcode implementation that uses NPEA. If you need NPE A for other functionality, you can use implementations optimized specifically for the Intel XScale core.

High-Level API Call Flow

The general sequence of calls to the API is similar whether you are using the API for IPscc or wireless applications.

- Initialize the `IxCryptoAcc` API.

- Set up a number of contexts, one for each security association. Each context specifies the algorithms, mode, direction, and a callback function pointer.

- Send packets for encryption/decryption and/or authentication, specifying the context.

- The NPE microcode loads the context and performs the operation on the packet, storing the result back into DRAM. When the updated packet has been stored in DRAM, your registered callback function is called to signal the completion of the operation.

This asynchronous function-call flow allows you to submit a number of packets for processing at the same time. Most software implementations of cryptographic algorithms are function calls, which are synchronous operations. You must modify the software stack to replace these synchronous function calls with the asynchronous callback flow. However, using the asynchronous flow will improve the performance of your security application significantly.

Registering a Context

A context is a form of *security association* (SA). While the term SA is well-known in the context of IPSec services, the IxCryptoAcc component defines a context to contain a subset of a security association. IxCryptoAcc also makes use of contexts for non-IPsec accelerations such as WEP.

You define each cryptographic "connection" by registering it using the function ixCryptoAccCtxRegister(). When you register a context, you receive a context ID. IxCryptoAcc stores the context information in an internal database. Each time you perform a cryptographic operation and supply a context ID, IxCryptoAcc uses the context information stored in the database. ixCryptoAccCtxRegister() takes a number of parameters:

■ A pointer to an IxCryptoAccCtx structure which includes:

– The mode of operation for this context; for example, encrypt, decrypt, authenticate, encrypt and authenticate, and so on

– Cipher parameters, such as algorithm, cipher mode, and key length

– Authentication parameters, such as algorithm, digest length, and authentication key length

– In-place versus non-in-place operation. In-place operation means the result of the crypto processing is stored back into the same IX_OSAL_MBUF

■ Two IX_OSAL_MBUFs that the NPE microcode populates with the primary and secondary chaining variables

■ Two callback functions. One is called when context registration is complete, the other when the performance of an individual operation completes.

■ The function stores the context ID in an output parameter.

This function has a number of possible return values. Here is a selection of return values and the recommended course of action when you receive them.

- IX_CRYPTO_ACC_EXCEED_MAX_TUNNELS. You are using the maximum number of supported tunnels. You can either refuse to set up the tunnel or rebuild your system to allow more tunnels. To rebuild your system, you can redefine IX_CRYPTO_ACC_MAX_ACTIVE_SA_TUNNELS. The default value is 1,000. Each context uses approximately 152 bytes, so if you increase this define, IxCryptoAcc will consume more memory for context storage. If you need to optimize memory use and know you need to support less than 1,000 simultaneous contexts, you can reduce the definition.

- IX_CRYPTO_ACC_QUEUE_FULL. Too many outstanding IxCryptoAcc transactions, an internal queue has filled. You can retry to register the context after a short period.

To unregister a context, call ixCryptoAccCtxUnregister(). If the function returns IX_CRYPTO_ACC_RETRY, the component still has outstanding "in progress" perform operations for the context. You can try to unregister the context again later or when your perform callback function is called for that context.

Performing a Cryptographic/Authentication Operation

When you have created a context, you are ready to encrypt, decrypt, or authenticate a packet using the ixCryptoAccAuthCryptPerform() function. This section focuses on an IPsec usage of the perform operation. Later sections describe some of the exceptions when performing WEP operations. The perform function takes a large number of parameters. The following code shows the function prototype.

Prototype for ixCryptoAccAuthCryptPerform

```
1    IxCryptoAccStatus ixCryptoAccAuthCryptPerform(
2        UINT32            cryptoCtxId,
3        IX_OSAL_MBUF *    pSrcMbuf,
4        IX_OSAL_MBUF *    pDestMbuf,
5        UINT16                authStartOffset,
6        UINT16                authDataLen,
7        UINT16                cryptStartOffset,
8        UINT16                cryptDataLen,
9        UINT16                icvOffset,
10       UINT8 *               pIV)
```

Line 2

> `cryptoCtxId` is the ID of the context you previously registered.

Line 3

> `pSrcMbuf` is a pointer to the message buffer storing the data you want to operate on. If you specified in-place operation when you registered the context, this buffer will also be used to store the output. A pointer to this buffer is resent to you when `IxCryptoAcc` completes and calls your callback function. Typically you receive this buffer from another packet interface. You must ensure the buffer is large enough to allow an extra ICV when appropriate. By default, the `ixCryptoAccAuthCryptPerform` function does not check the buffer size, so you need to design your code to ensure the buffer is large enough. If you build the Intel IXP400 software with the `IX_DEBUG` flag enabled, `ixCryptoAccAuthCryptPerform` checks buffer sizes.

Line 4

> `pDestMbuf` is a pointer to a message buffer where the result goes if you did not specify in-place operation.

Line 5

> `authStartOffset` indicates the data offset in the buffer where you want `IxCryptoAcc` to start calculating/verifying authentication.

Line 6

> `authDataLen` is the number of bytes in the buffer to include when calculating/verifying authentication.

Line 7

> `cryptStartOffset` indicates the data offset in the buffer where you want `IxCryptoAcc` to start encrypting/decrypting.

Line 8

> `cryptDataLen` is the number of bytes in the buffer to include when encrypting/decrypting.

Line 9

> `icvOffset` is the offset position in the buffer data where the initial chaining variable (ICV) is stored for authentication. The ICV should not span multiple `MBUF`s in a chained `MBUF`.

Line 10

pIV is a pointer to an initialization vector (IV) for encryption/decryption.

The function can return a number of error values:

- IX_CRYPTO_ACC_QUEUE_FULL—too many outstanding IxCryptoAcc transactions. An internal queue has filled. You can retry the perform operation after a short period.

- IX_CRYPTO_ACC_CRYPTO_CTX_NOT_VALID—the supplied context ID is invalid.

- IX_CRYPTO_ACC_CIPHER_INVALID_BLOCK_LEN—the block length of the plaintext/ciphertext (cryptDataLen) is invalid. It should be a multiple of the block size for each algorithm. For example, DES/3DES require 64-bit blocks, AES 128-bits, and ARC4 8-bits.

- IX_CRYPTO_ACC_FAIL—the operation failed for some unspecified internal reason.

When the operation completes in the NPE, IxCryptoAcc runs the callback function you provided when you registered the context. The following is an implementation of a skeleton callback function.

Sample Perform Callback Function

```
1    void exampleCryptoCallback(   UINT32 cryptoCtxId,
2                                  IX_OSAL_MBUF *pSrcMbuf,
3                                  IX_OSAL_MBUF *pDestMbuf,
4                                  IxCryptoAccStatus status)
5    {
6        switch(status)
7        {
8        case IX_CRYPTO_ACC_SUCCESS:
9            // forward the packet in the message buffer
10           break;
11       case IX_CRYPTO_ACC_AUTH_FAIL:
12           // the packet authentication failed
13           authFailureHandle(pSrcMbuf);
14           break;
15       default:
16           // an internal or unknown failure occurred
17           // handle the disposal of the message buffers
18           break;
19       }
20   }
```

Lines 1–5

Declare a function that matches the prototype for a perform complete callback.

Lines 8–10

Handle a successful operation. Send the transformed packet for further processing. For a packet just encrypted, you typically transmit it on an interface. For a packet decrypted or authenticated, you typically forward it to the IP stack for processing.

Lines 11–14

Handle a packet authentication failure. The contents of the message buffers are indeterminate when this situation occurs.

Lines 15–18

An internal or unknown error occurred. Handle the return of the message buffers to the buffer memory pools.

Stopping the Cryptographic Service

Call the function `ixCryptoAccCryptoServiceStop()` to stop the service. Any perform operations "in progress" will complete before the service stops; therefore, your perform callback function can still be called after you stop the service. Any new perform requests will fail. All registered contexts will be unregistered.

Other Functions

You can print `IxCryptoAcc` status information for a specific context to a console using the `ixCryptoAccShow` or `ixCryptoAccShowWithId` functions. These functions can be useful when debugging your application. They show such information as the number of packets returned with operation failure; number of packets encrypted, decrypted, and authenticated; the current status of the queue; whether the queue is empty or full; and the current queue length.

You can use `ixCryptoAccHashKeyGenerate()` or its alias `ixCryptoAccHashPerform()` to generate a hash key using SHA-1 or MD5. You can use this function in situations where an HMAC authentication key of greater than 64 bytes is required for a crypto context. The function can also be used by SSL client applications as part of the SSL protocol MAC.

You can use `ixCryptoAccCtxCipherKeyUpdate()` to change the key value of a previously registered context. This operation is supported for CCM cipher mode contexts only and allows you to quickly change keys without going through the process of context deregistration and registration. You cannot change the key length. Any "in progress" operations for the context will still execute, but their output is undefined. To update keys for other cipher modes, you must unregister and reregister the context.

IPsec Applications

To use the acceleration features of `IxCryptoAcc` in an IPsec application, you typically replace the low-level cryptographic and authentication algorithms. `IxCryptoAcc` does not implement a full security application, such as IPSec; rather, it implements algorithmic building blocks. Outside `IxCryptoAcc` you still use an IPSec stack. For example, the stack performs policy lookups when it receives an IP packet. In encapsulating security payload (ESP) mode, the stack adds headers and trailers to plaintext being encrypted. In authentication header (AH) mode, the stack inserts AH between the IP header and payload. You must ensure the ICV portion of the AH is cleared before performing the ICV calculation, as the AH is included in the calculation. You would need to modify the low-level algorithms to use the `IxCryptoAcc` perform function and translate security associations to contexts for `IxCryptoAcc`.

To use an authentication key with key length greater than 64 bytes, you must hash the key before calling crypto context registration API. Call the `ixCryptoAccHashKeyGenerate()` function and pass in the original authentication key in a message buffer. When the operation completes, `IxCryptoAcc` calls your callback function. Copy the generated authentication key into a cryptographic context structure for `ixCryptoAccCtxRegister()`.

You need to perform two operations to implement AES-CCM operations for IPSec. AES-CCM for 802.11i is covered later in this chapter. For IPSec, first you perform an AES-CBC operation to get the CBC-MAC. Then perform an AES-CTR encryption operation to encrypt the payload and create the CBC-MAC to get the message integrity check (MIC). You need to register two crypto contexts and run two crypto perform service requests to encrypt and authenticate a packet. The Intel IXP400 software programmer's guide (Intel 2004c) contains significant detail on the implementation of IPsec AES-CCM.

WEP Applications

The Wired Equivalent Privacy (WEP) specification provides a certain level of security to wireless 802.11 connections at the data-link level. WEP uses the ARC4 cryptographic algorithm, a cyclic redundancy calculation (CRC-32) for the authentication calculation (the integrity check value). IxCryptoAcc provides two WEP-specific perform functions:

- ixCryptoAccXScaleWepPerform() is an optimized Intel XScale core assembly language implementation.

- ixCryptoAccNpeWepPerform() uses microcode running on NPE A to implement the algorithms.

These functions take parameters that are similar to the main ixCryptoAccAuthCryptPerform() function. They don't have authentication parameters, and they add a parameter for an ARC4 key.

The ixCryptoAccNpeWepPerform() function operates in the same asynchronous mode as the main perform function.

The ixCryptoAccXscaleWepPerform() function, however, is a synchronous function call. The operation has completed when the function returns. It doesn't use a callback function and supports only in-place buffers.

SSL and TLS Applications

Secure sockets layer (SSL) and transport layer security (TLS) applications can use IxCryptoAcc for algorithm acceleration.

The main difference between SSL/TLS applications and IPsec applications is in the order of authentication and encryption/decryption. SSL/TLS applications generate the MAC prior to encryption, but IPSec ESP applications generate the HMAC-based ICV on the encrypted IP packet. When decrypting, SSL/TLS applications verify the MAC after decryption, but IPSec ESP applications verify the ICV before decrypting the payload. IxCryptoAcc provides single operation cryptography and authentication for the IPSec order only. To support SSL/TLS applications, you need to create two contexts and invoke two separate operations, one for encryption and decryption and the other for authentication calculation and verification.

For encryption and decryption, both applications can use `ixCrypto-AccAuthCryptPerform()` for DES-CBC and 3DES-CBC acceleration. To accelerate the ARC4 cipher, applications also can use `ixCrypto-AccNpeWepPerform()` or `ixCryptoAccXscaleWepPerform()`. These functions support only 128-bit keys for contexts that do not use WEP-CRC calculation.

For authentication, TLS can use `ixCryptoAccAuthCryptPerform()` for calculation or verification; however, SSL does not use HMAC. Instead, you can use `ixCryptoAccHashKeyGenerate()` or its alias `ixCryptoAc-cHashPerform()` for basic SHA-1 or MD-5 hashing operations to implement SSL MAC calculation and verification.

802†.11i Applications

You can also use `IxCryptoAcc` to accelerate some of the algorithms of 802.11i, the second generation of wireless data-link security. `IxCrypto-Acc` supports the cipher mode for 802.11i, counter-mode/CBC-MAC protocol (CCMP). The function `ixCryptoAccAuthCryptPerform()` provides a single pass CCMP-MIC computation and verification with CTR mode encryption/decryption. This implementation supports the 802.11i IV and MIC sizes only. Non-802.11i applications must perform a two-step authentication and cipher.

`IxCryptoAcc` expects a 64-byte IV in a contiguous buffer, consisting of 16 bytes of a CTR-mode IV followed by 48 bytes of MIC-IV-HEADER. If the MIC-IV-HEADER constructed is less than 48 bytes, it should be padded with zero to 48 bytes, which is equivalent to three AES blocks. `IxCryptoAcc` pads the plaintext with zeros if required for the MIC computation. The pad is discarded once the MIC and encryption take place.

As in IPSec, `IxCryptoAcc` expects the application stack to create the necessary initialization vectors and headers, in this case the CTR-mode IV, MIC-IV, and MIC headers.

Integrating IxCryptoAcc

When integrating `IxCryptoAcc`, you need to replace function call implementations of the cipher and authentication algorithms with the asynchronous-perform callback method supported by `IxCryptoAcc` to get the full benefit of the acceleration. For an example of this conversion, see the example code implementation of patches to the FreeS/WAN VPN application on the Intel Developer Web site listed in "References." Follow the readme instructions and examine the `Ipsec_glue` files.

OpenSSL applications need to access cryptographic functions from user mode. Typically, these applications use the /dev/crypto driver, which can be implemented using the `IxCryptoAcc`. Alternatively, you can implement the open cryptographic framework (OCF) interface to use `IxCryptoAcc`. The /dev/crypto driver can then be used by an OpenSSL implementation without needing any changes.

To maximize the processor's cryptographic performance, take advantage of the ability to submit multiple simultaneous cryptographic operations and chain-cipher and authentication operations. Implement an IXP4XX network processor-specific driver, /dev/crypto-ixp4XX, using these operations and modify OpenSSL to use this driver.

Public Key Algorithms

The IXP46X product line contains silicon accelerators for public key exchange algorithms, such as Rivest/Shamir/Adleman (RSA), digital signature algorithm (DSA), and Diffie-Hellman. The Intel IXP400 software does not currently support an API for these features. For details of the register-level interface, see the appropriate developer's manual listed in "References."

HSS/HDLC

This API provides your applications with driver-level access to the high-speed serial (HSS) and high-level data link control (HDLC) co-processors available on NPE A. This API and its supporting NPE-based hardware acceleration enable the IXP4XX network processors to support packetized or channelized TDM data communications.

The channelized service provides your code with the raw serial data streams retrieved from the HSS port, while the packetized service provides packet payload data that the processor has processed according to the HDLC protocol.

The HSS co-processor enables the IXP42X network processors to communicate externally, in a serial-bit fashion, using TDM data. T1, E1, and MVIP bit-stream protocols are supported. The HSS co-processor can also interface with xDSL framers.

The HSS co-processor communicates with an external device using three signals per direction: a frame pulse, clock, and data bit. The data stream consists of frames—the number of frames per second depending on the protocol. Each frame is composed of time slots. Each time slot consists of 8 bits (1 byte) that contain the data and an indicator of the time slot's location within the frame.

The maximum frame size is 1,024 bits and the maximum frame pulse offset is 1,023 bits. The line clock speed can be set to one of the following values to support various E1, T1, or aggregated serial (MVIP) specifications:

- 512 kilohertz
- 1.536 megahertz
- 1.544 megahertz
- 2.048 megahertz
- 4.096 megahertz
- 8.192 megahertz

The frame size and frame offsets are all programmable depending on the protocol. Other programmable options include signal polarities, signal levels, clock edge, endian-ness, and choice of input/output frame signal.

Figure 9.1 illustrates a typical T1 frame with active-high frame sync `hss_tx_frame_out` and a posedge clock `pads_tx_clock` for generating data. The data signal `hss_tx_data_out` is then read on the positive edge of each clock. A T1 frame consists of 192 data bits—24 time slots of 8 bits each.

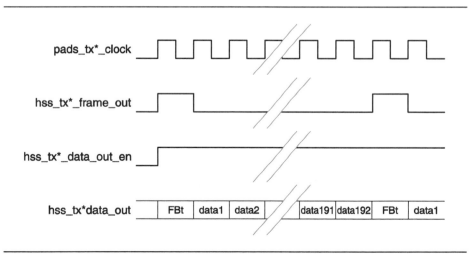

Figure 9.1 Typical T1 Frame

The time slots within a stream can be configured as:

■ Packetized, raw or HDLC, 64 kilobytes per second, and 56 kilobytes per second

■ Channelized voice 64 kilobytes, or channelized voice 56 kilobytes

■ Left unassigned

For packetized time slots, data is passed to the HDLC co-processor for processing as packetized data. The HDLC co-processor performs the bit-oriented HDLC processing, which identifies HDLC packets in the bit stream and provides them to your code as packets. It can also provide to your code "raw" packets, those that do not require HDLC processing. The HDLC co-processor can support up to four packetized services per HSS port. The following HDLC parameters are programmable:

■ The pattern to be transmitted when an HDLC port is idle

■ The HDLC data endianness

■ The CRC type (16-bit or 32-bit) to be used for this HDLC port

■ Channel-associated signalling (CAS) bit polarity and bit inversion

High-Level API Call Flow

Typically, you would use the HSS API in the following sequence:

1. Download the appropriate NPE microcode images to the NPEs. Initialize the NPEs and the `IxNpeMh` and `IxQMgr` components.

2. Call `ixHssAccInit` to initialize the component.

3. Call `ixHssAccPortInit` to configure each time slot in a frame to provide either packetized or channelized service.

4. Supply memory buffers for transmit and receive data. Packetized and channelized services use different types of memory buffers, covered later in this chapter.

5. Call `ixHssAccPktPortConnect` or `ixHssAccChanConnect()` to connect to the service. You also provide callback functions to be run when data is received.

6. Call `ixHssAccPktPortEnable` and `ixHssAccChanPortEnable` to enable the services on the port. Data can now flow, and your callback functions are called.

To disable the HSS component, call `ixHssAccPktPortDisable()` or `ixHssAccChanPortDisable`. These functions instruct the NPEs to stop handling data. Alternatively, you can call `ixHssAccPktPortDisconnect()` or `ixHssAccChanDisconnect()`, which clears all port configuration parameters and disables the port.

Receiving Channelized Data

Circular buffers are used to store received data for the channelized service. Your code allocates the buffers and provides them to the HSS API. For received data, you can allocate contiguous memory using `ixOsServCacheDmaAlloc()`. The pointer to this Rx data pool must be a physical address because NPE will directly write data into this memory area. To convert the virtual address to a physical address, use `IX_MMU_VIRTUAL_TO_PHYSICAL_TRANSLATION` before sending the pointer to the HSS interface.

The memory pool is divided into N circular buffers, one buffer per channel. N is the total number of channels in service. Currently, a channel corresponds to a timeslot, but future software releases might change this correspondence.

When you initialize the channelized service using `ixHssAccChanConnect()`, you must provide the pointer to the pool, the length of the circular buffers, and a `bytesPerTStrigger` parameter. You also provide a pointer to the `ixHssAccChanRxCallback` Rx callback function, which is called when `bytesPerTSTrigger` bytes have been received for all trunk time slots.

Figure 9.2 shows how the circular buffers are filled with data received through the HSS ports. When each of the N channels receives `bytesPerTStrigger` bytes, an interrupt service routine (ISR) calls your registered Rx callback function, with an `rxOffset` parameter to indicate where data is written into the circular buffer for each of the channels. If you don't provide a receive callback function, you can poll the HSS interface using the `ixHssAccChanStatusQuery()` function, which provides `rxOffset` as an output parameter.

When the end of the buffer is filled, `rxOffset` wraps back to the beginning of the circular buffer.

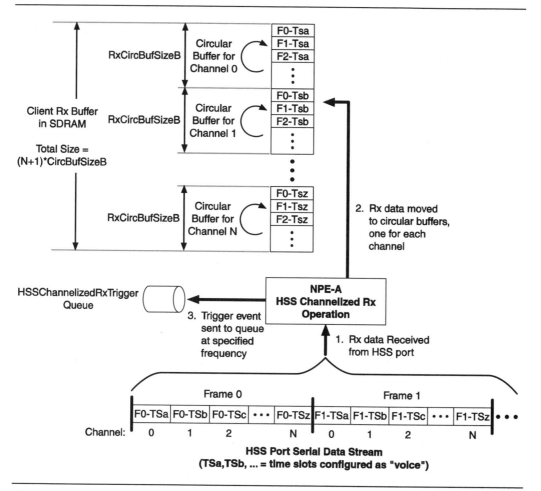

Figure 9.2   Channelized Receive Buffers

Make sure the Rx data is processed or moved elsewhere before being overwritten, and choose the size of the circular buffers carefully. The buffers must be large enough to give your code time to read and complete any in-place processing before the NPE rewrites over that memory.

Transmitting Channelized Data

When you initialize the channelized service using `ixHssAccChanConnect()`, you must provide storage for a circular buffer of pointers to data to be transmitted. When the channelized Rx callback is called or you call `ixHssAccChanStatusQuery()`, you also receive an indication from the

HSS service as to which transmit array offset is currently being transmitted by the HSS feature. Each transmit array offset contains a transmit pointer for each channel. Figure 9.3 shows the structure of the array of transmit pointers.

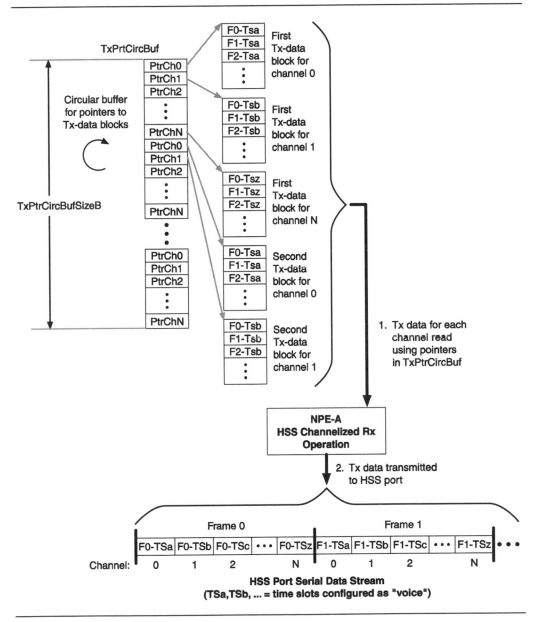

Figure 9.3 Channelized Transmit Buffers

You populate the Tx array with pointers to data for the channel. The underlying hardware reads the Tx array and transmits the data, which means you can transmit without having to copy the data.

The channelized service is quite sensitive to timing. You need to pay special attention designing this aspect of your system. Be sure to balance the latency and the size of the transmit and receive circular buffers with the real-time characteristics of your solution.

Receiving Packetized Data

The packetized service can support four HDLC channels per HSS port or one HDLC per T1/E1. The packetized interface is similar to the other packet-oriented interfaces on the IXP4XX network processor. You use the `ixHssAccPktPortConnect()` function to configure the packetized service. With this function, you can set receive and transmit-done callback functions along with a large number of other configurable parameters, such as idle pattern. For further details on the HDLC specific parameters, see the software programmer's guide (Intel 2004c).

You can also register a callback function that will be called when the packetized service is running low on buffers to store received packets. Call `ixHssAccPktPortRxFreeReplenish()` to provide buffers for packet storage.

A HSS Packetized Receive Callback

```
1    void pktRxCallback(     IX_OSAL_MBUF *buffer,
2                       unsigned numHssErrs,
3                       IxHssAccPktStatus pktStatus,
4                            IxHssAccPktUserId rxUserId)
5    {
6       IX_OSAL_MBUF *rxBuffer = buffer;
7       if (pktStatus != IX_HSSACC_PKT_OK)
8          // handle error case
9
10      while (rxBuffer != NULL)
11      {
12              processData(IX_OSAL_MBUF_MDATA(rxBuffer));
13          rxBuffer=IX_OSAL_MBUF_NEXT_BUFFER_IN_PKT_PTR
14                  (rxBuffer));
15          }
16      // free the chained buffer back to the OS pool
17          IX_OSAL_MBUF_POOL_PUT_CHAIN(buffer);
18    }
```

Lines 1–4

Declare a function that matches the prototype for a receive callback.

Line 7

Check the status of the packet.

Lines 10–16

This loop walks through the buffer chain calling a function `process-Data()` to process the data in each message buffer.

Line 17

Free the buffer back to the OS buffer pool. Alternatively, you could replenish the buffer using `ixHssAccPktPortRxFreeReplenish` if processing is complete.

Transmitting Packetized Data

Transmit an `IX_OSAL_MBUF` using the `ixHssAccPktPortTx()` function. You specify the HSS port and HDLC channel along with an `MBUF` that can be chained. The Tx-done callback function you registered when connecting to the port will be called when transmission of the packet has completed.

The HSS port transmits the idle pattern that you configured with `ixHssAccPktPortConnect()` if it has no queued packets for transmission.

Packetized Disconnect

You can disconnect the packetized service channel by using the `ixHssAccPktPortDisable()` function to stop the packetized service and the `ixHssAccPktPortDisconnect()` function to disconnect the service.

You should not try to transmit any packets or replenish any buffers after disconnecting the service.

ATM/UTOPIA

The ATM/UTOPIA software consists of three separate components.

- IxAtmdAcc—AtmD is the main driver component. It contains features to support the configuration, transmission, and reception of ATM adaptation layer 5 packets (AAL5); raw ATM cells, which we call ATM adaptation layer 0 (AAL0); and operations and maintenance (OAM).

- IxAtmm—AtmM is a component that demonstrates the management of port and ATM virtual connections (VCs). It contains functions that manage the buffer allocations for AtmD. As a demonstration, you may decide to replace AtmM with implementations of your own for some features.

- IxAtmSch—The Intel IXP400 software implements cell scheduling on the Intel XScale core. AtmSch is a demonstration implementation of an ATM cell scheduler. It is not a general-purpose scheduler, but may be sufficient for your application. The features of this scheduler are enumerated later in this chapter. If you do need to implement a more fully featured scheduler, implement it using the AtmSch scheduler API as AtmD can then make use of your alternative scheduler without any changes.

The following sections discuss the ATM subcomponents in more detail. For a description of the general concepts of ATM and UTOPIA, see ATM Theory and Applications (McDysan and Spohn 1999).

IxAtmdAcc

The main features supported by the AtmD component include:

- Up to 12 ports on the UTOPIA Level-2 interface

- The transmission of AAL-5 CPCS PDUs on a port/VC. The processor contains hardware acceleration for the AAL-5 CRC calculation, freeing a significant number of core processor cycles for your application.

- Raw cell (AAL-0-48) PDU transmission service, which accepts PDUs containing an integral number of 48-byte or 52-byte cells for transmission on a particular port/VC. For 48-byte cells, it adds a header, including header error check (HEC). For 52-byte cells, it adds only an HEC.

■ The transmission of OAM PDUs. It accepts PDUs containing an integral number of 52-byte OAM cells for transmission on a particular port, independent of the VC.

■ Your ability to connect it to a custom ATM scheduler, which implements traffic shaping using the IxAtmSch API. You can supply a different scheduler implementation for each port.

■ The reception of fully formed AAL-5 CPCS PDUs, with error detection for CRC errors, priority queuing, and corrupt-packet delivery.

■ The reception of AAL-0 PDU containing 48-byte or 52-byte cells received on a particular port and VC. When you want just payload 48-byte cells, it checks the HEC and removes the cell header.

■ The reception of OAM PDUs containing a single, 52-byte OAM cell. It checks the HEC and CRC-10.

■ Up to 32 VCC channels for transmit services and up to 32 channels for AAL-0/AAL-5 receive services.

■ One dedicated OAM transmit channel (OAM-VC) per port. It supports one dedicated OAM receive channel (OAM-VC) for all ports. This channel supports reception of OAM cells from any port on any VC.

■ The ability for you to query it for statistics such as cells received with invalid cell size, parity errors, invalid HEC, and the number of idle cells.

■ An interface that you can use in either polled or interrupt mode.

Configuring a Port

To configure a UTOPIA port using AtmD, perform the following three steps:

1. Call ixAtmdAccPortInit() supplying a port ID.

2. Call ixAtmdAccUtopiaConfigSet() providing a structure with parameters to configure the UTOPIA port. This structure allows you to set the mode (MPHY or SPHY), enable parity and HEC generation, and set the physical PHY address, among many other parameters. The mode you use must correspond to the NPE microcode image you have downloaded.

3. Call ixAtmdAccUtopiaPortEnable() to enable the port.

Configuring the Receive Service

To receive PDUs on a particular port, perform the following three steps:

1. Configure the receive service. To do this, call `ixAtmdAccRxConnect()` providing a port number, virtual path index (VPI), virtual channel index (VCI), and a pointer to the function you want called when a PDU is received.

2. Supply receive buffers for that connection using `ixAtmdAccRxFreeReplenish()`.

3. Call `ixAtmdAccRxStart()` for that connection. When PDUs are received for that connection, your callback function is called with a status and a pointer to a message buffer containing the PDU.

AtmD also supports a callback function that you can provide when connecting, which will be called when the number of receive buffers is running low. You can then implement this callback function to supply new receive buffers.

AtmD will chain a number of buffers together if the PDU is too large for any one buffer.

Configuring the Transmit Service

To transmit PDUs on a particular port, perform the following three steps:

1. Provide scheduler functions for the port using the function `ixAtmdAccScheduledModeEnable()`. You provide callbacks to scheduler functions. The AtmSch API defines the types of these functions. AtmSch provides example implementations. Once registered, you cannot unregister the scheduler. If you don't supply a scheduler for a port, all cells are transmitted immediately without scheduling or shaping

2. Create a transmit connection by calling `ixAtmdAccTxConnect()`, supplying port, VPI, VCI, and a callback function to handle free buffers when transmission is complete.

3. Call `ixAtmdAccTxPduSubmit()`, which internally submits the message buffer to the scheduler. For AAL5 PDUs, AtmD pads and calculates the CRC. The buffer must contain enough storage for the AAL5 trailer. When all of the cells of the PDU have been transmitted, your callback function is passed the message buffer of the transmitted PDU.

When the underlying hardware is running low on cells, it notifies AtmD to request a table from the scheduler, which in turn decides how to shape and interleave cells for all VCs on a port. The scheduler returns a schedule table to AtmD, which AtmD then interprets and provides individual cells to the underlying hardware.

IxAtmdAcc provides a number of features to manage transmit-done scenarios. You can either use a polled or a callback scheme.

The callback scheme allows you to register a callback function that AtmD calls when a number of transmit buffers have been completely transmitted. This callback function is called for buffers on any connection. You can register the built-in ixAtmdAccTxDoneDispatcher() function as the callback or you can call the dispatcher function in your own callback. The ixAtmdAccTxDoneDispatcher() function then looks up the associated connection and calls the connection-specific transmit-done callback.

Alternatively, you can poll the number of transmit-done buffers using the ixAtmdAccTxDoneLevelQuery() function, and then you can call iixAtmdAccTxDoneDispatch() explicitly.

Disconnecting a Transmit Service

To disconnect a transmit connection, call ixAtmdAccTxTryDisconnect(). The function will return IX_ATMDACC_RESOURCES_STILL_ALLOCATED if some PDUs previously submitted are still being transmitted. All attempts to send new PDUs on the connection will fail. When the resources have completed, ixAtmdAccTxVcTryDisconnect() returns success.

Receiving PDUs using a Threshold and Callback

You can register a receive callback function using ixAtmdAccRxCallbackRegister(). You can specify a threshold number of PDUs; when that threshold is reached, your function will be called. You can register the built-in ixAtmdAccRxDispatch() function or call that function in your own callback function. ixAtmdAccRxDispatch() then iterates over all of the received PDUs, examines the connection for which they were received, and calls the appropriate connection-specific receive-callback function registered for that connection.

Receiving PDUs Using Polling

Alternatively, you can call `ixAtmdAccRxLevelQuery()` to poll the number of unprocessed PDUs received. You can then decide to call `ixAtmdAccRxDispatch()` directly, which iterates over the buffered PDUs, calling the appropriate connection-associated receive-callback function.

Disconnecting a Receive Service

To disconnect a receive service, call the `ixAtmdAccRxVcTryDisconnect()` function. `AtmD` returns all receive buffers by calling the receive callback for that connection with status set to `IX_ATMDACC_MBUF_RETURN`. It returns `IX_ATMDACC_RESOURCES_STILL_ALLOCATED` while receive buffers for the connection are still in `AtmD`. When `AtmD` has returned all the buffers, the subsequent call returns `IX_SUCCESS`.

Buffers for IxAtmdAcc

`AtmD` imposes the following constraints on the `IX_OSAL_MBUFs` you supply:

- ■ You must allocate these buffers in the lower 256 megabytes of physical memory. `AtmD` uses the top four bits of the physical address internally.

- ■ When you submit a chained buffer for transmission, you must set the packet length in the first buffer to the length of the PDU.

- ■ Do not replenish chained buffers.

- ■ The PDU in a buffer must be a multiple of 48 bytes or 52 bytes for OAM/AAL0.

- ■ The maximum supported depth of a buffer chain is 256 message buffers.

IxAtmm

The IxAtmm component is an ATM-port, virtual-connection (VC), and VC-access manager. It does not provide support for ATM OAM services and it does not directly move any ATM data. It is supplied in the Intel IXP400 software as a demonstration. You can modify or replace it as required. IxAtmm has the following features:

■ It configures up to 12 UTOPIA ports.

■ It initializes the demonstration scheduler and registers it with AtmD.

■ It configures a callback-based, threshold-notification scheme for transmitted buffers.

■ It manages two streams of received PDUs: an event-driven, high-priority stream and a low-priority, timer-based stream.

■ It checks the validity of a channel connection examining the traffic descriptor.

Configuring the UTOPIA Interface

AtmM simplifies the configuration of the UTOPIA interface. Use ixAtmmUtopiaInit() to configure up to 12 UTOPIA ports supplying only the PHY mode and PHY addresses for each port. It makes the subsequent calls to the AtmD port configuration interface. It also allows you to configure a single UTOPIA PHY in loopback mode.

Port Management

AtmM simplifies setting up ports and unidirectional virtual channels on ports. To configure a port, call ixAtmmPortInitialize() supplying the receive and transmit port rates. The transmit port rate is used to determine peak cell rate on a port. For example, in a DSL application you can set the port rate when the DSL line training has completed and you know the speed of the link. If the DSL link retrains, you can reset the port using ixAtmmPortModify().

You can create a virtual channel on a port using `ixAtmmVcRegister()`. You provide an ATM traffic descriptor, and `AtmM` calls the connection admission control (CAC) function on the scheduler to determine if the ATM port can supply the level of service required by the traffic descriptor. The Intel IXP400 software supports virtual channel connections (VCC) only. Virtual path connections (VPCs) are not supported.

You can deregister a VC using `ixAtmmVcDeregister()`.

Transmit and Receive Services

`AtmM` also provides some simplification of the following services of `AtmD`:

■ It registers a callback function for the transmit-low notification from `AtmD`. This callback implementation requests a schedule table from `AtmSch` and forwards it to `AtmD`. Essentially, `AtmM` provides the glue code between `AtmD` and `AtmSch`.

■ It configures the transmit-done, handling-return buffers to the appropriate connection when the number of available buffers exceeds a threshold.

■ It configures two receive-handling mechanisms, a low-threshold callback for high-priority connections, and a timer poll for low-priority connections.

With the exception of the `AtmD`/`AtmSch` glue functionality, `AtmM` stays out of the direct data path when transmitting and receiving buffers.

IxAtmSch

`IxAtmSch` is an "example" ATM scheduler component provided with the Intel IXP400 software. It may be sufficient for many applications. However, you can replace this scheduler with a more powerful scheduler of your own if you want to. If you do this, you should re-implement the same `AtmSch` API.

Limitations of the Default Scheduler

The default scheduler can only support 32 VCs of type unassigned bit rate (UBR). It can support one VC per port of real-time variable bit rate (rt-VBR), near-real-time variable bit rate (nrt-VBR), or constant bit rate (CBR). You can essentially simulate CBR using an rt-VBR VC with PCR=SCR. Table 9.1 summarizes the supported modes and traffic descriptors of the built-in scheduler. This simplified scheduler uses a small percentage of the data path data cycles. A more complex scheduler may use a larger portion of those cycles. Finally, the cell delay variation threshold (CDVT) implementation does not comply with the ATM-TM-4.1 standard.

Table 9.1   Summary of Default Scheduler Modes

Traffic Type	# VCs	CDVT	PCR	SCR	MCR	MBS
rt-VBR	1 per port	Yes	Yes	Yes	No	Yes
nrt-VBR	1 per port	No	Yes	Yes	No	No
UBR	Up to 32	No	Yes	No	No	No
CBR	1 per port	Yes	Yes	= PCR	No	No

Make sure the port rate you use when configuring the scheduler corresponds to the actual rate the cells are being pulled through the UTOPIA interface. For example, a DSL PHY might sometimes train to a lower than port rate. If the PHY is faster or slower than the configured port rate, the scheduling will not be accurate.

The Scheduler API

The following API functions are described at a high level because you may need to replace some or all of these functions with an alternative scheduler. For additional information on any of these functions, see the Intel IXP400 software programmer's guide (Intel 2004c).

- ■ AtmSchInit. You call this function once to initialize the component. It must be called before any other function on the API.

- ■ ixAtmSchPortModelInitialize(port, portRate, minCells-ToSchedule). You call this function to initialize a specific port, supplying the transmit or upstream portRate in cells per second. The final parameter minCellsToSchedule sets the lower limit on the size of a schedule table. This parameter effectively sets the CDVT for the port. For example, if only one PDU is queued and the scheduler is asked for a schedule table, the scheduler will generate a table with this number of cells and one data cell, and pad the rest with idle cells. If a PDU arrives just after the scheduler generates the table, the PDU will be delayed by `minCellsToSchedule` idle cells. You can modify the port rate on an initialized port using `ixAtmSchPortRateModify()`.

■ `ixAtmSchVcModelSetup(port, trafficDesc, vcId)`. You can use this function to set up a VC on a port. The function takes a traffic descriptor, which describes the type of traffic contract you want for the VC. The descriptor includes traffic parameters such as PCR, SCR, and MBS. The function also performs a CAC function to decide if the VC can get its required traffic descriptor given the VCs already setup on the port. The function returns `IX_ATMSCH_RET_NOT_ADMITTED` if the required VC cannot be supported with the remaining free resources. You can remove a VC with `ixAtmSchVcModelRemove()`.

■ `ixAtmSchVcQueueUpdate(port, vcId, numberOfCells)`. You call this function when you want to transmit a PDU of length `numberOfCells` on a VC. This information is stored and used when the system next requests a schedule table for the whole port.

■ `ixAtmSchTableUpdate(port, maxCells, IxAtmScheduleTable-**rettable)`. Call this function when you want the scheduler to look at all the submitted cells on all the VCs for the port and determine the sequence of cells and idle cells to transmit when all of the VC traffic descriptors are taken into account. The function returns a schedule table pointer in the `rettable` output parameter. If the port has no queued cells for transmission, `ixAtmSchTableUpdate()` returns `IX_ATMSCH_RET_QUEUE_EMPTY`.

The Schedule Table

The schedule table contains an array of structures.

The Schedule Table Entry

```
1    typedef struct
2    {
3        IxAtmConnId connId; /* connection Id for the VC */
4        unsigned int numberOfCells; /* number of cells */
5    } IxAtmScheduleTableEntry;
```

Lines 3–4

The connId corresponds to the VC. A connId set to IX_ATM_IDLE_CELLS_CONNID indicates idle cells should be transmitted. The numberOfCells field signifies the number of consecutive cells to transmit on connId.

Figure 9.4 shows the translation of a schedule table into cells going out on the line at the bottom of the diagram. Read the cell transmission from right to left.

Choosing the Optimal Size of Schedule Table

When you develop an ATM application and choose a value for the max-Cells parameter of ixAtmSchTableUpdate(), you need to balance two factors. If you set maxCells high, you generate a large cell table. When new PDUs arrive, they are delayed by a period of time equivalent to the length of that schedule table. However, if you set maxCells low, you call the scheduler more frequently and it uses more CPU cycles on average. You need to experiment with the maxCells parameter to find the right balance between transmit latency and CPU efficiency for your application.

ATM Drivers

The ATM components IxAtmdAcc, IxAtmSch, and IxAtmm together provide a low-level ATM driver for the IXP4XX network processor. To integrate this functionality into an application, you typically need to wrap these low-level drivers into an OS-specific ATM driver. For more information on Linux ATM drivers, see the Linux-ATM project on the Source-Forge Web site listed in "References." An open-source ATM SAR driver is available on the SourceForge Web site (Zeffertt).

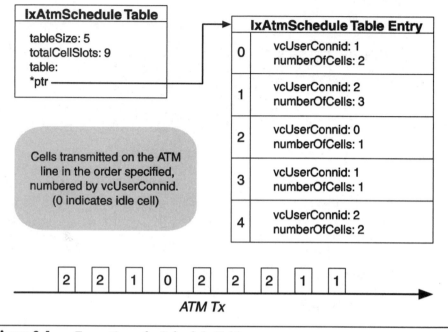

Figure 9.4   Execution of a Schedule Table

TimeSync

The IXP46X product line supports IEEE 1588[†] precision time protocol (PTP). This component allows you to configure the hardware assist block, which supports the time-critical parts of IEEE 1588. It does not implement the protocol.

You can use IEEE 1588 to synchronize terminal devices in an Ethernet network, in the sub-microsecond range. Other protocols, such as network time protocol (NTP), do not support the accuracy or convergence speeds. For detailed background on IEEE 1588, you should read the standards document (IEEE 2002a).

The hardware assist captures the timestamps at each of the MII interfaces on NPE-A/B/C for both incoming and outgoing PTP protocol messages, which are multicast over UDP/IP packets in IPv4 format.

The hardware implements a 64-bit register to keep track of the system time. The register increments based on a frequency scaling value, which is accumulated on every clock cycle in the system into a 32-bit register. Scaling register overflows increment the system time. You can then modify the scaling factor to reduce the time drift.

The Intel IXP400 software for the IXP46X product line contains an API to control this feature. The API allows you to:

■ Get and set the system time

■ Configure and query the PTP ports

■ Set and get the tick rate (frequency scaling value)

■ Poll for detected transmit/received IEEE 1588 messages

■ Get and set a target time

■ Enable/disable an interrupt/callback to be called when system time is greater than target time

■ Poll for the condition where system time is greater than target time

■ Enable/disable an interrupt and callback for the auxiliary time-stamp signal

■ Poll the time stamp in the auxiliary snapshot register

■ Reset the IEEE 1588 hardware block

Operating System Abstraction Layer (OSAL)

An Operating System Abstraction Layer (OSAL) is provided as part of the Intel IXP400 software version 1.5 and higher. The OSAL provides a set of abstracted operating-system services. We have provided implementations of these services for VxWorks, Linux kernel mode, and Windows CE. All access-layer components abstract their OS dependencies to this layer. Though primarily intended for use by the Intel IXP400 software access-layer components, these services are also available for use by your application-layer software. The OSAL layer includes the following modules:

■ Core operating system services module

■ Buffer pool management module

■ Virtual memory mapping of peripherals and endian adaptation.

For details of the OSAL API, please see the Intel IXP4XX software programmer's guide (Intel 2004c).

Core Operating System Services Module

The OSAL's core operating system services module defines the following functionality:

- Memory allocation
- Thread management
- Interrupt handling
- Thread synchronization
- Delay functions
- Time-related functions and macros
- Interthread communication
- Logging services

Each function is described in more detail below.

Memory Allocation

The memory allocation API provides mechanisms to allocate and free memory. In particular, it provides the ability to allocate memory for use by device drivers. This memory is aligned on 32-byte boundaries. Macros are provided to manage the coherence of the memory when both the NPEs and the Intel XScale core are accessing the memory.

Thread Management

The module allows you to create, destroy, and control execution of threads in the operating system. The threads are mapped to different constructs in each operating system. For VxWorks, an OSAL thread is created as a VxWorks task. In Linux, an OSAL thread is mapped to a Linux kernel thread. And for Windows CE, an OSAL thread is mapped to a thread within the device.exe process.

Interrupt Handling

This module provides functions to manage interrupts on your system. The API provides the capability to register a callback function to a specific interrupt and to enable or disable interrupts.

Thread Synchronization

This module provides an API to control synchronization of execution between threads. Synchronization between threads can be used to notify a thread of an event or to control access to a shared resource. Most functions map directly to functions that are provided in the operating system. We do, however, provide a "fast" mutex capability that makes use of an Intel XScale core instruction. It provides the capability to acquire a mutex with much lower overhead than the traditional operating system-based mutex.

Time-related Functions

This API provides time-management and delay functions. Several class-of-timer-related functions are provided:

■ *Sleep*. Delay the execution of a thread for a specified time. There are two types of sleep: the first is a simple piece of code running in a loop for the required duration, the second uses operating system calls to put the thread to sleep for the required duration. The operating system then schedules other threads to run.

■ *Yield*. This function is a specific call made to the operating system to request that the operating system run the thread scheduler.

■ *Time*. Get the system time (millisecond resolution) or the value of a time stamp counter (microsecond resolution).

Interthread Communication

The interthread communication provides the ability to send messages from one thread to another. The messages are sent across a queue, so you can send multiple messages to another task before the other task starts to run and read the messages.

Logging Services

The logging API provides a simple mechanism to record debug information at runtime. It is particularly useful as it can be called from an interrupt handler or thread.

Buffer Management Module

The Intel IXP400 software makes extensive use of memory buffers (IX_OSAL_MBUF) to pass data to and from the NPEs. This module facilitates the creation and management of buffer pools used by your application.

The OSAL buffer management module implements the following functionality:

■ Buffer pool management (pool initialization and allocation)

■ Buffer management (buffer allocation and freeing)

As most operating systems do not provide buffers in the same format used by the NPEs, you must provide a pool of message buffers (IX_OSAL_MBUFs) to transmit and receive data to the NPEs. Macros are provided to set the data pointers within the buffers. You would normally assign the buffer data pointer to the data you want to transmit, which allows you to transmit data without the need to perform any copying of data.

I/O Memory and Endianness Module

The I/O memory management defines a set of macros that allows you to gain and release access to memory-mapped hardware in an operating system-independent fashion. Depending on the target platform and OS, gaining access can vary from no special behavior (statically mapped I/O), to I/O dynamically mapped through operating system specific functions. For example, in VxWorks, all resources in IXP4XX network processors have fixed virtual addresses. Fixed addresses are achieved by using a static memory management (MMU) mapping. As a result, no special action is required to access the IXP4XX network processor resources. On the other hand, the Linux operating system requires the use of ioremap() to map the memory at run time, as the Linux LSP does not provide static mapping for all IXP4XX network processor resources.

The module also provides abstraction of the endian mapping of a particular resource. Macros are provided to read and write to Intel IXP400 software resources regardless of the operating system's endian architecture.

Backwards Compatibility

The OSAL layer was introduced in the Intel IXP400 software version 1.5. Previous Intel IXP400 software releases used different abstraction layers (OSSL and IxOsServices), which are still provided for backward compatibility. We recommend that you use the OSAL layer for all new development.

NPE Downloader

The Intel IXP400 software provides an API to download microcode images to the NPE. The microcode, which runs on the NPE, is known as an NPE image. The capabilities of all NPE images are documented in the software programmer's guide (Intel 2004c). Each image is defined by an identifier of the form IX_NPEDL_NPEIMAGE_NPEx_yyyyy. Where x is the NPE identifier A, B, or C, and yyyyy is the feature that the image provides. Ideally, all functions would be provided in one image per NPE, but due to resource constraints within the NPEs, it is more common to provide several images with differing capabilities per NPE. You should choose the image that matches your application needs. The image identifiers are defined in the src/include/IxNpeMicrocode.h header file. The following demonstrates how simple it is to load the NPE with a microcode image.

NPE Download

```
1
2      #include <IxNpeDl.h>
3
4      if (IX_SUCCESS != ixNpeDlNpeInitAndStart(
5                              IX_NPEDL_NPEIMAGE_NPEA_HSS0));
6      {
7          printf ("Error initialising and starting NPE A!\n");
8          return (IX_FAIL);
9      }
```

Line 2

Include the NPE download public header file.

Line 4

This function is used to download an NPE image and start execution of the NPE.

Line 5

This example image identifier is for NPE A and provides high-speed serial services. Other image identifiers are available in `src/include/IxNpeMicrocode.h`.

Lines 6–9

Check the return code for errors and print a message if an error is returned.

Build Structure

The NPE microcode images are maintained in a proprietary binary data structure. Prior to downloading the NPE with an image, you must make the data available to the download function. The two ways you can make the images available to the downloader are:

- Direct inclusion of NPE image data into the Intel IXP400 software library.
- Run-time provision of image data loaded from a file system.

The standard approach for VxWorks and Windows CE is to include the microcode image data directly into the library. The build system automatically includes the data. You do not need to do anything except the steps outlined in the previous code sample.

For Linux, the microcode image data should not be directly linked to the kernel in any way due to GPL licensing considerations. We have provided a mechanism to provide the microcode data from a Linux user space command shell. The following code shows the steps required to load the Intel IXP400 software library, the microcode, and the NPE Ethernet device driver:

```
> insmod ixp400.o
> cat IxNpeMicrocode.dat > /dev/ixNpe
> insmod ixp400_eth.o
```

In this case, the NPE Ethernet driver downloads and starts the NPEs using the function `ixNpeDlNpeInitAndStart()` described above. The `IxNpeMocrocode.dat` is provided as part of the Intel IXP400 software, version 1.5 and higher.

Message Handler

The IXP4XX network processors contain a silicon block known as the message handler. The Intel IXP400 software uses this block to exchange configuration messages between the Intel XScale core and the NPEs. The block is intended for use only by the Intel IXP400 software. As the message exchanges between the core and the NPEs are infrequent, it is most effective to simply trigger the message communications exchange between NPE and the core using the Intel XScale core message handler interrupt. Even though your application cannot make use of the message handler features directly, we do have a small favor to ask: please initialize the component as shown below.

NPE Message Handler Initialization

```
10    #include <IxNpeMh.h>
11
12    if(ixNpeMhInitialize(
13                        (IX_NPEMH_NPEINTERRUPTS_YES)
14       != IX_SUCCESS)
15    {
16        printf("Unable to start NPE Message handler!\n);
17        return (IX_FAIL);
18    }
```

Line 10

Include the definitions for the NPE message handler.

Line 12

Initialize the NPE message handler.

Line 13

Indicate that the NPE message handler should bind to the message handler interrupt. You must use this "option."

Lines 14–16

These lines provide some standard error checking return code.

Queue Manager

The IXP4XX network processors contain a silicon block known as the queue manager. The block provides 64 first in, first out (FIFO) hardware queues. The Intel IXP400 software makes use of these queues to transfer information between the Intel XScale core and the NPEs. The information is usually in the form of a descriptor with details of the data to operate on. The queue manager hardware block implements two groups of 32 queues, known as the lower and upper groups. Each queue group (lower and upper) is mapped to a separate Intel XScale core interrupt.

Each Intel IXP400 software access component configures the appropriate queue to generate an event when a specific queue condition occurs, such as when a queue becomes full. Your application is not required to directly configure or modify any of the queues.

The queue manager software component consists of a dispatch loop. The purpose of this dispatch loop is to iterate through the queues. When an event is pending on a queue, the appropriate Intel IXP400 software component is notified of the event. This event may, in turn, trigger a user-level call back, which your application has previously registered. An extremely important point is that all application level callbacks are called in the same stack context as the queue-manager dispatch loop. That is, if the dispatch loop is called from an interrupt handler, the application callbacks are also called at interrupt level.

Your application is responsible for calling or registering the queue manager dispatch loop as an interrupt handler.

Dispatch Loop API

A number of dispatch loop implementations are currently available in the Intel IXP400 software. The entry point into each dispatch loop is defined in the `IxQMgr.h` header file.

- ■ `ixQMgrDispatcherLoopRunA0()`. This function is the original dispatch loop implementation for the first release (A0) of the IXP42X silicon. It contains some specific workarounds for that silicon release. You should not use this version unless you have an A0 version of the IXP42X network processor.

■ ixQMgrDispatcherLoopRunB0(). This standard dispatch loop is used by most applications. It iterates through all the queues in a group, operating on all queue entries in a specific queue before moving on to the next queue. The function returns after it has iterated through all queues.

■ ixQMgrDispatcherLoopRunB0LLP(). This dispatch loop implements an Intel IXP400 software feature known as *live lock prevention*. It was developed to help systems prioritize voice traffic from the high-speed serial (HSS) device over traffic from the Ethernet interfaces. You should use this dispatch loop when the live lock prevention feature has been enabled.

The Intel IXP400 software provides an easy way to get a pointer to the correct dispatcher, ixQMgrDispatcherLoopGet(). For IXP42X network processor A0 silicon, the function returns a function pointer to ixQMgrDispatcherLoopRunA0. For IXP42X network processor B0 silicon and all IXP45X and IXP46X network processors, the default is a function pointer to ixQMgrDispatcherLoopRunB0. If the live lock prevention option is enabled, a function pointer to ixQMgrDispatcher-LoopRunB0LLP is returned.

Dispatch Loop Calling Context

Your application must provide the calling context for the dispatch loop. The choices are:

■ *Event-based interrupt.* The interrupt is driven through QM1 (lower queue group) or QM2 (upper queue group) interrupt. In this case, the system is interrupted only when there is traffic to service. This mode is suitable for low traffic rates and provides the lowest latency—as soon as traffic occurs, the Intel XScale core is interrupted. In this mode of operation, high data rates result in a very large number of interrupts being serviced. Depending on the speed of your processor, this large number of interrupts may overwhelm the operating system, whereby the operating system spends a significant amount of time handling the interrupts and less time on other useful functions such as routing the traffic or running your application.

■ *Timer-based interrupt mode.* In this case, the dispatch loop is called from a timer-based interrupt. Rather than generate an interrupt directly from the queue manager hardware, the dispatch is called at fixed intervals, regardless of the traffic activity. This option is more appropriate when your application is servicing high traffic rates such as the 100BaseT Ethernet interfaces. One disadvantage is that the system calls the dispatch loop at frequent intervals even if there are no queues to be serviced, but it does have the advantage that the system is not overwhelmed by queue manager hardware interrupts when there is a burst of traffic.

■ *Task-level polling mode.* In this case, the servicing of the queue manager is dictated by the priority of the thread in which it is called. This option provides considerable granularity in setting the relative priority of the queue manager dispatch loop.

The following code fragments show how to call the dispatch loop for each case described above. In most cases, the interrupt timer-based implementation has achieved the highest networking performance.

Queue Manager Interrupt Based Dispatch

```
1    IxQMgrDispatcherFuncPtr dispatcherFunc = 0;
2
3    ixQMgrInit();
4    ixFeatureCtrlSwConfigurationWrite
5            (IX_FEATURECTRL_ORIGB0_DISPATCHER,
6             IX_FEATURE_CTRL_SWCONFIG_DISABLED);
7
8    ixQMgrDispatcherLoopGet(&dispatcherFunc);
9
10   ixOsalIrqBind(IXP400_INT_LVL_QM1,
11               (VOIDFUNCPTR)dispatcherFunc,
12               (void *)IX_QMGR_QUELOW_GROUP);
13
14   ixOsalIrqBind(IXP400_INT_LVL_QM2,
15               (VOIDFUNCPTR)dispatcherFunc,
16               (void *)IX_QMGR_QUEUPP_GROUP);
17
```

Line 1

Declare the variable to save the dispatch function pointer.

Line 3

The queue manager component must be called before any other components are initialized.

Lines 5–6

Enable the live lock prevention feature within the queue manager component. This feature is optional and does not depend on the calling context you choose for the dispatch loop in your system.

Line 8

Set up the dispatch function pointer. The call returns the appropriate dispatch loop for your IXP4XX network processor.

Lines 10–12

Bind the dispatch loop function entry point for the lower group of queues to the appropriate queue-manager interrupt (QM1).

Lines 14–16

Bind the dispatch loop function entry point for the upper group of queues to the appropriate queue-manager interrupt (QM2). At press time, the upper group of queues are only used by ATM services, and you do not need to call the dispatch loop of this group of queues if you are not using ATM services.

Timer-Based Dispatch

This method calls the dispatcher loop from a hardware-based timer interrupt. Our example shows how to do this in VxWorks where `AuxClk` functions are used to call the function at interrupt level from timer 1 interrupts.

```
18    IxQMgrDispatcherFuncPtr dispatcherFunc = 0;
19
20      ixQMgrInit()
21      ixQMgrDispatcherLoopGet(&dispatcherFunc);
22      ixpAuxClkDisable();
23      ixpAuxClkRateSet (1000);
24      ixpAuxClkConnect ((FUNCPTR)dispatcherFunc,
25                        IX_QMGR_QUELOW_GROUP);
26      ixpAuxClkEnable();
27
```

Line 18

Declare the variable to save the dispatch function pointer.

Line 20

The queue manager component must be called before any other components are initialized.

Line 21

Set up the dispatch function pointer. The call returns the appropriate dispatch loop for your IXP4XX network processor.

Line 22

Disable the VxWorks auxiliary clock function.

Line 23

Set the auxiliary rate to 1,000 times per second. The dispatch loop will be called once every millisecond.

Lines 24–25

Bind the dispatch loop function to the auxiliary timer. On systems that do not have an auxiliary clock function you can bind a function directly to the timer interrupt (IXP425_INT_LVL_TIMER2) using the ixOsalIrqBind() function call. This function resets and clears the interrupt and calls the dispatch loop function. Make sure you set up the timer to generate an interrupt at the required interval.

Line 26

Enable the VxWorks auxiliary clock function.

Thread-Based Dispatch Loop

In this implementation, the dispatch loop is called from the task level. Two parameters control how much access the dispatch gets to the CPU: the priority of the thread and how long it sleeps between iterations.

```
28    IxQMgrDispatcherFuncPtr dispatcherFunc = 0;
29    IxOsalThread threadId;
30      ixQMgrInit();
31      ixOsalThreadCreate( &threadId ,
32                          NULL,
33                          dispatchTask,
34                          (void *)0 );
```

```
35      ixOsalThreadStart ( &threadId);
36
37      ..
38      static void dispatchTask(void)
39      {
40        while (1)
41        {
42          ixOsalSleep(1);
43          (*dispatcherFunc) (IX_QMGR_QUELOW_GROUP);
44        }
45      }
```

Line 28

Declare the variable to save the dispatch function pointer.

Line 29

Declare the variable to save the thread/task identifier.

Line 30

The queue-manager component must be called before any other components are initialized.

Line 31

Create a thread and save the identifier in threadId.

Line 32

This example sets the thread attributes structure to null and uses the default values. You can override the thread priority by setting up the thread attributes structure.

Line 33

Set a pointer to the function, which is the entry point to the thread that is being created.

Line 34

The thread does not require any arguments; so we set it to zero.

Line 35

Start the thread running.

Line 38

Set the entry point to the thread that has just been created and started.

Line 40

Start an infinite loop; this thread should never exit.

Line 42

This function sleeps for one millisecond.

Line 43

Call the dispatch loop function.

UART Support

The Intel IXP400 software provides generic support for the UARTs available on the IXP4XX network processors; however, the UARTS are fully supported by each operating system with native device drivers. The operating system drivers provide a standard serial port abstraction specific for each operating system. At this point, you probably do not need to use the Intel IXP400 UART software component.

The UARTs are modeled on the de facto industry standard 16550 UART. There are, however, some minor differences in the implementation and register map, which necessitate minor modification to the drivers that support the standard UART. Should you need to develop a device driver for the UART, you should start with a 16550 UART driver closest to your target and modify it to accommodate the differences. The differences to the standard implementation are as follows:

■ *UART FIFO depth.* The IXP4XX network processors provide a FIFO of 64 bytes; the de facto standard is 16 bytes.

■ *Interrupt-enabled register.* This register contains two additional bits: one to enable the UART (UUE bit), and the other to enable a receiver time out interrupt (RTOIE bit).

The UARTs support the clear to send (CTS) and request to send (RTS) flow control signals, but do not support any of the extended modem signals, such as data set ready, data terminal ready, data carrier detect, or ring indicator. If you require these additional signals, the GPIO pins are ideal.

USB Device Functions

The IXP4XX network processors provide a USB 1.1 device interface. This interface allows an IXP4XX network processor-based platform to connect to a PC host. The USB access component provides a device-driver layer to this hardware. This component does not cover the USB 1.1 host device available on the IXP45X and IXP46X network processors. A USB 1.1 host controller driver is currently under development. The USB 1.1 device API provides the following device functions:

- USB 1.1 device hardware initialization
- Data transfer to and from all endpoints (control, bulk, and isochronous)
- Stall an endpoint

The USB access component provides a very low-level interface to the device. The Intel IXP400 software provides a USB device driver compliant with the Remote Network Driver Interface Specification (RNDIS) for VxWorks, Linux, and Windows CE. The RNDIS is a Microsoft specification (Microsoft 2004). This driver provides the *device side* of an RNDIS connection. Microsoft XP provides the *host side* implementation of the RNDIS driver. When you connect a PC to an IXP4XX network processor-based platform via a USB cable, the driver provides an emulated Ethernet interface over the USB cable. The generic communication device class (CDC) driver was not available when Intel first developed the RNDIS device driver, so it was not implemented. The RNDIS driver is provided in `ixp400_xscale/src/codelets/usb`.

The RNDIS device driver provides the following features for each of the operating systems supported:

- Provides a native Ethernet type device driver for the operating system. The interface connects to the IP stack and must have an IP address assigned to it.
- Manages USB device descriptors.
- Facilitates the USB bus enumeration of the IXP4XX network processor-based device.

The RNDIS interface appears just like any other network interface. It provides an 11-megabit per second interface, although due to protocol overhead and the polled nature of USB, the interface can sustain a data transfer of approximately 5.5 megabits per second.

Chapter 10

Performance Tuning

We should forget about small efficiencies, say about 97% of the time; premature optimization is the root of all evil.

— Donald Knuth

Performance tuning is one of the black arts of embedded system development. You will almost certainly spend some portion of your development schedule on optimization and performance activities. Unfortunately, these activities usually seem to occur when the ship-date is closing in and everyone is under the most pressure.

However, help is at hand. We have helped a number of customers tune many diverse applications. From these real-life experiences we have developed a useful toolbox of tricks and techniques for performance tuning, which are summarized in this chapter. These best-known methods appear in "pattern" form. While many of the patterns are generally applicable on any performance-tuning work, some are specific to Intel XScale® core and the Intel® IXP4XX network processors. We have organized the optimization and performance tuning patterns under the following headings:

- General Approaches
- Networking Techniques
- Code and Design
- Intel XScale Core and Intel IXP4XX Network Processor-Specific
- Operating System Specific

What are Patterns?

Each performance improvement suggestion is documented in the form of a pattern (Alexander 1979) (Gamma et al. 1995). A pattern is "a solution to a problem in a context," a literary mechanism to share experience and impart solutions to commonly occurring problems. Each pattern contains these elements:

- *Name*—for referencing a problem/solution pairing.

- *Context*—the circumstance in which we solve the problem that imposes constraints on the solution.

- *Problem*—the specific problem to be solved.

- *Solution*—the proposed solution to the problem. Many problems can have more than one solution and the "goodness" of a solution to a problem is affected by the context in which the problem occurs. Each solution takes certain forces into account. It resolves some forces at the expense of others. It may even ignore some forces.

- *Forces*—the often contradictory considerations we must take into account when choosing a solution to a problem.

A pattern language is the organization and combination of a number of interrelated patterns. Where one pattern references another pattern we use the following format: "(*see* Pattern Name)."

You may not need to read each and every pattern. You certainly do not need to apply all of the patterns to every performance optimization task. You might, however, find it useful to scan all of the context and problem statements to get an overview of what is available in this pattern language.

General Approaches

This first set of patterns proposes general approaches and tools you might use when embarking on performance tuning work. These patterns are not specific to any processor or application.

Defined Performance Requirement

Context. You are a software developer starting a performance improvement task on an application or driver.

Problem. Performance improvement work can become a never-ending task. Without a goal, the activity can drag on longer than productive or necessary.

Solution. At an early stage of the project or customer engagement, define a relevant specific, realistic, and measurable performance requirement. Document that performance requirement as a specific detailed application and configuration with a numerical performance target.

- ■ "Make it as fast as possible" is not a specific performance requirement.

- ■ "The application must be capable of 10-gigabit per second wire-speed routing of 64-byte packets with a 266-megahertz CPU" is not a realistic performance requirement.

Forces. You might be inclined to avoid defining a requirement because:

- ■ A performance target can be hard to define.

- ■ Waiting to have a goal might affect your product's competitiveness.

- ■ A performance target can be a moving target; competitors do not stand still. New competitors come along all the time.

- ■ Without a goal, the performance improvement work can drag on longer than productive.

Performance Design

Context. You are a software developer designing a system. You have a measurable performance requirement (*see* Defined Performance Requirement).

Problem. The design of the system does not meet the performance requirement.

Solution. At design time, describe the main data path scenario. Walk through the data path in the design workshop and document it in the high level design.

When you partition the system into components, allocate a portion of the clock cycles to the data-path portion of each component. Have a target at design time for the clock-cycle consumption of the whole data path. Ganssle (1999) gives notations and techniques for system design performance constraints.

During code inspections, hold one code inspection that walks through the most critical data path.

Code inspections are usually component-based. This code inspection should be different and follow the scenario of the data path.

If you use a polling mechanism, ensure the CPU is shared appropriately.

It can also be useful to analyze the application's required bus bandwidth at design time to decide if the system will be CPU or memory bandwidth/latency limited.

Forces. You might be deterred from making code inspections because:

■ It can be difficult to anticipate some system bottlenecks at design time.

■ The design of the system can make it impossible to meet the performance requirement. If you discover this late in the project, it might be too difficult to do anything about it.

Premature Code Tuning Avoided

Context. You are implementing a system, and you are in the coding phase of the project. You do have a good system-level understanding of the performance requirements and the allocation of performance targets to different parts of the system because you have a performance design (*see* Performance Design).

Problem. It is difficult to know how much time or effort to spend thinking about performance or efficiency when initially writing the code.

Solution. It is important to find the right balance between performance, functionality, and maintainability.

Some studies have found 20 percent of the code consumes 80 percent of the execution time; others have found less than 4 percent of the code accounts for 50 percent of the time (McConnell 1993).

KISS—Keep it simple. Until you have measured and can prove a piece of code is a system-wide bottleneck, do not optimize it. Simple design is easier to optimize. The compiler finds it easier to optimize simple code.

If you are working on a component of a system, you should have a performance budget for your part of the data path (*see* Performance Design).

In the unit test, you could have a performance test for your part of the data path. At integration time, the team could perform a performance test for the complete assembled data path.

> *The best is the enemy of the good. Working toward perfection may prevent completion. Complete it first, then perfect it. The part that needs to be perfect is usually small.*
>
> — Steve McConnell

For further information, see Chapters 28 and 29 of Code Complete (McConnell 1993) and question 20.13 in the comp.lang.c FAQ Web site (Summit 1995).

Forces. You find the following things troublesome:

- ■ Efficient code is not necessarily "better" code. It might be difficult to understand and maintain.

- ■ It is almost impossible to identify performance bottlenecks before you have a working system.

- ■ If you spend too much time doing micro-optimization during initial coding, you might miss important global optimizations.

- ■ If you look at performance too late in a project, it can be too late to do anything about it.

Step-by-Step Records

Context. You are trying a number of optimizations to fix a particular bottleneck. The system contains a number of other bottlenecks.

Problem. Sometimes it is difficult when working at a fast pace to remember optimizations made only a few days earlier.

Solution. Take good notes of each experiment you have tried to identify bottlenecks and each optimization you have tried to increase performance. These notes can be invaluable later. You might find you are stuck at a performance level with an invisible bottleneck. Reviewing your optimization notes might help you identify incorrect paths taken or diversionary assumptions.

When a performance improvement effort is complete, it can be very useful to have notes on the optimization techniques that worked. You can then put together a set of best-known methods to help other engineers in your organization benefit from your experience.

Forces. Writing notes can sometimes break the flow of work or thought.

Slam-Dunk Optimization

Context. You have made a number of improvements that have increased the efficiency of code running on the Intel XScale core.

Problem. The latest optimizations have not increased performance. You have hit some unidentified performance-limiting factor. You might have improved performance to a point where environmental factors, protocols, or test equipment are now the bottleneck.

Solution. It is useful to have a code modification identified that you know should improve performance, for example:

- An algorithm on the data path that can be removed temporarily such as IP checksum.

- Increase the processor clock speed.

In one application, we implemented a number of optimizations that should have improved performance but did not. We then removed the IP checksum calculation, and performance still did not increase. These results pointed to a hidden limiting factor, an unknown bottleneck. When we followed this line of investigation, we found a problem in the way we configured a physical layer device, and when we fixed this hidden limiting factor, performance improved immediately by approximately 25 percent.[‡] We retraced our steps and reapplied the earlier changes to identify the components of that performance improvement.

Forces. Increasing the processor clock speed improves performance only for CPU bound applications.

---

‡ See "Disclaimer" at the end of this chapter.

Best Compiler for Application

Context. You are writing an application using a compiler. You have a choice of compilers for the processor architecture you are using.

Problem. Different compilers generate code that has different performance characteristics. You need to select the right one for your application and target platform.

Solution. Experiment with different compilers and select the best performing compiler for your application and environment.

Performance can vary between compilers. For example, we ran the Dhrystone[†] MIPS benchmark on a 533-megahertz Intel IXP425 Network Processor. The following compilers are listed in order of their relative performance, at the time of writing.

■ Greenhills[†] v3.61 (Green Hills Software, Inc.)

■ ADS[†] v1.2 (ARM Ltd.)

■ Tornado[†] 2.2 Diab (Wind River Systems)

■ Tornado 2.2 GCC (Wind River Systems)

The Intel XScale core GNU-PRO compiler, when measuring the Java[†] CaffineMark benchmark, generates approximately 10-percent better performance than the open source GCC compiler. For more information about the GNU-PRO compiler, refer to the Intel Developer Web site listed in "References."

Intel is currently working to improve the GNU-PRO compiler and is expecting to further optimize its code generation for the Intel XScale core.

Forces. When selecting a compiler, you might find that:

■ Some compilers are more expensive than others.

■ Some compilers and operating systems might not match. For example, the compiler you want to use generates the wrong object file format for your tool chain or development environment.

■ A particular compiler might optimize a particular benchmark better than another compiler, but that is no guarantee it will optimize your specific application in the same way.

■ You might be constrained in your compiler choice because of tools support issues. If you are working in the Linux kernel, you might have to use GCC. Some parts of the kernel use GCC-specific extensions.

Compiler Optimizations

Context. You have chosen to use a C compiler (*see* Best Compiler for Application).

Problem. You have not enabled all of the compiler optimizations.

Solution. Your compiler supports a number of optimization switches. Using these switches can increase global application performance for a small amount of effort. Read the documentation for your compiler and understand these switches.

In general, the highest-level optimization switch is the -O switch. In GCC, this switch takes a numeric parameter. Find out the maximum parameter for your compiler and use it. Typical compilers support three levels of optimization. Try the highest. In GCC, the highest level is -O3. However, in the past, -O3 code generation had more bugs than -O2, the most-used optimization level. The Linux kernel is compiled with -O2. If you have problems at -O3 you might need to revert to -O2.

Moving from -O2 to -O3 made an improvement of approximately 15 percent in packet processing in one application tested. In another application, -O3 was slower than -O2.[‡]

You can limit the use of compiler optimizations to individual C source files.

Introduce optimization flags, one by one, to discover the ones that give you benefit.

Other GCC optimization flags that can increase performance are:

■ `-funroll-loops`

■ `-fomit-frame-pointer -mapcs`

■ `-align-labels=32`

---

‡ See "Disclaimer" at the end of this chapter.

Forces. You find the following things troublesome:

■ Optimizations increase generated code size.

■ Some optimizations might not increase performance.

■ Compilers support a large number of switches and options. It can be time consuming to read the lengthy documentation.

■ Optimized code is difficult to debug.

■ Some optimizations can reveal compiler bugs. For example, `-fomit-frame-pointer -mapcs` reveals a post-increment bug in GCC 2.95.X for the Intel XScale core.

■ Enabling optimization can change timings in your code. It might reveal latent undiscovered problems.

Data Cache

Context. You are using a processor that contains a data cache. The core is running faster than memory or peripherals.

Problem. The processor core is spending a significant amount of time stalled waiting on an external memory access. You have identified this problem using the performance monitoring function on your chosen processor to quantify the number of cycles for which the processor is stalled.

In some applications, we have observed a significant number of cycles are lost to data-dependency stalls.

Solution. In general, the most efficient mechanism for accessing memory is to use the data cache. Core accesses to cached memory do not need to use the internal bus, leaving it free for other devices. In addition, accessing data in cache memory is faster than accessing it from the SDRAM.

The cache unit can make efficient use of the internal bus. On the IXP4XX network processor, the core fetches an entire 32-byte cache line, making use of multiple data phases. This fetch reduces the percentage of overhead cycles required for initiating and terminating bus cycles, when compared with issuing multiple bus cycles to read the same 32 bytes of data without using the cache.

The cache supports several features that give you flexibility in tailoring the system to your design needs. These features affect all applications to some degree; however, the optimal settings are application-dependent. It is critical to understand the effects of these features and how to fine-tune them for the usage-model of a particular application. We cover a number of these cache features in later sections.

In one application that was not caching buffer descriptors and packet data, developers enabled caching and saw an approximate 25-percent improvement in packet-processing performance.[‡]

Tornado 2.1.1 `netBufLib` does not allocate packet descriptors and packet memory from cached memory. Later versions of Tornado fixed this issue for the IXP42X product line.

Choose data structures appropriate for a data cache. For example, stacks are typically more cache efficient than linked-list data structures.

In most of the applications we have seen, the instruction cache is very efficient. It is worth spending time optimizing the use of the data cache.

Forces. Consider the following things:

- If you cache data-memory that the core shares with another bus master, you must manage cache flush/invalidation explicitly.

- If you use caching, you need to ensure no two-packet buffers ever share the same cache line. Bugs that are difficult to diagnose may result.

- Be careful what you cache. *Temporal locality* refers to the amount of time between accesses to the data. If you access a piece of data once or access it infrequently, it has low temporal locality. If you mark this kind of data for caching, the cache replacement algorithm can cause the eviction of performance-sensitive data by this lower priority data.

- The processor implements a round-robin line-replacement algorithm.

[‡] See "Disclaimer" at the end of this chapter.

Networking Techniques

The following patterns can be applied to networking performance in general. These techniques are not typically specific to the IXP42X product line.

Bottleneck Hunting

Context. You have a running functional system. You have a performance requirement (*see* Defined Performance Requirement). A customer is measuring performance lower than that requirement.

Problem. You can have a number of performance bottlenecks in the designed system, but unless you identify the current limiting factor, you might optimize the wrong thing. One component of the system might be limiting the flow of network packets to the rest of the system.

Solution. Performance improvement really starts with bottleneck hunting. It is only when you find the performance-limiting bottleneck that you can work on optimizations to remove the bottleneck. A system typically has a number of bottlenecks. You first need to identify the current limiting bottleneck then remove it. You then need to iterate through the remaining bottlenecks until the system meets its performance requirements.

First, determine if your application is CPU or I/O bound. In a CPU-bound system, the limiting factor or bottleneck is the amount of cycles needed to execute some algorithm or part of the data path. In an I/O-bound system, the bottleneck is external to the processor. The processor has enough CPU cycles to handle the traffic, but the traffic flow is not constant enough to make full use of the available processor cycles.

To determine if the system is CPU or I/O bound, try running the processor at a number of different clock speeds. If you see a significant change in performance, your system is probably CPU bound.

Next, look at the software components of the data path; these might include:

■ Low-level device drivers specific to a piece of hardware. These device drivers could conform to an OS-specific interface.

■ A network interface service mechanism running on the Intel XScale core. This mechanism might be a number of ISRs or a global polling loop.

- Adapter components or glue code that adapts the hardware-specific drivers or the underlying Intel® IXP400 software APIs to an RTOS or network stack.

- Encapsulation layers of the networking stack

- The switching/bridging/routing engine of the networking stack or the RTOS

- Intel IXP400 software access APIs. These functions provide an abstraction of the underlying microcode and silicon.

- IXP42X NPE microcode

If some algorithm in a low-level device driver is limiting the flow of data into the system, you might waste your time if you start tweaking compiler flags or optimize the routing algorithm.

It is best to look at the new or unique components to a particular system first. Typically, these are the low-level device drivers or the adapter components unique to this system. Other projects have already used the routing-algorithm, the Intel IXP400 software, and the NPE microcode.

Concentrate on the unique components first, especially if these components are on the edge of the system. In one wireless application we discovered the wireless device driver was a bottleneck that limited the flow of data into the system.

Many components of a data path can contain packet buffers. Packet counters inserted in the code can help you identify queue overflows or underflows. Typically, the code that consumes the packet buffer is the bottleneck.

This process is typically iterative. When you fix the current bottleneck, you then need to loop back and identify the next one.

Forces. Be aware of the following:

- Most systems have multiple bottlenecks.

- Early bottleneck hunting—before you have a complete running system—increases the risk of misidentified bottlenecks and wasted tuning effort.

Evaluating Traffic Generator and Protocols

Context. You are using a network-traffic generator and protocols to measure the performance of a system.

Problem. The performance test or protocol overheads can limit the measured performance of your application.

Solution. Identifying the first bottleneck is a challenge. First, you need to eliminate your traffic generators and protocols as bottlenecks and analyze the invariants.

Typical components in a complete test system might include:

- Traffic sources, sinks, and measurement equipment

- The device under test (DUT) for which you are tuning the performance

- Physical connections and protocols between traffic sources and the DUT

Your test environment might use a number of different types of traffic sources, sinks, and measurement equipment. You need to first make sure they are not the bottleneck in your system.

Equipment, like Smartbits[†] and Adtech[†] testers, is not typically a bottleneck. However, using a PC with FTP software to measure performance can be a bottleneck. You need to test the PC and FTP software without the DUT to make sure your traffic sources can reach the performance you require.

Running this test can also flush out bottlenecks in the physical media or protocols you are using.

In addition, you need to make sure the overhead inherent in the protocols you are using makes the performance you require feasible. For example:

- You cannot expect 100 megabits per second over Ethernet with 64-byte packets due to inter-frame gap and frame preamble. You can expect to get at most 76 megabits per second.

- You cannot expect to get 8 megabits per second over an ADSL link; you can expect to get at most 5.5 megabits per second.

■ You cannot expect to get 100 megabits per second on FTP running over Ethernet. You must take IP protocol overhead and TCP acknowledgements into account.

■ You cannot expect 52 megabits per second on 802†.11a/g networks due to CTS/RTS overhead and protocol overhead.

Characteristics of the particular protocol or application could also be causing the bottleneck. For example, if the FTP performance is much lower (by a factor of 2) than the large-packet performance with a traffic generator (Smartbits), the problem could be that the TCP acknowledgement packets are getting dropped. This problem can sometimes be a buffer management issue.

FTP performance can also be significantly affected by the TCP window sizes on the FTP client and server machines.

Forces. Test equipment typically outperforms the DUT.

Environmental Factors

Context. You are finding it difficult to identify the bottleneck.

Problem. Environmental factors can cause a difficult-to-diagnose bottleneck.

Solution. Check the environmental factors.

When testing a wireless application, you might encounter radio interference in the test environment. In this case, you can use a Faraday cage to radio-isolate your test equipment and DUT from the environment. Antenna configuration is also important. The antennas should not be too close (<1 meter). They should be erect, not lying down. You also need to make sure you shield the DUT to protect it from antenna interference.

Check shared resources. Is your test equipment or DUT sharing a resource, such as a network segment, with other equipment? Is that other equipment making enough use of the shared resource to affect your DUT performance?

Check all connectors and cables. If you are confident you are making improvements but the measurements are not giving the improvement you expect, try changing all the cables connecting your DUT to the test equipment. As a last resort, try a replacement DUT. We have seen a number of cases where a device on the DUT had degraded enough to affect performance.

Polled Packet Processor

Context. You are designing the fundamental mechanism that drives the servicing of network interfaces.

Problem. Some fundamental mechanisms can expose you to more overhead and wasted CPU cycles. These wasted cycles can come from interrupt preamble/dispatch and context switches.

Solution. You can categorize most applications as interrupt or polling driven or a combination of both.

When traffic overloads a system, it runs optimally if it is running in a tight loop, polling interfaces for which it knows there is traffic queued.

If the application driver is interrupt-based, look to see how many packets you handle per interrupt. To get better packet-processing performance, handle more packets per interrupt by possibly using a polling approach in the interrupt handler.

Some systems put the packet on a queue from the interrupt handler and then do the packet processing in another thread. In this kind of a system, you need to understand how many packets the system handles per context switch. To improve performance, increase the number of packets handled per context switch.

Other systems can drive packet processing, triggered from a timer interrupt. In this case, you need to make sure the timer frequency and number of packets handled per interrupt is not limiting the networking performance of your system. In addition, this system is not optimally efficient when the system is in overload.

Systems based on Linux are usually interrupt-based.

Forces. Be sure to consider the following:

- Reducing wasted CPU cycles can complicate the overall architecture or design of an application.

- Some IP stacks or operating systems can restrict the options in how you design these fundamental mechanisms.

- You might need to throttle the amount of CPU given to packet processing to allow other processing to happen even when the system is in overload.

- Applying these techniques might increase the latency in handling some packets.

Edge Packet Throttle

Context. The bottleneck of your system is now the IP forwarding or transport parts of the IP stack.

Problem. You might be wasting CPU cycles processing packets to later drop them when a queue fills later in the data path.

Solution. When a system goes into overload, it is better to leave the frames back up in the RX queue and let the edges of your system, the NPE and PHY devices, throttle reception. You can avoid wasting core cycles by checking a bottleneck indicator, such as queue full, early in the data path code.

For example, on VxWorks[†], you can make the main packet-processing task (netTask) the highest priority task. This technique is one easy way to implement a "self-throttling" system. Alternatively, you could make the buffer-replenish code a low-priority task, which would ensure receive buffers are only supplied when you have available CPU.

Forces. Be aware of the following:

■ Checking a bottleneck indicator might weaken the encapsulation of an internal detail of the IP stack.

■ Implementing an early check wastes some CPU cycles when the system is in overload.

Detecting Resource Collisions

Context. You make a change, and performance drops unexpectedly.

Problem. A resource collision effect could be causing a pronounced performance bottleneck. Examples of such effects we have seen are:

■ TX traffic is being generated from RX traffic; Ethernet is running in half-duplex mode. The time it takes to generate the TX frame from an RX frame corresponds to the inter-frame gap. When the TX frame is sent, it collides with the next RX frame.

■ The Ethernet interface is running full duplex, but traffic is being generated in a loop, and the frame transmissions occur at times the MAC is busy receiving frames.

Solution. These kinds of bottlenecks are difficult to find and can only be checked by looking at driver counters and the underlying PHY devices. Error counters on test equipment can also help.

Forces. Counters might not be available or easily accessible.

Code and Design

This section covers some general code-tuning guidelines that are applicable to most processors. In many cases, these optimizations can decrease the readability, maintainability, or portability of your code. Be sure you are optimizing code that needs optimization (*see* Premature Code Tuning Avoided).

Reordered Struct

Context. You have identified a bottleneck segment of code on your application data path. The code uses a large struct.

Problem. The struct spans a number of cache lines.

Solution. Reorder the fields in a struct to group the frequently accessed fields together. If all of the accessed fields fit on a cache line, the first access pulls them all into cache, potentially avoiding data-dependency stalls when accessing the other fields.
Organize all frequently written fields into the same half-cache line.

Forces. Reordering structs might not be feasible. Some structs might map to a packet definition.

Supersonic ISR

Context. Your application uses multiple interrupt service routines (ISR) to signal the availability of data on an interface and trigger the processing of that data.

Problem. Interrupt service routines can interfere with other ISR and packet processing code.

Solution. Keep ISRs short. Design them to be re-entrant.
An ISR should just give a semaphore, set a flag, or en-queue a packet. You should de-queue and process the data outside the ISR. This way, you obviate the need for interrupt locks around data in an ISR.

Interrupt locks in a frequent ISR can have hard-to-measure effects on the overall system.

For more detailed interrupt design guidelines, see Doing Hard Time (Douglass 1999).

Forces. Consider the following things when designing your ISR:

■ Posting to a semaphore or queue can cause extra context switches, which reduce the overall efficiency of a system.

■ Bugs in ISRs usually have a catastrophic effect. Keeping them short and simple reduces the probability of bugs.

Assembly-Language-Critical Functions

Context. You have identified a C function that consumes a significant portion of the data path.

Problem. The code generated for this function might not be optimal for your processor.

Solution. Re-implement the critical function directly in assembly language. Use the best compiler for the application (*see* Best Compiler for Application) to generate initial assembly code, then hand-optimize it.

Forces. Keep the following things in mind:

■ Modern compiler technology is beginning to out-perform the ability of humans to optimize assembly language for sophisticated processors.

■ Assembly language is more difficult to read and maintain.

■ Assembly language is more difficult to port to other processors.

Inline Functions

Context. You have identified a small C function that is called frequently on the data path.

Problem. The overhead associated with the entry and exit to the function can become significant in a small function, frequently called on by the application data path.

Solution. Declare the function inline. This way, the function gets inserted directly into the code of the calling function.

Forces. Be aware of the following:

■ Inline functions can increase the code size of your application and add stress to the instruction cache.

■ Some debuggers have difficulty showing the thread of execution for inline functions.

■ A function call itself can limit the compiler's ability to optimize register usage in the calling function.

■ A function call can cause a data dependency stall when a register waiting for an SDRAM access is still in flight.

Cache-Optimizing Loop

Context. You have identified a critical loop that is a significant part of the data-path performance.

Problem. The structure of the loop or the data on which it operates could be "thrashing" the data cache.

Solution. You can consider a number of loop/data optimizations:

■ Array merging—the loop uses two or more arrays. Merges them into a single array of a struct.

■ Induction variable interchange

■ Loop fusion

For more details, see the Intel IXP400 software programmer's guide (Intel 2004c).

Forces.

■ Loop optimizations can make the code harder to read, understand, and maintain.

Minimizing Local Variables

Context. You have identified a function that needs optimization. It contains a large number of local variables.

Problem. A large number of local variables might incur the overhead of storing them on the stack. The compiler might generate code to set up and restore the frame pointer.

Solution. Minimize the number of local variables. The compiler may be able to store all the locals and parameters in registers.

Forces. Removing local variables can decrease the readability of code or require extra calculations during the execution of the function.

Explicit Registers

Context. You have identified a function that needs optimization. A local variable or a piece of data is frequently used in the function.

Problem. Sometimes the compiler does not identify a register optimization.

Solution. It is worth trying explicit register hints to local variables that are frequently used in a function.

It can also be useful to copy a frequently used part of a packet that is also used frequently in a data path algorithm into a local variable declared register. An optimization of this kind made a performance improvement of approximately 20 percent in one customer application.[‡]

Alternatively, you could add a local variable or register to explicitly "cache" a frequently used global variable. Some compilers do not work on global variables in local variables or registers. If you know the global is not modified by an interrupt handler and the global is modified a number of times in the same function, copy it to a register local variable, make updates to the local, and then write the new value back out to the global before exiting the function. This technique is especially useful when updating packet statistics in a loop handling multiple packets.

Forces. The register keyword is only a hint to the compiler.

Optimized Hardware Register Use

Context. The data path code does multiple reads or writes to one or more hardware registers.

Problem. Multiple read-operation-writes on hardware registers can cause the processor to stall.

Solution. First, break up read-operation-write statements to hide some of the latencies when dealing with hardware registers. For example:

---

‡ See "Disclaimer" at the end of this chapter.

Read-Operation-Writes on HW Registers

```
1        *reg1ptr |= 0x0400;
2        *reg2ptr &= ~0x80;
```

Optimized Read-Operation-Writes

```
3        reg1 = *reg1ptr;
4        reg2 = *reg2ptr;
5        reg1 |= 0x0400;
6        reg2 &= ~0x80;
7        *reg1ptr = reg1;
8        *reg2ptr = reg2;
```

This modified code eliminates one of the read dependency stalls.

Second, search the data path code for multiple writes to the same hardware register. Combine all the separate writes into a single write to the actual register. For example, some applications disable hardware interrupts using multiple set/resets of bits in the interrupt enable register. In one such application, when we manually combined these write instructions, performance improved by approximately 4 percent.[‡]

Forces. Manually separated read-operation-write code expands code slightly. It can also add local variables and could trigger the creation of a frame pointer.

Avoiding the OS Packet-Buffer Pool

Context. The application uses a system packet buffer pool.

Problem. Memory allocation or calls to packet buffer pool libraries can be processor intensive. In some operating systems, these functions lock interrupts and use local semaphores to protect simultaneous access to shared heaps.

Pay special attention to packet-buffer management at design time. Are buffers being allocated on the application data path? Where in the design are packet buffers replenished into the Intel IXP400 software access layer?

Solution. Avoid allocating or interacting with the RTOS packet buffer pool on the data path. Pre-allocate packet buffers outside the data path and store them in lightweight software pools/queues.

---

‡ See "Disclaimer" at the end of this chapter.

Stacks or arrays are typically faster than linked lists for packet buffer pool collections, as they require less memory accesses to add and remove buffers. Stacks also improve data cache utilization.

Forces. OS packet-buffer pools implement buffer collections. Writing another light collection duplicates functionality.

C-Language Optimizations

Context. You have identified a function or segment of code that is consuming a significant portion of the Intel XScale core's clock cycles on the data path. You might have identified this code using profiling tools (*see* Profiling Tools) or a performance measurement (*see* PMU Performance Measurement).

Problem. A function or segment of C-code needs optimization.

Solution. You can try a number of C-language level optimizations:

- Pass large function parameters by reference, never by value. Values take time to copy and use registers.

- Avoid array indexing. Use pointers.

- Minimize loops by collecting multiple operations into a single loop body.

- Avoid long if-then-else chains. Use a switch statement or a state machine.

- Use `int` (natural word-size of the processor) to store flags, rather than `char` or `short`.

- Use `unsigned` variants of variables; and parameters where possible. Doing so might allow some compilers to make optimizations.

- Avoid floating point calculations on the data path.

- Use decrementing loop variables; for example, `for (i=10; i--;) {do something}` or even better `do { something } while (i--)`. Look at the code generated by your compiler in this case. The Intel XScale core has the ability to modify the processor condition codes using `adds` and `subs` rather than `add` and `sub` saving a `cmp` instruction in loops. For more details, see the Intel IXP400 software programmer's guide (Intel 2004c).

- Place the most frequently true statement first in if-else statements.

■ Place frequent case labels first.

■ Write small functions, but balance size with complexity and performance. The compiler likes to reuse registers as much as possible and cannot do it in complex nested code. However, some compilers automatically use a number of registers on every function call. Extra function call entries and returns can cost a large number of cycles in tight loops.

■ Use the function `return` as opposed to an output parameter to return a value to a calling function. Return values on many processors are stored in a register by convention.

■ For critical loops, use Duff's device, a devious, generic technique for unrolling loops. See question 20.35 in the comp.lang.C FAQ (Summit 1995).

For other similar tips, see Chapter 29 in Code Complete (McConnell 1993).

Forces. Good compilers make a number of these optimizations.

Intel XScale® Core and Intel® IXP4XX Network Processor Specifics

The following patterns provide specific help for code running on the Intel XScale core and the IXP4XX network processors.

Devices' Silicon Features

Context. You have identified the processing power of the Intel XScale core as the bottleneck in your application.

Problem. You are using cycles on the Intel XScale core that could be offloaded by the NPEs and other on-chip offload facilities.

Solution. Get to know the IXP4XX product line and microcode feature set. IXP4XX network processors contain a number of processor elements that can operate in parallel to the Intel XScale core. Three NPEs and a DSP co-processor can offload some processing from the Intel XScale core and can increase the performance of your application. Some of these features include:

■ NPE Ethernet learning/filtering

■ NPE crypto algorithm offload

- Intel XScale core DSP co-processor MAC instructions
- DSP voice CODEC implementations
- NPE software DMA
- NPE ATM packet SAR
- NPE HDLC processing

If you believe an application requires offloading some features to the NPE, identify this potential feature request early in the development cycle. For new applications that are bound to the Intel XScale core's CPU, it might be feasible for Intel to design new offload functionality into the NPE. Features to consider for offloading include IP checksum and TTL update—estimated to improve routing performance by 4 percent—and 802.11 to 802.3 frame conversion. This kind of work needs some time to evaluate and implement.

Check to make sure you have the latest Intel IXP400 software access layer release. Each release typically contains a number of performance improvements.

Extensive documentation is available for the IXP42X product line and software. Read the ARM reference manual (Seal 2000) and the appropriate developer's manual listed in "References."

Forces. Take the following considerations into account:

- Integrating offloaded features can take some effort. Typically, you need to replace or glue in the offloaded feature to an existing code base or software stack.

- New NPE features can be implemented only by Intel or some ecosystem partners.

PMU Performance Measurement

Context. You have a functional system that does not meet its performance requirements.

Problem. Some general processor related issues might be affecting the performance of your applications in a number of software components.

Solution. Use the Intel XScale core's PMU to identify some macro performance characteristics of your whole application. Some of these performance characteristics include:

■ Instruction cache efficiency

■ Data cache efficiency

■ Data/bus request buffer full

■ Stall/write-back statistics

■ Instruction/data TLB efficiency

This kind of analysis can help you to identify a subtle bottleneck. For more details on these characteristics, see the appropriate developer's manual listed in "References."

For PMU sample code, see profiling the Intel XScale core (Intel 2002b). The Intel IXP400 software now provides a C-function API to simplify access to the PMU.

In most applications, this test can identify problems with data dependency stalls, but it is a good idea to test all of the characteristics as soon as possible to discount some possible factors early. For example, we have not seen instruction cache being an issue in any applications at the time of writing.

At higher clock speeds (400 megahertz and 533 megahertz), you might find a significant number of "cycles lost due to data-dependency stalls." If you measure this number on a 533-megahertz IXP4XX network processor and it is above 50 percent, you should investigate this area further. Many of the later sections of this chapter focus on strategies to reduce lost cycles waiting for data.

A word of warning: it can be dangerous to try to optimize these characteristics individually. In one test case, an optimization improved packet-processing performance, but made the "cycles lost due to data-dependency stalls" measurement worse.

Forces. Be aware that:

■ High-level PMU measurements can be misleading.

■ Optimizing PMU performance indicators might not optimize networking performance.

Disabled Counters/Statistics

Context. The Intel IXP400 software access layer is part of the data path. You have completed integration testing of your application.

Problem. The Intel IXP400 software access layer keeps a number of counters and statistics to facilitate integrating and debugging of both the access layer and the system as a whole. These counters usually incur a read and write or increment in main, or possibly cached, memory.

The access layer also contains code that checks parameters for legal values. This feature facilitates the integration and debugging of both Intel IXP400 software and the system as a whole. These checks usually test conditions that never occur once the system and customer code has been fully tested and integrated.

Solution. You can disable many of the internal Intel IXP400 software counters and statistics by defining the NDEBUG macro. Doing so also removes many of the internal parameter debug checks. You can enable or disable debug features on a per-component basis by modifying the compile flags in the component makefile and rebuilding the component.

In one application, use of this pattern increased packet-processing throughput by up to 4 percent.

Forces. Be aware that:

■ Disabling counters and statistics removes useful debugging information.

■ Removing parameter checks can obfuscate an issue, making it harder to detect incorrect parameter checks in customer code.

Stall Instructions

Context. You have run some tests using performance measurements (*see* PMU Performance Measurement) that indicate a large number of Intel XScale core cycles are being lost due to data dependency stalls.

Problem. You might find over 50 percent of the cycles are lost to stalls on a 533-megahertz processor. You need to identify the pieces of code that are causing these stalls.

Solution. One simple way to identify "hot instructions" is to use a program counter sampler. The sampler would run at a regular interval and count the number of times each instruction or program-counter executes while running the networking performance test.

If you run the test for a significant period of time, you should see a large number of samples on the instructions that stall most often.

Performance-profiling techniques (Intel 2002b) contain significant PMU example code, including a program counter (PC) sampler. Intel IXP400 software also includes a C-function API to simplify access to the PMU.

To reduce the impact of these stalls you could use the PLD instruction (*see* Intel XScale® Core PLD Instruction). You could also move code that won't cause a stall before the code that does.

Forces. Adding sampling code can affect the behavior of the system under test.

Profiling Tools

Context. You are at an early stage of performance improvement. You have not identified a specific bottleneck but you have proven the current bottleneck is the speed of execution of the code on the Intel XScale core.

Problem. You have a working system that is not meeting a performance requirement. You suspect raw algorithmic processing power is the current bottleneck; you need to identify the bottleneck code.

Solution. A number of profiling tools exist to help you identify code hotspots. Typically, they identify the percent of time spent in each C-function in your code base.

■ Rational Quantify[†] contains performance profiler, which is a useful tool for finding where application bottlenecks are. The usage model is very similar to that used to gather code coverage. You instrument your code and then execute that code on the board.

■ Intel supplies an excellent performance profiler, called the VTune™ Performance Analyzer, for many Intel product lines. At time of writing, the VTune™ Performance Analyzer is not yet available for the IXP4XX product line.

■ Gprof is available for many Linux-based systems.

■ Some ICEs contain profiling features such as visionClick[†].

Forces. Consider the following when selecting a tool:

■ Profiling tools can affect the performance of the system.

■ Some tools might not be available for your RTOS.

- Some profiling tools cost money.

- Each of these tools has a learning curve but could pay back the time and money investment.

Intel XScale Core PLD Instruction

Context. You have identified a stall instruction (*see* "Stall Instructions").

Problem. You want to reduce the time the processor spends stalled due to a data dependency.

Solution. The IXP4XX network processor has a true prefetch load instruction called PLD. The purpose of this instruction is to preload data into the data and mini-data caches.

Data prefetching allows hiding of memory transfer latency while the processor continues to execute instructions. The judicious use of the prefetch instruction can improve throughput performance of the IXP4XX network processor.

Look at the line of C-code that generates the stall instruction (*see* "Stall Instructions").

Insert an explicit assembly language PLD instruction some time before the stall instruction (*see* "Stall Instructions"). On a 533-megahertz IXP4XX network processor, you could issue the PLD 70 to 90 clock cycles before the stall.

Data prefetch can be applied not only to loops but to any data references within a block of code. Prefetch also applies to data writing when the memory type is enabled as write-allocate.

The IXP4XX network processor prefetch load instruction is a true prefetch instruction because the load destination is the data or mini-data cache and not a register. The prefetch load is a hint instruction and does not guarantee the data will be loaded.

Using prefetches requires careful experimentation. In some cases performance improved, and in others the performance degraded.

Overuse of prefetches can use shared resources and degrade performance. If the bus traffic requests exceed the system resource capacity, the processor stalls. The IXP4XX network processor data transfer resources are:

- Four fill buffers

- Four pending buffers

- Eight half-cache line write buffer

SDRAM resources are typically:

- Four memory banks
- One page buffer per bank referencing a 4-kilobyte address range
- Four transfer request buffers

Spread prefetch operations over calculations so as to allow free flow of bus traffic and to minimize the number of necessary prefetches.

Forces. Be aware that:

- Overuse of prefetches can use shared resources and degrade performance.

- The placement of a PLD instruction can be CPU speed specific. The latency to external memory when measured in cycles changes when you change the CPU speed.

Separate SDRAM Memory Banks

Context. You have completed a performance measurement (*see* "PMU Performance Measurement"). This data has identified a significant percentage of cycles lost due to data dependency stalls.

Problem. SDRAMs are typically divided into four banks. Thrashing occurs when subsequent memory accesses within the same memory bank access different pages. The memory page change adds three to four bus-clock cycles to memory latency.

Solution. You can resolve this type of thrashing by either placing the conflicting data structures into different memory banks or paralleling the data structures such that the data resides within the same memory page. Either action can reduce the latency reading data from memory and reduce the extent of many stalls.

Allocate packet buffers in their own bank. The SDRAM controller can keep a page partially open in four different memory banks. You could also split packet buffers across two banks.

It is also important to ensure instruction and data sections are in different memory banks, or they might continually thrash the memory page selection.

In one networking application, this technique increased packet-processing performance by approximately 10 percent. In another, it had no effect.

Forces. Write code to use different banks for code and data, or spread packets across multiple banks. Either action will complicate your BSP and configuration code.

Line-Allocation Policy

Context. You are using data cache for data or packet memory. You have enabled the cache.

Problem. The cache line-allocation policy can affect the performance of your application.

Solution. The Intel XScale core makes a decision about placing new data into the cache based on the *line-allocation policy*.

If the line-allocation policy is read-allocate, all load operations that miss the cache request a 32-byte cache line from external memory and allocate it into either the data cache or mini-data cache. Store operations that miss the cache do not cause a line to be allocated.

With a read/write-allocate policy, load or store operations that miss the cache request a 32-byte cache line from external memory if the cache is enabled.

In general, regular data and the stack for your application should be allocated to a read-write allocate region. Most applications regularly write and read this data. Again, it is worth experimenting.

Write-only data—or data that is written and subsequently not used for a long time—should be placed in a read-allocate region. Under the read-allocate policy, if a cache-write miss occurs, a new cache line is not allocated, and hence does not evict critical data from the data cache.

In general, read-allocate seems to be the best performing policy for packet data. One application had an improvement of approximately 10 percent when packet memory was set up read-allocate.

Forces. The appropriate cache line-allocation policy can be application-dependent. It is worth experimenting with both types of line-allocation policies.

Cache Write Policy

Context. You are using data cache for data or packet memory. You have enabled the cache.

Problem. The cache-write policy can affect the performance of your application.

Solution. Cached memory also has an associated write policy. A write-through policy instructs the data cache to keep external memory coherent by performing stores to both external memory and the cache. A write-back policy only updates external memory when a line in the cache is cleaned or needs to be replaced with a new line.

Generally, write-back provides higher performance because it generates less data traffic to external memory. However, if your application is making a small number of modifications, for example to packet data or message buffers, write-through may be more efficient.

In a multiple-bus/master environment, you might have to use a write-through policy or explicit cache flushes if data is shared across multiple masters.

Forces. The appropriate cache-write policy can be application-dependent. It is worth experimenting with both types of write policies.

Write Coalescing

Context. You are optimizing performance for a processor based on the Intel XScale core. A performance-critical part of the application does multiple writes to memory locations close together.

Problem. Multiple writes consume clock cycles.

Solution. Write coalescing allows you to bring together a new store operation with an existing store operation already resident in the write buffer. The new store is placed in the same write buffer entry as an existing store when the address of the new store falls in the four-word, aligned address of the existing entry.

The K bit in the auxiliary control register (CP15, register 1) is a global enable/disable for allowing coalescing in the write buffer. When this bit is disabled, no coalescing occurs regardless of the value of the page attributes. If this bit is enabled, the page attributes X, C, and B are examined to see if coalescing is enabled for each region of memory.

Write coalescing can be used only on memory that is free of side effects.

Forces. If you enable coalescing in the write buffer, writes can occur out of program order to external memory. You might need to perform explicit drain operations of the write buffer if an external device depends on write ordering.

Cache-Aligned Packet Buffers

Context. Your application/driver caches packet buffers and buffer descriptors.

Problem. You need to use the cache as effectively as possible. On some systems, the descriptors might be larger than a cache line.

Solution. Allocate IX_OSAL_MBUFs, clBlks (BSD) and packet data on cache line boundaries. This action maximizes the use of cache when accessing these data structures.

You must make sure the descriptors and packet storage for different packets do not share the same cache line. If they are cacheable, these conditions can be the cause of subtle difficult-to-find bugs.

Using this pattern can also simplify the addition of an instruction (*see* Intel XScale® Core PLD Instruction).

Forces. You might waste some memory if the size of these data structures in your operating system is not divisible by the cache line size. Typically, this memory wastage is worth the increase in performance.

On-Chip Memory

Context. Your data path code makes frequent reference to a specific table or piece of data.

Problem. Accesses to this data are causing stalls because the cache is heavily used and the data is being frequently evicted. Due to the Intel XScale core's round-robin replacement cache policy, all cache data that is not locked is eventually evicted.

Solution. You can lock tags associated with 32-byte lines in the data cache, thus creating the appearance of data RAM. Any subsequent access to this line hits the cache unless the line is invalidated.

You have two choices when locking tags into the data cache. The method you choose depends on the application.

One method is used to lock data that resides in external memory into the data cache and the other method is used to re-configure lines in the data cache as data RAM.

Locking data from external memory into the data cache is useful for lookup tables, constants, and any other data that is frequently accessed. Re-configuring a portion of the data cache as data RAM is useful when an application needs scratch memory—bigger than the register file can provide—for frequently used variables. These variables could be strewn across memory, making it advantageous for software to pack them into data RAM memory.

To reduce cache pollution between two processes and avoid frequent cache flushing during context switch, the OS could potentially lock critical data sections in the cache.

You can also lock blocks of instructions into the instruction cache. However, a case has not been found yet where the instruction cache was being overloaded to this extent.

Forces. Locking data into the cache reduces the amount of cache available to the processor for general processing.

Mini-DCache

Context. You are optimizing performance on a processor based on the Intel XScale core. The data cache is heavily utilized.

Problem. Frequently used data is being constantly evicted by temporarily cached memory such as packet data.

Solution. Use the mini-dcache. It is a 2-kilobyte block of fast memory. You can use it to reduce the pressure on the main dcache.

You can map the following kinds of data to mini-dcache:

- Put your stack or interrupt stack into the mini-dcache. One application saw an approximate 10-percent performance improvement using this technique. Another application saw no improvement.

- Put packet data into the mini-dcache. One application saw an approximately 5-percent performance improvement using this technique.

- Use the mini-dcache for frequently used tables.

Forces. Consider the following when deciding to use the mini-dcache:

- The mini-dcache might not be available in future iterations of the Intel XScale core.

- Utilizing the mini-dcache might mean BSP changes.

Optimized Libraries

Context. You are optimizing an application for the Intel XScale core. Your data path uses some of the standard C library functions, for example, `memcpy`, and `memcmp`.

Problem. Some compilers come with default C implementations of the standard C libraries. These might not run optimally on the Intel XScale core.

Solution. Intel XScale core-optimized implementations of some of the standard C libraries are available from both Intel and the Internet.

For example, Red Hat has a number of libc functions, specific to the Intel XScale core available on their Web site, listed in "References." A `memcpy` optimized for the little-endian PXA250 and PXA210 processors, based on the Intel XScale core, is detailed in the appendix of PXA Optimization (Intel 2002a).

An efficient `memcpy` is usually processor-specific—sometimes even target-specific depending on factors such as memory widths—so it's most sensible for RTOS infrastructure to supply a generic `memcpy` that's adequate and let the compiler/processor/target override it with its own, if necessary.

Another good example is a count-leading-zeros (CLZ) operation. The Intel XScale core has a CLZ instruction, but many systems implement it as a C-function.

Intel now publishes optimized floating-point libraries for the Intel XScale core and the IXP4XX network processors on the Intel Developer Web site, listed in "References." The floating-point performance has been measured at approximately 5.5 megaflops for the ARM floating-point routines, and about 7 megaflops for the Intel routines (measured on a 400-megahertz processor).

On a related note, make sure you do not re-implement functions that are already available in the standard C library. The performance difference between a C-implementation of `memset` and one specific to the Intel XScale core can be a factor of 30.

Modulo/Divide Avoided

Context. You are writing code for a processor based on the Intel XScale core.

Problem. The processor does not directly support `modulo` or `divide` instructions. When compiled, the code generates a call to a library support function.

Solution. You can translate some `modulo` or `divide` calculations into bit masks or shifts.

For example, `modulo` for dimensions that are a power of 2 can use a mask, such as instead of (var % 8) use (var & 7). Likewise, you can convert some divisions by constants into shift and add instructions.

Most compilers should be capable of generating this optimization, but it might be worth examining generated code for any `modulo` or `divide` on your data path.

Forces. Bit masks/shifts are less readable code than division or modulo.

Operating System Specific

This section describes performance-tuning techniques specific to a number of operating systems.

VxWorks-Specific Improvements

Context. The following techniques are specific to VxWorks. Typically, you would apply these techniques in the board support package (BSP)—when configuring the cache attributes of the memory map—or the END driver.

Problem. You are tuning a VxWorks-based system. It doesn't perform at required levels.

Solution. Try any or all of the following optimizations:

- Use the Intel-supplied OSAL API to allocate mbufs for the Intel IXP400 software. This API allocates VxWorks compatible, cache friendly mbufs at the cost of some memory padding.

- Increase the size of the network data buffer stack instead of using multiple buffer pools.

- Write wrappers for `netTupleGet` and `clChainFree`. Call the wrappers from all END drivers. The free function should add the packet buffer to its own chain free and only return to the system pool when the system pool is lower than a configured threshold or the internal chain is full. The `alloc` function should allocate from the internal chain and call `netTupleGet`—a very heavyweight function—only if the internal chain is empty. The `alloc` should reset data pointers, lengths, and fields.

- Search for all usage of `netJobAdd` in your application and the networking stack software you are using. Inspect the code to determine if it calls `netJobAdd` for every packet. If it does, change the code to de-queue a number of packets, chain them together, and submit them all. This kind of packet batching can also make better use of cache by ensuring the functions stay in instruction cache.

- Disable non-critical features. For example, turn off `netStatLib` from `config.h` to increase IP stack performance.

- Use PNE. Wind River claims the Platform NE software improves the performance of the standard VxWorks IP-routing capability. For details, see the PNE performance white paper (Wind River, 2003).

Linux-Specific Improvements

Context. The following techniques are specific to Linux. Typically, you would apply these techniques at a device-driver level.

Problem. You are tuning a Linux based system that doesn't perform at required levels.

Solution. Try any or all of the following optimizations:

- Understand the Linux IP stack (Herbert 2004). You might do an optimization to reduce the cycles used in part of your application to have the internal throttling features of Linux defer some processing to a kernel thread, using many of the cycles you saved in optimization.

- Avoid the system buffer pools. Where possible, use your own private buffer pools with single producer and single consumer to avoid a significant amount of interrupt locking.

- Preload the `skbuf` header as early as possible, but not too early (*see* Intel XScale® Core PLD Instruction).

- On receive, fill in the packet timestamp. Otherwise, `netif_rx` will try to fill in the value and the computation is cycle consuming. If you can handle more than one packet per interrupt, use one timestamp value for all.

■ Implement a custom transmit-scheduling discipline. The IXP4XX network processor contains its own internal transmit queue for bursts of traffic. So you might not need to use the Linux default queueing algorithms. Implement the `enqueue` and `requeue` functions to call your device driver `hard_start_xmit` function directly.

■ Do not overload the kernel `softirq` queue.

■ Modify the IP stack to preload the IP header before the IP checksum calculation. You can find this code in the Linux kernel at `net/core/dev.c`.

Windows CE-Specific Improvements

Context. The following techniques are specific to Windows CE. Typically, you would apply these techniques in a BSP.

Problem. You are tuning a Windows CE platform and the network performance does not perform at required levels.

Solution. Try any or all of the following optimizations:

■ Understand the context switch overhead in the networking stack and device driver. The Windows CE kernel MMU map is divided into kernel space and user-process space. Significant performance improvement can be achieved by loading dynamic link libraries into the kernel space.

■ Loading the dynamic link libraries high in memory significantly reduces the Intel XScale core translation look aside buffer (TLB) misses. Loading dynamic libraries into high memory is enabled by setting `IMGLOADNETHIGH=1` in `\PLATFORM\INTEL_IXDP425\IXDP425.BAT`. The list of modules that are loaded high is defined in the `IXDP425.BAT` file and `\PLATFORM\INTEL_IXDP425\KERNEL\HAL\loadhighmodules.txt`. You should consider adding your own dynamic link libraries to these lists to improve the performance of your application.

Disclaimer

The techniques discussed in this chapter are suggested solutions to the problems proposed, and as such, they are provided for informational purposes only. Neither the authors nor Intel Corporation can guarantee that these proposed solutions will be applicable to your application or that they will resolve the problems in all instances.

The performance tests and ratings mentioned in this chapter are measured using specific computer systems and/or components, and the results reflect the approximate performance of Intel products as measured by those tests. Any difference in system hardware or software design or configuration can affect actual performance. Buyers should consult other sources of information to evaluate the performance of systems or components they are considering purchasing.

For more information on performance tests and on the performance of Intel products, visit the Web site http://www.intel.com or call (U.S.) 1-800-628-8686.

Chapter **11**

Frequently Asked Questions

If we really understand the problem, the answer will come out of it, because the answer is not separate from the problem.

— J. Krishnamurti

At this point, you probably have some questions. To anticipate and answer them, this chapter contains a selection of frequently asked customer questions we have gathered over a number of years. We have repeated some questions and answers from the main text of the book for convenience. Periodically, you should check the Intel Developer Web site, the address for which is listed in "References," for additions to the frequently asked questions for the Intel® IXP4XX product line. If you don't find your questions answered in either place, send us e-mail and maybe we can add yours to the list.

Software-Related FAQs

The following section is a collection of FAQs related to software aspects of the IXP4XX network processors.

Why do I need the Intel® IXP400 software?

The Intel IXP400 software provides the binary image of the network processor engine (NPE) microcode and the operating system-independent Intel XScale® core APIs to communicate to the NPEs.

How can I check the version number of my Intel IXP400 software?

The Intel IXP400 software source code contains a version number in `\ixp400_xscale_sw\src\include\IxVersionId.h`. The version is defined by `#define IX_VERSION_ID`.

What type of programmability is there with the microengines?

The Intel IXP4XX network processors do not contain microengines. Microengines are processing elements on the IXP2XXX product line. The IXP4XX network processors contain NPEs.

Are the NPEs customer programmable?

No. You cannot program the NPEs. They are fixed-function-processing units for which Intel provides APIs. Intel provides the microcode for these NPEs in the Intel IXP400 software.

Do the IXP4XX network processors support little-endian mode, big-endian mode, or both?

You can configure the Intel XScale core in either little-endian or big-endian mode. We support VxWorks[†] and Linux in both modes, and, of course, Windows[†] CE is a little endian-only operating system.

How can I reduce the size of the Intel IXP400 software library?

You can remove unwanted components by deleting the component name from the Intel IXP400 software makefile `BI_ENDIAN_COMPONENTS` definition and rebuilding the library.

Why does security (DES/3DES/AES) performance vary by application?

Ethernet NPE B hosts the security co-processors. That same NPE also hosts the Ethernet co-processor, which has the media-independent interface (MII) functionality. Because security and MII share the same NPE, performance can vary with MII Ethernet traffic. For example, routing a large number of small, 64-byte IP packets affects the performance of simultaneous cryptographic processing.

How does the Intel IXP400 software support wireless equivalent privacy (WEP)?

The IxCryptoAcc API provides acceleration for the necessary RC4 and CRC routines as defined by the 802.11 WEP specification. IxCryptoAcc supports WEP in two ways: via an NPE-based engine on NPE-A, or with optimized code running on the Intel XScale core. You choose which one to use when submitting the data to the API to be cryptographically processed. The NPE-based WEP engine requires exclusive use of NPE A. If you need NPE A for other purposes, you should choose the Intel XScale core-based WEP implementation instead.

What is the maximum data frame size handled by the Intel IXP4XX network processor UTOPIA, HSS, and Ethernet interfaces?

Each interface supports different data frame sizes.

- *ATM AAL-5.* This interface can support PDUs up to 65,535 bytes or up to 256-chained mBufs, whichever is smaller. The PDU includes any padding needed to align on a 48-byte boundary and any AAL-5 trailer data.

- *Ethernet.* You can configure IxEthAcc to support Ethernet (jumbo) frames up to 16,320 bytes.

- *HSS-HDLC.* The maximum HLDC frame length supported is 16 kilobytes.

Can I change the length of the queues in the queue manager?

The queue manager hardware block is used to communicate between the Intel XScale core and the NPEs. The Intel IXP400 software manages the queues, and there should be no reason to modify the length of the queues.

On Linux, do the access layers run in user mode or kernel mode?

The access layers run in kernel mode, as they need direct access to the hardware. NPE-specific device drivers must make use of the Intel IXP400 software.

Do Intel Integrated Performance Primitives (IPPs) for the PXA family of devices also run on IXP4XX network processors?

The PXA and IXP product lines contain different Intel XScale cores. Please contact Intel for information on specific Intel IPPs.

Why is my networking performance lower for PCI NIC cards running on Linux when I have more than 64 megabytes of SDRAM?

The IXP4XX network processor PCI controller provides visibility of the lower 64 megabytes of SDRAM to the PCI bus. In systems with more than 64 megabytes of SDRAM, you must copy the network packet buffers from higher memory into a buffer that is visible to the NIC card. Copying packet data lowers system performance.

How do I perform PCI I/O transactions?

The IXP4XX network processors do not have a memory-mapped window from the core to PCI I/O space. You must use the APIs provided in each BSP to generate PCI I/O transactions. This requirement can be an issue if you are porting device drivers that assume PCI I/O space is directly mapped to processor memory space.

How many voice channels does the Intel IXP400 DSP software support?

The Intel IXP400 DSP software library supports up to four voice channels. For the most computationally expensive configuration, G.729a, with echo canceller, you can assume that two channels consume 50 percent of a 266-megahertz device and four channels consume 50 percent of a 533-megahertz device.

Does the Intel IXP400 software use the Intel XScale® core mini-instruction cache or mini-data cache?

The Intel IXP400 software does not make use of the mini-instruction or mini-data cache. The decision to use either of the mini caches is a system optimization left up to you.

Why are there multiple operating system service layers?

Intel IXP400 software release 1.5 introduced an operating system abstraction layer called OSAL. OSAL offers the same services as those found in the legacy OSSL and IxOsServices found in previous releases. This restructuring was carried out based on customer feedback. The original intent for the two layers was OSAL was targeted at users of the Intel IXP400 software, and IxOsServices was intended to be used by the Intel IXP400 software. Over time, this distinction became blurred and resulted in some customer confusion.

Can data be moved directly from one Ethernet NPE to another?

The Intel IXP400 software does not support the direct transmission of data from one NPE to another without the Intel XScale core's involvement. The Intel XScale core must be used to receive an event on one port and send it to the other. It's important to note that the packet data does not have to be copied or moved; the Intel XScale core just manages packet descriptors. The Ethernet codelet is a good example showing the reception of data on one NPE and the transmission of that same data on the other. An IXP425 network processor running at 266 megahertz is capable of switching Ethernet frames at 100 megabits per second full duplex.

Why was the fast path removed?

Fast path provided the ability to send data received from the ATM NPE, perform ATM processing, and send the appropriate data to an Ethernet NPE. There is significant application overhead in integrating such a capability. That problem, combined with the fact that no customers were using the feature, led Intel to remove it.

Can I put the DMA access layer on two NPEs at the same time?

No. You can enable the DMA access layer on only one NPE. That NPE then behaves as a DMA engine, and no other functionality can be provided by that NPE.

Hardware Related FAQs

The following section is a collection of FAQs related to the IXP4XX network processors and hardware platforms.

Is there a development platform for the IXP4XX product line?

Yes, two development platforms are available:

- *IXDP425 development platform*—supports IXP42X network processors

- *IXDP465 development platform*—supports the IXP45X and IXP46X network processors

How can you boot the IXP4XX network processor?

You must boot the IXP4XX network processors from a device attached to chip select 0. This device is typically flash memory.

What is the "AHB" in the IXP4XX network processor diagrams?

The AHB is the advanced, high-performance bus, based on a 32-bit, 133-megahertz AMBA-standard bus technology that supports burst transfers, split-transactions, pipeline operations, and multiple masters. The AHB allows data transfers between its masters and the SDRAM controller.

Why do the DRAM controllers have multiple ports?

Both the SDRAM and DDR memory controllers have multiple ports connecting them to the AHB buses. The purpose for this is to optimize the throughput of the memory. For example, having multiple AHB buses connected to the SDRAM controller allows it to set up an NPE memory access while a memory access from the Intel XScale core is in progress. The memory itself should not be considered dual ported.

Do IXP4XX network processors support synchronous flash devices such as Intel StrataFlash® Synchronous Memory?

Yes, the processors can interface and work with synchronous flash such as the Intel StrataFlash® K3 synchronous memory chip. The IXP46X and IXP45X network processors include support for burst mode transfers.

Can a PCI device—connected to the PCI controller of the IXP4XX network processors—access SDRAM devices connected to the SDRAM controller?

Yes. The PCI controller can transfer data via the AHB bus to and from a SDRAM device connected to the SDRAM.

Is it possible to have an external DMA engine transfer data from the expansion bus to an external SDRAM device connected to the SDRAM controller?

The IXP46X and IXP45X network processors support external masters on the expansion bus. The IXP42X network processors do not support this feature.

Why are there two performance monitoring units (PMUs) in the IXP4XX network processor?

The two PMUs are an Intel XScale core PMU and an IXP4XX network processor bus PMU. Each PMU collects different data. The Intel XScale core PMU collects core-specific data, such as the data cache miss ratio. The AHB PMU collects detailed statistics on the performance of the internal memory buses and the DRAM controllers. The AHB-related counters can be used to identify the traffic loading from the NPEs versus the Intel XScale core. You can use the DRAM counters to see if your application is making good use of the DRAM page policy. If not, you should consider the "separate SDRAM memory banks" optimization outlined in Chapter 10.

Can the DMA access layer pull Ethernet frames directly from an Ethernet NPE?

No. The DMA access layer offloads from the Intel XScale core the task of moving data from a non-NPE-based peripheral to another non-NPE-based peripheral including SDRAM. The ixEthAcc component of the Intel IXP400 software is, in essence, an Ethernet DMA engine as it pulls in Ethernet frames and places them in SDRAM without the intervention of the core.

How many ATM PHYs do the IXP4XX network processors support?

The Intel IXP400 software supports a maximum of 12 PHYs.

How many simultaneous channels does a high-speed serial (HSS) port support?

The IXP4XX network processor contains two HSS ports. You can use the `ixHssAcc` component in the Intel IXP400 software to access, configure, and control the HDLC and HSS co-processors of the HSS ports. Each of the HSS ports supports two types of services: packetized (HDLC) services and channelized services (voice). The HSS packetized service supports one HDLC channel per T1/E1 interface. The HSS channelized service supports a maximum of 32 channels. You can select these 32 channels from any one of the 128 time slots spread across the HSS interface.

How many time slots does an HSS port support?

The HSS packetized services support TDM signals and up to four HDLC termination points per port—one per E1/T1 trunk. Each termination point supports up to 32 time slots. Consequently, the maximum supported time slots per HSS port is 128.

Can the WAN/voice NPE of the IXP4XX network processor simultaneously use both HSS ports and the UTOPIA port?

No. If your platform is using both HSS interfaces at the same time, the NPE cannot support the UTOPIA interface. If you are using one HSS interface, however, you can also use the UTOPIA interface.

The IXP4XX network processor documentation says that the PCI controller and the expansion bus can run at a maximum of 66 megahertz. How can I get the processors to generate a 66-megahertz clock output?

The IXP4XX network processors do not provide a 66-megahertz clock. The maximum speed of the internal clock generated by the processors is 33 megahertz. To run the PCI controller or the expansion bus at 66 megahertz, an external clock is required.

Can PCMCIA or a compact flash module directly interface with the IXP4XX network processor?

Yes, you can make a 16-bit PC card—PCMCIA compact flash—connection through the expansion bus, which has a 16-bit data bus.

What is the function of the queue manager in the IXP4XX network processor? How do I manage it?

The queue manager (QM) provides hardware queuing functionality to the network processor engines and the XScale core. Its primary role is to facilitate data flow from the NPEs to/from the Intel XScale core by passing 32-bit pointers to data structures that require processing and reside in SDRAM. It maintains 64 independent queues as circular buffers in an internal 8-kilobyte SRAM and implements the status flags and pointers required for each queue. The `ixQmgr` component of the Intel IXP400 software allows configuration and control of the QM. That access layer also defines what queues are dedicated to the NPEs or to the core.

Does the expansion bus support 32-bit, read-and-write accesses?

The expansion bus has a 16-bit physical interface that internally supports 32-bit reads. However, it does not support 32-bit writes. You can issue only 8-bit and 16-bit writes.

How can I generate a reset from the IXP4XX network processor when a watchdog timeout occurs?

The Intel IXP400 software does not provide an external reset pin to be asserted during this condition. The watchdog timeout function can be set up to generate an FIQ interrupt. The FIQ handler should then drive a GPIO pin low.

How long after PWRON_RESET_N *goes to logic 1 does the boot access start?*

The access of the boot device starts when RESET_IN_N goes to logic 1 and PLL_LOCK goes to logic 1. A minimum of 10 nanoseconds is needed to hold RESET_IN_N at state 0 before it goes to state 1, and a maximum of 10 microseconds is needed before PLL_LOCK changes state to 1. Then the first instruction of the boot access starts.

The processor boots up intermittently. What is a common cause of this?

If you are using the JTAG interface, you must pull `JTAG_TRST_N` high with a 10,000-ohm resistor. If the interface is unused, you must pull `JTAG_TRST_N` low with a 10,000-ohm resistor. Failure to do so may result in the processor booting intermittently.

How should I connect `RCOMP`?

You must tie `IXP_RCOMP`, the RCOMP reference ball, to ground through a 34-ohm 1 percent resistor.

Can I connect a 33-megahertz device and a 66-megahertz device to the PCI bus at the same time?

You can connect the devices but, the PCI standard does not facilitate devices operating at different frequencies. The bus speed automatically drops to the speed of the slowest device.

On the IXP46X network processor, do I need pullup or pulldown resistors on the UTOPIA or Ethernet signals?

The UTOPIA and Ethernet signals on the IXP46X network processor do not require pullup or pulldown resistors if you write to the expansion bus registers to disable the UTOPIA and Ethernet interfaces.

Why can't I plug my PCI card into the IXDP425 development platform? The connector appears to be the wrong way around.

The PCI connector is keyed to allow you to insert 3.3-volt PCI cards. If your card supports only 5-volt operation, you cannot insert it into IXDP425 platform.

Why does my BSP hang when trying to access the PCI block?

If you do not provide a PCI clock to the IXP4XX network processor, any access to the PCI controller from the Intel XScale core causes the processor to hang. You must provide a PCI clock if you plan to use the PCI controller.

Which PCI transactions are generated on the bus for 16-bit PCI memory reads from the Intel XScale core?

The IXP4XX network processor generates a single 32-bit read on the PCI bus and discards the data it does not require. In most cases, this behavior does not cause an issue; however, some devices might not respond to the 32-bit read if it contains 16-bit registers.

How do I program flash with a boot loader?

The simplest way to program flash for the first time is to use an in-circuit emulator (ICE). Most ICE vendors supply applications to program the flash. If you already have RedBoot in flash, it can be used to upgrade the flash image.

Can I use the Intel JFlash utility to program flash devices on IXP4XX network processor based platforms?

Not at present, but we are working on it. For now, we recommend you use a JTAG ICE to program the flash devices on your board.

Glossary

Access point is a stationary device on an 802.11 wireless network. The access point receives and retransmits data, extending the range of wireless computers on the network. Access points can also connect to an Ethernet network, linking wireless computers to other computers connected with cables.

Analog terminal adapters convert the signals from a regular analog phone into a stream of VoIP packets on an Ethernet interface.

Authentication is the process of determining that someone trying to access resources on a network has permission to do so. Usually you use a login name and password to control access to network resources.

Codelet is the term we use to describe code Intel has developed to serve as an example on how to use a particular Intel IXP400 software component.

Execute in place is the direct execution of kernel images stored in flash.

Fence memory operations guarantee all memory operations issued prior to the fence execute before any memory operations issued after the fence.

Firewall protects the network devices inside the home or small-office from external Internet attacks. It detects attacks by analyzing incoming packets and filtering the offending packets.

Flash Memory provides nonvolatile storage for the boot loaders, operating systems, and configuration details.

Gateways are networking products that are typically deployed as the demarcation point between a private local area network (LAN) and the public wide area network (WAN). A residential or small office, home office (SOHO) gateway typically contains router and firewall functionality.

Internet appliance is a browser-based consumer Internet device with a fixed display such as LCD or CRT keyboard and mouse input.

Line-allocation policy dictates how the cache decides to put new data into the cache. If the line-allocation policy is read-allocate and the cache is enabled, all load operations in cacheable pages that miss the cache request a cache line from external memory and allocate it into the data cache. If read/write-allocate is in effect, load or store operations that miss the cache request a cache line and allocate it into the data cache.

Message buffers or packet descriptors are structures that overlay packets in memory. Message buffers allow the developer to chain a number of segments of memory together to form a single packet.

Network attached storage (NAS) device is a network file server that contains or attaches to one or more disks and provides access to them over a network.

Router is a networking product that contains more than one communications interface. It receives packets from those interfaces and makes a decision to forward the packet to another interface based on the IP protocol information in the packet.

RTP stack is a protocol stack that supports the real-time transport protocol. RTP is an Internet protocol for transmitting real-time data such as audio and video. The protocol is defined in the Internet Engineering Task Force – RFC 3550.

Split transactions are bus transactions where a bus target decides to split the transaction into request and reply phases, allowing other bus masters to use the bus between these phases. This feature gives a higher bandwidth but usually means higher latency than a bus held for a full transaction. Hennessy and Patterson (2003) give more details on processor bus architectures.

Software architecture is the overall design structure, goals, requirements, and development strategies for a software intensive system.

Scrubbing is a process where a boot loader writes a known value into all of the memory.

Security association is a policy defining how two or more entities communicate over a particular security protocol. The policy specifies the transform and shared secret keys for the protected data flow.

SLIC/CODEC devices perform all battery, over voltage, ringing, supervision, coding, and hybrid and test (BORSCHT) functions. They convert the analog signal to and from digital PCM.

Station is a node or a mobile computer in a wireless network.

Temporal locality refers to the amount of time between accesses to a piece of data. If you access the data once or access it infrequently, it has low temporal locality.

Universal asynchronous receiver-transmitter (UART) interfaces are usually connected to an RS232 serial port via a transceiver device.

Voice residential gateway integrates the functions of an analog terminal adapter and a gateway into one product.

VoIP phones are standalone phones that can connect directly to an IP network instead of the standard analog telephone network.

VoIP enabled PBXs are used in a business environment where a large number of phones must be adapted to VoIP. It also provides local services such as voice mail.

Write policy defines what happens in the cache when a write operation occurs. A write-through policy instructs the data cache to keep external memory coherent by performing stores to both external memory and the cache. A write-back policy updates external memory only when a line in the cache is flushed or needs to be replaced with a new line.

References

This book contains a number of references to manuals written by Intel for specific Intel network processors. These manuals are constantly changing; they are being updated or written as new network processors are released. You can find the appropriate manual at:

http://www.intel.com/design/network/products/npfamily/ixp4xx.htm

The list provided here helps you find the books and Web sites referenced in this book.

Alexander, Christopher. 1979. *The Timeless Way of Building*. Oxford: Oxford University Press.

Ball, Stuart. 2002. *Embedded Microprocessor Systems: Real World Design*. 3rd ed. Burlington, MA: Newnes.

Beck, Kent. 1999. *Extreme Programming Explained*. Boston: Addison-Wesley.

Douglass, Bruce. 1999. *Doing Hard Time: Developing Real-Time Systems with UML, Objects, Frameworks and Patterns*. Boston: Addison-Wesley.

FASS Web site.
http://www.disy.cse.unsw.edu.au/Software/FASS/.

Foote, Brian, and Joseph Yoder. 1997. Big Ball of Mud. *Proceedings of the Fourth Conference on Pattern Languages of Programs.* Available on the Web in portable document format at: http://st-www.cs.uiuc.edu/~plop/plop97/Proceedings/foote.pdf.

Gamma, Erich, Richard Helm, Ralph Johnson, and John Vlissides. 1995. *Design Patterns: Elements of Reusable Object-Oriented Software.* Boston: Addison-Wesley.

Ganssle, Jack. 1999. *The Art of Designing Embedded Systems.* Burlington, MA: Newnes.

Hennessy, John, and David Patterson. 2003. *Computer Architecture: A Quantitative Approach.* 3rd ed. Burlington, MA: Morgan-Kaufmann.

Herbert, Thomas. 2004. *The Linux TCP/IP Stack: Networking for Embedded Systems.* Hingham, MA: Charles River Media.

IEEE Computer Society. 2002a. *1588[†] Standard for a Precision Clock Synchronization Protocol for Networked Measurement and Control Systems.* Purchasable at http://standards.ieee.org.

——. 2002b. *802.3[†].* Information about this standard is available in portable document format at:

http://standards.ieee.org/getieee802/download/802.3-2002.pdf

IEEE Registration Authority.
http://standards.ieee.org/regauth/oui/oui.txt.

Intel Communications Alliance Web site.
http://www.intel.com/design/network/ica/.

Intel Corporation. 2002a. *Intel[®] PXA250 and PXA210 Processors Optimization Guide,* Santa Clara, CA: Intel Corporation. Portable Document Format.

——. 2002b. *Performance Profiling Techniques on Intel XScale[®] Microarchitecture Processors,* Santa Clara, CA: Intel Corporation. Portable Document Format.

——. 2003. *Intel/Linksys Case Study.* Available on the Web in portable document format at:
http://developer.intel.com/design/network/casestudies/linksys.pdf.

——. 2004a. *Intel[®] IXP400 Digital Signal Processing (DSP) Software.* v. 2.4. Available on the Web in portable document format at:
http://www.intel.com/design/network/manuals/273811_v2_4.pdf.

———. 2004b. Intel® IXP400 Software Releases. http://www.intel.com/design/network/products/npfamily/ixp425swr1.htm.

———. 2004c. *Intel® IXP400 Software Version 1.5 Programmers' Guide*. Available on the Web in portable document format at: http://www.intel.com/design/network/manuals/252539_v1_5.htm.

———. 2004d. *Intel Processors in Industrial Control and Automation Applications*. Available on the Web in portable document format at: http://www.intel.com/design/network/papers/30405401.pdf.

Intel Developer Web site. http://developer.intel.com.

Intel Developer Web site. FreeS/WAN patches. http://www.intel.com/design/network/products/npfamily/ixp400_osc.htm.

Intel Developer Web site. System Reference Designs. http://developer.intel.com/design/network/products/npfamily/ixdpg425.htm.

Johnson, Erik J, and Aaron Kunze. 2003. *IXP2400/2800 Programming: The Complete Microengine Coding Guide*. Hillsboro: Intel Press.

Iyer, Sanjay, and Linley Gwennap. 2004. *A Guide to Communications Processors*. 2nd ed. Mountain View, CA: The Linley Group.

Kernel source code. www.kernel.org

Kruchten, P. 1995. The 4+1 View Model of Architecture. *IEEE Software*, 12(6): 42-50. Los Alamitos: IEEE Computer Society Press.

Malik, Vipin. 2001. The Linux MTD, JFFS HOWTO. Available on the Web at: ftp://ftp.uk.linux.org/pub/people/dwmw2/mtd/cvs/mtd/mtd-jffs-HOWTO.txt.

Massa, A J. 2002. *Embedded Software Development with eCos*. Upper Saddle River: Prentice Hall.

McConnell, Steve. 1993. *Code Complete: A Practical Handbook of Software Construction*. Redmond, WA: Microsoft Press.

McDysan, David, and Darren Spohn. 1999. *ATM Theory and Applications*. Emeryville, CA: McGraw-Hill.

Meyers, Scott. 1997. *Effective C++: 50 Specific Ways to Improve Your Programs and Design*. 2nd ed. Boston: Addison-Wesley Professional.

Microsoft Corporation. 2004. *Remote Network Driver Interface Specification (RNDIS)*. Available on the Web at: http://msdn.microsoft.com/library/default.asp?url=/library/en-us/wceddk5/html/wce50conRNDISDriverImplementationGuide.asp.

MontaVista. 2005. http://www.mvista.com.

NSLU2 Web site. http://www.nslu2-linux.org/.

Perlman, Radia. 1992. *Interconnections Bridges and Routers*. Boston: Addison-Wesley.

Pont, Michael. 2001. *Patterns for Time-Triggered Embedded Systems: Building Reliable Applications with the 8051 Family of Microcontrollers*. Boston: Addison-Wesley.

Red Hat. 2004. http://www.redhat.com.

———. 2005. RedBoot. http://sources.redhat.com/ecos/.

Schneier, Bruce. 1996. *Applied Cryptography: Protocols Algorithms and Source Code*. 2nd ed. Hoboken: Wiley.

Seal, David. 2000. *ARM Architecture Reference Manual*. 2nd ed. Boston: Addison-Wesley.

SnapGear. 2005. SnapGear Embedded Linux Distribution Home Page. http://www.snapgear.org/.

Snort Web site. http://www.snort.org/.

Software Engineering Institute Web site. 2004. http://www.sei.cmu.edu/ata.

SourceForge. http://www.sourceforge.net/.

———. ATM on Linux. http://linux-atm.sourceforge.net/.

———. *IXP4XX Open Source Developer's Guide*. http://ixp4xx-osdg.sourceforge.net/.

———. Linux 2.6 Support for the IXP400 Access Library. http://ixp4xx-osdg.sourceforge.net/linux-2.6.html

Summit, Steve. 1995. comp.lang.c FAQ Web site. http://www.eskimo.com/~scs/C-faq/top.html. Content from *C Programming FAQs: Frequently Asked Questions*. Boston: Addison-Wesley.

The ATM Forum. 1995. *UTOPIA Level 2 Specification*. Available on the Web in portable document format at: ftp://ftp.atmforum.com/pub/approved-specs/af-phy-0039.000.pdf.

The Tolly Group. 2004. *Performance Analysis of VPN Devices*. Available on the Web in portable document format at: http://www.intel.com/design/network/products/npfamily/tolly_204132.pdf.

USB Implementers Forum. 1998. *Universal Serial Bus Revision 1.1 Specification*. Available on the Web in zip file format at: http://www.usb.org/developers/docs.

Wind River Systems. 2003. *Meeting the Demand for a Higher Performance Routing Stack*. Available on the Web in portable document format at: http://www.windriver.com/whitepapers/wp_pne.pdf

———. 2005. http://www.windriver.com.

Zeffertt, Alex. (no date). *ixp425sar: An ATM device driver for the IXP425*. http://ixp425.sourceforge.net/.

Index

66 *As the pace of technology introduction increases, it's difficult to keep up. Intel Press has established an impressive portfolio. The breadth of topics is a reflection of both Intel's diversity as well as our commitment to serve a broad technical community.*

I hope you will take advantage of these products to further your technical education. **99**

Patrick Gelsinger
Senior Vice President and Chief Technology Officer
Intel Corporation

**Turn the page to learn about titles
from Intel Press for system developers**

Get Up to Speed on the Latest Intel Network Processor Family

IXP2400/2800 Programming

The Complete Microengine Coding Guide
By Erik J. Johnson and Aaron R. Kunze
ISBN 0-9717861-6-X

Intel Senior Network Software Engineers Erik Johnson and Aaron Kunze bring their key insights to programming for the Intel® IXP2XXX Network Processor family. Software and firmware engineers developing products based on the IXP2400, IXP2800, or IXP2850 network processors will find this guide to be an invaluable resource. Whether you are new to programming Intel® network processors or already familiar with the IXP1200, this book helps you come up to speed quickly on the IXP2XXX family of processors.

IXP2400/2800 Programming takes you through a set of tasks typically faced by network software engineers, from basic receive and transmit operations to more complex packet processing. Each task is decomposed, using a working code example in both microengine C and microengine assembly, into what the appropriate parts of the software and hardware can do, explaining why the task is important to the design and implementation. The various tradeoffs that are possible within the software and hardware are fully analyzed as well. The book progresses in steps from simple, single-threaded programs to a complete multithreaded reference application using the microblock programming paradigm. Application and programming notes are used throughout the book to accelerate the pace for readers already familiar with IXP1200 programming. Complete and working code examples from the book are included on the accompanying CD-ROM, along with the Intel® IXA Software Developer's Kit.

> 66 *Every developer who wants to program the IXP2XXX should read this book.* 99
>
> Steve Yates, President & Chief Technology Officer, ADI Engineering

Designing High-Performance Networking Applications

Esential Insights for Developers of IXP2XXX Network Processor-based Systems

By Uday R. Naik and Prashant R. Chandra

ISBN 0-9743649-8-3

Software architects and network system engineers will appreciate this nuts-and-bolts explanation of tested methodology for developing data plane applications from senior architects of the Intel® IXA Portability Framework. Many adopters of this new technology struggle with performance analysis and software reuse for network applications, so this book shows you how to get the most benefit from these methods. Case studies of applications in defined market segments show you how to use the microblock framework of Intel IXA to build specifically targeted data plane applications and how to use proven analysis methodology to estimate performance before you build the application.

Know the best methods before you start...

Intel® Internet Exchange Architecture and Applications

A Practical Guide to Intel's Network Processors

By Bill Carlson

ISBN 0-9702846-3-2

In this invaluable developer resource, Bill Carlson provides an overview of the Intel® Internet Exchange Architecture (Intel® IXA) and an in-depth technical view of the standards required by hardware and software developers of next-generation OEM networking equipment. This book is not only for hardware and software engineers; it also explains to support professionals, management, and salespersons how the IXP2XXX processors are replacing ASICs. *Intel® Internet Exchange Architecture and Applications* describes a typical network processor architecture and provides a detailed example of a DSLAM using the multi-protocol software framework.

❝ Engineers should read this book then use it for a reference to streamline the coding process. ❞

Douglas A. Palmer, PhD

Special Deals, Special Prices!

To ensure you have all the latest books
and enjoy aggressively priced discounts,
please go to this Web site:

www.intel.com/intelpress/bookbundles.htm

Bundles of our books are available,
selected especially to address the needs
of the developer. The bundles place
place important complementary
topics at your fingertips, and the
price for a bundle is substantially less
than buying all the books individually.

About Intel Press

Intel Press is the authoritative source of timely, highly relevant, and innovative books to help software and hardware developers speed up their development process. We collaborate only with leading industry experts to deliver reliable, first-to-market information about the latest technologies, processes, and strategies.

Our products are planned with the help of many people in the developer community and we encourage you to consider becoming a customer advisor. If you would like to help us and gain additional advance insight to the latest technologies, we encourage you to consider the Intel Press Customer Advisor Program. You can **register** here:

> www.intel.com/intelpress/register.htm

For information about bulk orders or corporate sales, please send email to
bulkbooksales@intel.com

Other Developer Resources from Intel

At these Web sites you can also find valuable technical information and resources for developers:

developer.intel.com	general information for developers
www.intel.com/IDS	content, tools, training, and the Early Access Program for software developers
www.intel.com/netcomms	solutions and resources for developers of networking and communications products
www.intel.com/software/products	programming tools to help you develop high-performance applications
www.intel.com/idf	worldwide technical conference, the Intel Developer Forum

INTEL PRESS